INTERNATIONAL POLITICAL ECONOMY SERIES

General Editor: Timothy M. Shaw, Professor of Political Science and International Development Studies, and Director of the Centre for Foreign Policy Studies, Dalhousie University, Halifax, Nova Scotia

Recent titles include:

Pradeep Agrawal, Subir V. Gokarn, Veena Mishra, Kirit S. Parikh and Kunal Sen
ECONOMIC RESTRUCTURING IN EAST ASIA AND INDIA: Perspectives on Policy Reform

Deborah Bräutigam
CHINESE AID AND AFRICAN DEVELOPMENT: Exporting Green Revolution

Steve Chan, Cal Clark and Danny Lam (*editors*)
BEYOND THE DEVELOPMENTAL STATE: East Asia's Political Economies Reconsidered

Jennifer Clapp
ADJUSTMENT AND AGRICULTURE IN AFRICA: Farmers, the State and the World Bank in Guinea

Robert W. Cox (*editor*)
THE NEW REALISM: Perspectives on Multilateralism and World Order

Ann Denholm Crosby
DILEMMAS IN DEFENCE DECISION-MAKING: Constructing Canada's Role in NORAD, 1958–96

Diane Ethier
ECONOMIC ADJUSTMENT IN NEW DEMOCRACIES: Lessons from Southern Europe

Stephen Gill (*editor*)
GLOBALIZATION, DEMOCRATIZATION AND MULTILATERALISM

Jeffrey Henderson (*editor*), assisted by Karoly Balaton and Gyorgy Lengyel
INDUSTRIAL TRANSFORMATION IN EASTERN EUROPE IN THE LIGHT OF THE EAST ASIAN EXPERIENCE

Jacques Hersh and Johannes Dragsbaek Schmidt (*editors*)
THE AFTERMATH OF 'REAL EXISTING SOCIALISM' IN EASTERN EUROPE, Volume 1: Between Western Europe and East Asia

David Hulme and Michael Edwards (*editors*)
NGOs, STATES AND DONORS: Too Close for Comfort?

Staffan Lindberg and Árni Sverrisson (*editors*)
SOCIAL MOVEMENTS IN DEVELOPMENT: The Challenge of Globalization and Democratization

Anne Lorentzen and Marianne Rostgaard (*editors*)
THE AFTERMATH OF 'REAL EXISTING SOCIALISM' IN EASTERN
EUROPE, Volume 2: People and Technology in the Process of Transition

Stephen D. McDowell
GLOBALIZATION, LIBERALIZATION AND POLICY CHANGE: A Political
Economy of India's Communications Sector

Juan Antonio Morales and Gary McMahon (*editors*)
ECONOMIC POLICY AND THE TRANSITION TO DEMOCRACY: The
Latin American Experience

Ted Schrecker (*editor*)
SURVIVING GLOBALISM: The Social and Environmental Challenges

Ann Seidman, Robert B. Seidman and Janice Payne (*editors*)
LEGISLATIVE DRAFTING FOR MARKET REFORM: Some Lessons from
China

Caroline Thomas and Peter Wilkin (*editors*)
GLOBALIZATION AND THE SOUTH

Kenneth P. Thomas
CAPITAL BEYOND BORDERS: States and Firms in the Auto Industry,
1960–94

Geoffrey R. D. Underhill (*editor*)
THE NEW WORLD ORDER IN INTERNATIONAL FINANCE

Henry Veltmeyer, James Petras and Steve Vieux
NEOLIBERALISM AND CLASS CONFLICT IN LATIN AMERICA: A
Comparative Perspective on the Political Economy of Structural Adjustment

Robert Wolfe
FARM WARS: The Political Economy of Agriculture and the International Trade
Regime

How Sanctions Work

Lessons from South Africa

Edited by

Neta C. Crawford
Assistant Professor of Political Science
Department of Political Science
University of Massachusetts, Amherst

and

Audie Klotz
Associate Professor of Political Science
Department of Political Science
University of Illinois, Chicago

St. Martin's Press
New York

HOW SANCTIONS WORK

St. Martin's Press, Scholarly and Reference Division, 175 Fifth Avenue, New York, N.Y. 10010

First published in the United States of America in 1999

This book is printed on paper suitable for recycling and made from fully managed and sustained forest sources.

Printed in Great Britain

ISBN 0–312–21854–0 clothbound
ISBN 0–312–21856–7 paperback

Library of Congress Cataloging-in-Publication Data
How sanctions work : lessons from South Africa / edited by Neta C. Crawford and Audie Klotz.
p.   cm. — (International political economy series)
Includes bibliographical references and index.
ISBN 0–312–21854–0 (cloth). — ISBN 0–312–21856–7 (pbk.)
1. Sanctions (International law)—Case studies.   2. South Africa–
–Foreign relations—1978–1989.   I. Crawford, Neta.   II. Klotz,
Audie, 1962   .   III. Series.
JZ6373.H69   1998
341.5'82—dc21   98–38459
                                                                    CIP

Contents

List of Tables

List of Maps

Acknowledgments

This project would not have been possible without financial and institutional support from the Thomas J. Watson Jr. Institute for International Studies at Brown University, which allowed us to gather together as a group in Providence, RI. We also thank the International Studies Association for a workshop grant which enabled us to present early drafts of the papers at its April 1996 annual conference. The discussants and participants at both meetings, including Tom Biersteker, Margaret Doxey, Jendayi Frazer, Arlene Getz, Willard Johnson, Norma Kriger, Kim Nossal, David Rowe, and Newell Stultz, offered invaluable insights. The individual chapter authors also generously shared their knowledge and judgment with us and each other. We greatly appreciate the enthusiasm and patience of Tim Shaw, Aruna Vasudevan and Keith Povey throughout the editing and publication processes. Neta Crawford gratefully acknowledges the overall support of Jill Breitbarth, the research assistance of Amy Nash, and the financial support of the University of Massachusetts, Amherst, and the Humanitarianism and War Project of Brown University, which allowed her to make research trips to South Africa and meet some of the chapter authors on their home ground. Audie Klotz gratefully acknowledges financial support from the Campus Research Board of the University of Illinois at Chicago and thanks Dave Black, Cecelia Lynch, Kim Nossal and Tim Shaw for sage advice at critical moments.

Amherst and Arlington, Massachusetts   NETA C. CRAWFORD
Chicago, Illinois   AUDIE KLOTZ

Notes on the Contributors

David R. Black is Associate Professor of Political Science at Dalhousie University. His articles and book chapters include work on the role of "middle powers" in southern Africa; Canada in North–South relations; the "new" South Africa in Africa; and the role of rugby in South African politics and society. He is co-editor, with Larry Swatuk, of *Bridging the Rift: The New South Africa in Africa* (Boulder, CO: Westview, 1997) and co-author, with John Nauright, of *Rugby and the South African Nation* (Manchester: Manchester University Press, 1998).

Xavier Carim is Deputy Director of Multilateral Trade Relations at the Department of Trade and Industry, Government of South Africa. He has a masters degree from Rhodes University. Before entering government service in 1995, Mr. Carim was a research associate at the Centre for Southern African Studies at the University of the Western Cape, where he was the coordinator of the *Southern African Perspectives* working paper series.

Neta C. Crawford is an Assistant Professor of Political Science at the University of Massachusetts at Amherst. She is the author of *Soviet Military Aircraft* (Lexington: Lexington, 1987). Her articles in books and scholarly journals are about US foreign and military policy, security regimes, media coverage of Africa, decolonization as an international norm, international ethics, security studies, South Africa's foreign and military policy, and the humanitarian consequences of sanctions against South Africa. Dr. Crawford is currently completing a book, *The Making of World Politics: Argument, Belief and Culture*.

David Fig teaches sociology at the University of Witwatersrand, in Johannesburg, and holds a doctorate in International Relations from the London School of Economics. Formerly Director of the Group for Environmental Monitoring (a Johannesburg-based non-governmental organization working for environmental justice in South Africa), he sits on the National Parks Board and the National Science and Technology Forum, and serves on the Management Advisory Team of the Consultative National Environmental Policy Process. Dr. Fig has written extensively on South–South relations, environmental, foreign policy and labor issues, and is currently writing a history of the nuclear industry in South Africa.

Gilbert M. Khadiagala is an Associate Professor at the School of Advanced International Studies, Johns Hopkins University. He is the author of *Allies in Adversity: The Frontline States in Southern African Security, 1975–1993* (Athens, OH: Ohio University Press, 1994) and *Mediating Conflicts in Eastern Africa* (forthcoming).

Audie Klotz is Associate Professor of Political Science at the University of Illinois at Chicago. She is the author of *Norms in International Relations: The Struggle against Apartheid* (Ithaca, NY: Cornell University Press, 1995), which received the 1996 Edgar S. Furniss Prize. She has also written articles on African foreign affairs, sanctions, and international relations theory.

Olivier Lebleu has worked as a financial consultant for several South African corporations, including Investec Bank, Seardel, Sappi, and Sasol. He earned his masters degree at Columbia University's School of International and Public Affairs.

Tshidiso Maloka is a Lecturer in History at the University of Cape Town, where he works on the social history of mining and labor migrancy in southern Africa. He is presently special adviser to the premier of Gauteng Province in South Africa and was a postdoctoral research fellow at Princeton University in 1996. Dr. Maloka has also written about the role of chieftanship in contemporary African politics.

Mzamo P. Mangaliso is an Associate Professor in the School of Management at the University of Massachusetts at Amherst, where he has also directed the MBA program. A South African by birth, he obtained his undergraduate degree from the University of Fort Hare, an MBA from Cornell University, and a PhD from the University of Massachusetts. Dr. Mangaliso worked in South Africa as a metallurgical research assistant at the Harmony Gold Mines in the Free State and as a chemical analyst and soap production manager for Lever Brothers in Durban. His articles have appeared in the *Journal of Management, Journal of Business Ethics, Entrepreneurship,*

and *Innovation and Change.* He has co-edited two conference pro-
ceedings, *Learning Is Managing* (Madison, WI: Omni, 1995) with
Joan Weiner, and *Managing in a Global Economy* (Madison, WI:
Omni, 1995) with David D. Palmer.

Nomazengele A. Mangaliso is Associate Professor of Sociology at
Westfield State College, Westfield, Massachusetts. She teaches various
courses, including Principles of Sociology, Sociological Theory, Social
Change, Collective Behavior and Complex Organizations. She is
the author of *The South African Mosaic: A Sociological Analysis of
Post-Apartheid Conflict* (Lanham, MD: University Press of America,
1994). Her recent chapters in books include "The Paradoxical
Outcome of Discrimination: The United States and the South African
Experience," in *The United States and South Africa: The Historical
Field of Cultural Interaction* (London: Verso, 1997), and "Gender
and Nation-Building in South Africa," in *Feminist Nationalism* (New
York: Routledge, 1997). She resides in Amherst, Massachusetts,
with her husband, Mzamo, and two daughters, Bande and Unati.

Meg Voorhes is Director of the South Africa Service at the Investor Responsibility Research Center, a not-for-profit organization
in Washington, DC. Ms. Voorhes, who has a BA degree from
Wesleyan University and a masters from the School of Advanced
International Affairs at Johns Hopkins University, has written extensively about the political situation and multinational investment
in South Africa since joining IRRC in 1979. From 1984 to 1994
she served as a consultant to the College and University Consortium on South Africa. Her recent publications include *Multinational
Business in South Africa* (IRRC, 1996), written with Peter DeSimone,
and she is currently editor of *South Africa Investor*, published monthly
by IRRC.

Abbreviations

AEB	Atomic Energy Board
AEC	Atomic Energy Commission
Amcham	American Chamber of Commerce in South Africa
ANC	African National Congress
Armscor	Armaments Development and Production Corporation
CAAA	Comprehensive Anti-Apartheid Act
CDA	Combined Development Agency
COSATU	Congress of South African Trade Unions
CSIR	Council for Scientific and Industrial Research
CSS	Central Statistical Service
CWIU	Commercial Workers Industrial Union
ECOSOC	Economic and Social Council [of the UN]
Eskom	Electricity Supply Commission
FDI	Foreign Direct Investment
FLS	Frontline States
FOSATU	Federation of South African Trade Unions
Frelimo	Front for the Liberation of Mozambique
GDP	gross domestic product
GfK	(West German) Nuclear Research Center
GM	General Motors
HEU	Highly Enriched Uranium
HNP	*Herstigte* [Reconstituted] National Party
IAEA	International Atomic Energy Agency
ILO	International Labour Organization
IMF	International Monetary Fund
IOC	International Olympic Committee
IRRC	Investor Responsibility Research Center
JSE	Johannesburg Stock Exchange
MNC	Multinational Corporation
NATO	North Atlantic Treaty Organization
NP	National Party
NPT	Non-Proliferation Treaty
NUMSA	National Union of Metal Workers
OAU	Organization of African Unity
OPEC	Organization of Petroleum Exporting Countries
PAC	Pan-African Congress

R&D	research and development
RSA	Republic of South Africa
SAAF	South African Air Force
SACOS	South African Council of Sport
SACU	Southern African Customs Union
SACTU	South African Congress of Trade Unions
SADC	Southern African Development Community
SADCC	Southern African Development Coordination Conference
SADF	South African Defence Force
SANDF	South African National Defence Force
SAMCOR	South African Motor Corporation
SANROC	South African Non-Racial Olympic Committee
SAONGA	South African Olympic and National Games Association
Sasol	South African Oil and Gas Corporation
SC	(UN) Security Council
SCSA	Supreme Council of Sport in Africa
SDR	standard drawing right
SRB	Shipping Research Bureau
SWA	South West Africa (i.e., Namibia)
TIAA-CREF	Teachers Insurance and Annuity Association – College Retirement Equities Fund
UCOR	Uranium Enrichment Corporation of South Africa
UDF	United Democratic Front
UDI	Unilateral Declaration of Independence
UK	United Kingdom
UN	United Nations
UNITA	Union for the Total Independence of Angola
US(A)	United States (of America)

Map 1 South Africa

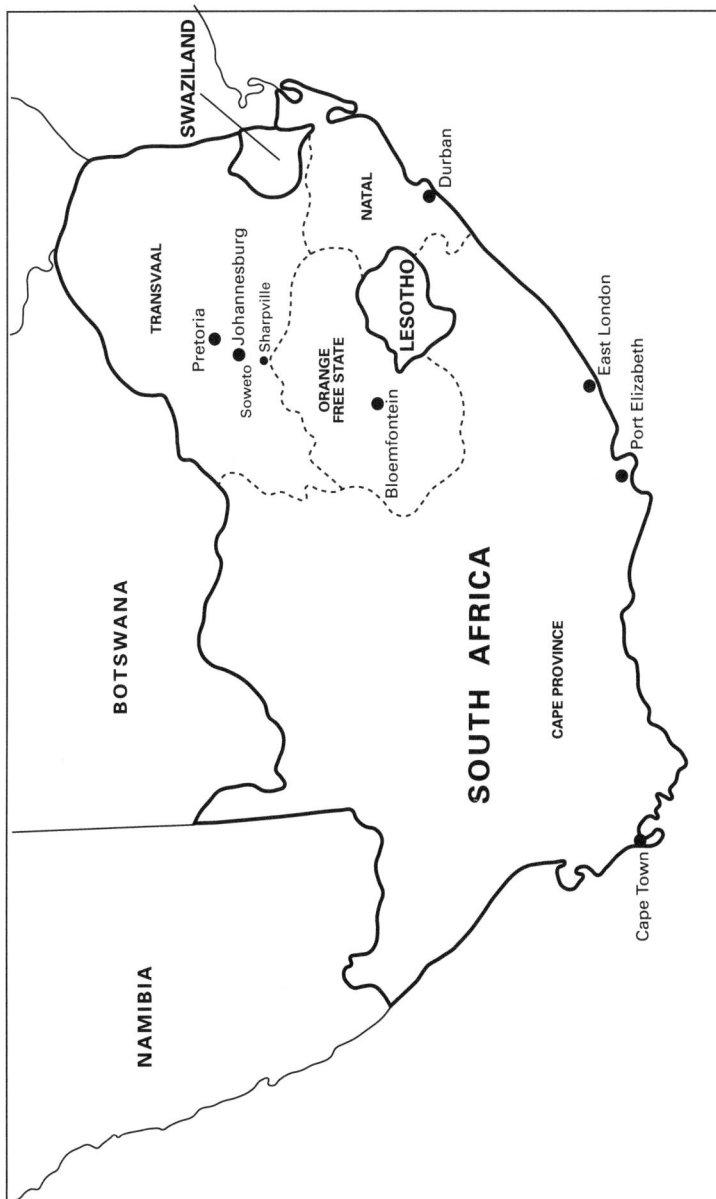

Part I

Introduction

1 Trump Card or Theater? An Introduction to Two Sanctions Debates[1]

Neta C. Crawford

This book responds to two ongoing and interrelated debates about sanctions against South Africa. The broader debate is over the efficacy of sanctions as a tool of influence. The second debate focuses on the role of sanctions in promoting South Africa's democratic transition (for a chronology, see the Appendix). The two debates have become intertwined because the South African case is an excellent one for understanding the role of sanctions.

First, as the discussion below shows, nearly every theoretical argument about the potential impact of sanctions on a target was made with respect to South Africa. Second, South Africa's mixed economy (based on industry, agriculture, and mining raw materials) enables the evaluation of the impact of sanctions on different economic sectors. Third, various types of sanctions – strategic, economic, and social – were levied against apartheid South Africa. Finally, multiple tools of influence were used, besides sanctions, in the effort to change South Africa's foreign and domestic policies. Specifically, South Africa is the paradigm case of constructive engagement – the effort to change another government's policies by embrace rather than isolation. In addition, international diplomacy, mediation, and negotiation were used in an effort to promote democratic reforms within South Africa, halt South Africa's occupation of Namibia, and end its war in Angola. Moreover, sanctions and diplomacy were only part of a larger anti-apartheid strategy. The African National Congress (ANC), the South African Communist Party, trade unions, religious groups, and literally hundreds of other activist organizations inside South Africa waged a determined struggle for change over the course of several decades while guerrilla movements and South Africa's neighbors used military force to resist South African aggression and to force domestic restructuring. Thus, South Africa is an appropriate, some might say critical, case for

3

understanding how strategic, economic, and social isolation affects the politics, economy, and social relations of the targets of sanctions, as well as third parties.

DO SANCTIONS WORK?

International sanctions, for centuries utilized for political and military leverage, are frequently used to promote democratization and to enforce norms against aggression and domestic repression. In recent years, diplomatic, economic, and military sanctions have been imposed against Angola, China, Cuba, Haiti, Iran, Iraq, Myanmar, Nigeria, Rwanda, and Yugoslavia. Yet, despite frequent recourse to this tool there is no consensus on whether or how sanctions work to change the behavior of states or elites within target states.[2]

The conventional wisdom is that sanctions are at best blunt instruments, if they are not simply counterproductive or harmful to the economies of those imposing the restrictions.[3] Many of the arguments associated with the view that sanctions do not work were articulated in an advertisement by Mobil Oil Corporation that appeared in the *New York Times*. Mobil asserted that "Unilateral sanctions may be satisfying theater: that is, we feel better punishing an offender's behavior. But they usually don't accomplish what they set out to do – namely, to deter and rehabilitate."[4]

Such skepticism has historical roots. The League of Nations, concerned with deterring international aggression, regarded sanctions as an alternative to the use of force. The perceived failure of the League's reaction to Italy's 1935 invasion of Ethiopia, where sanctions were tried, emphasized for critics the difficulties of collective action among sanctioners and poor signaling to Italy.[5] Morgan and Schwebach argue that while sanctions may be effective on occasion, "most studies in political science have concluded that sanctions do not 'work,' at least not in the sense of bringing about a desired change in the policy of the target country" and that "foolish sanctioners may pay dearly for little gain."[6] Pape argues that sanctions are rarely successful. He suggests that the "key" reason sanctions fail and are unlikely to be used with greater effect in the future is the "nature of the target." He argues that elites in authoritarian states can slough the costs of sanctions off onto weaker segments of the society while nationalism and democracy make states more resilient in the face of sanctions.[7] Further, media images of

Haiti, Iraq, and the former Yugoslavia in the 1990s raised the question of sanctions being a cause of humanitarian crises, not their solution.[8] Others, disputing any significant role for sanctions, argue that policies of economic contact and dialogue such as "constructive engagement" are more likely to influence target states.[9] Similarly, some argue that economic isolation is counterproductive since it may slow the target's economic growth; in this view growth, especially industrialization, promotes political liberalization.[10] And some argue that sanctions need to be backed by the threat of force to be effective and that sanctions are a poor alternative to military force.[11]

Part of the difficulty with drawing conclusions about the utility of sanctions is conceptual. First there is no standard definition of international sanctions, nor a clear set of arguments about how they might work, and differing notions of success.[12] In this volume, sanctions are defined as the denial of customary interactions (strategic, economic, or social); they are intended to promote social, political, or economic change in a target state. As the denial of customary interactions, sanctions speak louder than words: imposition of sanctions communicates the threat of more sanctions and also the promise of release from embargoes if the target meets certain conditions. Sanctions are potentially effective prior to their imposition as threats (perhaps even obviating the need to impose sanctions) and while they are under way as *both* a form of denial and as an incentive, assuming the target understands how to behave to get the sanctions lifted.[13] Sanctions, or the threat of their imposition, are successful to the extent that they contribute to promoting the change desired by those who imposed or support sanctions.[14]

Second, much of the literature focuses on *economic* sanctions imposed by states against states. This conceptualization is too narrow. Sanctions may be undertaken by international organizations, alliances, single countries, corporations, universities, municipalities, or individuals. Further, the denial of customary interaction may take the form of embargoes of material and financial resources and products to the target, boycotts of target-state products, seizures of financial or real-estate assets held outside the target's borders, and isolation of the target in material economic and social – diplomatic, cultural, and intellectual – realms. The target of sanctions may be simply the "state," but sanctions are better understood if targets are disaggregated.

Another difficulty is a dearth of careful case studies which disaggregate states and look beyond economic sanctions. Political arguments regarding the effects of sanctions are often anecdotal while scholarly analyses often offer inconsistent, if not contradictory, lessons.[15] The policy debate on whether and when to implement sanctions, and when to lift them, would be enriched by a careful understanding of the direct, indirect, and counterproductive consequences of sanctions on the domestic politics, economy, and society of a target state, as well as its neighbors.[16] This is why we undertook a detailed study of one case and hope that others will look at other cases in greater detail. The authors included in this volume focus on how sanctions actually worked (and did not work) in the South African case through an analysis of the immediate and long-term consequences of sanctions against South Africa and its neighbours.[17]

The piecemeal implementation of sanctions against apartheid South Africa, and the consequences of sanctions, cannot be understood without reference to the apartheid state and economy and the anti-apartheid movement. The following discussion places sanctions against South Africa in their historical-political context and recalls the many, sometimes contradictory, arguments that were made about the utility of sanctioning South Africa.

THE SOUTH AFRICAN CONTEXT

Racial discrimination in apartheid South Africa came into being gradually over the centuries of white settlement that began when the Dutch East India Company founded a colony on the Cape in 1652.[18] Dutch settlers were joined by English colonials who fought and won control of South Africa at the end of the nineteenth century. White control followed independence from Britain and the descendents of Dutch setters regained political power when the Afrikaner-dominated National Party (NP), which governed South Africa until 1994, won all-white elections in 1948.[19] One of the National Party's main goals was to codify centuries of *de facto* white domination. The legislative cornerstones of apartheid – including the Mixed Marriages Act of 1949 (prohibiting marriage between people of different races), the Population Registration Act and Group Areas Act, both of 1950, the Reservation of Separate Amenities and Bantu Education Bills both of 1953 – constructed distinct racial categories, and sought to ensure that racial groups were kept physically separate; and that black, Asian, and coloured South Africans receive inferior education and remain weak in political and economic terms. Only white South Africans were allowed to vote; black South Africans were physically relocated to separate African "homelands" created for that purpose, and black South Africans were permitted in white areas only for work under the pass laws that were used to control the movement of black South Africans.

The anti-apartheid movement had deep roots in South African politics but achieved widespread international recognition when the police met a peaceful protest against the pass-law system in Sharpeville with force on 21 March 1960: the South African police killed 69 and wounded more than 200 protesters. The government declared a state of emergency later that month and then banned anti-apartheid political organizations, notably, the ANC and the Pan-African Congress (PAC), detaining many of their leaders. Government repression continued and the armed wing of the banned ANC, Umkhonto we Sizwe, or MK, began a sabotage campaign. In July 1963, Nelson Mandela, who had been arrested earlier, and other members of the ANC were charged with leading guerrilla action and eventually given long prison terms.

State repression and anti-apartheid resistance escalated. Many members of the ANC and other banned groups who were not imprisoned left the country and organized resistance, including sanctions, from exile while those who remained worked underground in South Africa. Black workers became more militant and engaged in several large strikes in the 1970s. In June 1976, a student protest against "Bantu" education in Soweto was met by police force. At the end of several days of protest, 1000 students were killed by police and many more were injured. The practice of forced removals of black, Asian, and colored people so that white South Africans could obtain the most desirable areas for farming, residence, and business continued through the 1980s. Wealth continued to be concentrated in white hands, and by 1970 the richest 20 percent of the population owned 75 percent of the wealth. In 1980, though whites were about 15 percent of the population, they earned almost two-thirds of the income and controlled over 80 percent of the land. In 1989, Wilson and Ramphele wrote: "Thousands of South African babies are dying of malnutrition and associated diseases; two million children are growing up stunted for lack of sufficient calories in one of the few countries in the world that exports food."[20]

As the political and economic situation in South Africa became more charged, the National Party came under greater pressure and divisions among Afrikaners intensified. One of the most salient rifts was between *"verligtes"* and the *"verkramptes."* The *verligte*, or "the enlightened ones" were less conservative than the *verkramptes*, "the cramped ones." The *verkrampte* view was that the Afrikaner, in opposition to the other races and the English-speaking whites, alone deserved to govern South Africa and reforms should be resisted. *Verligtes* tended to support some accommodation with English-speaking white South Africans and were more willing to make reforms to ease world pressure on South Africa. Although *verligte* and *verkrampte* Afrikaners tended to agree on the fundamental questions of South African politics, namely, on preserving the political supremacy of the whites in South Africa, differences between the *verligtes* and the *verkramptes* grew severe enough to cause a split within the NP in 1968 leading to the formation of the *Herstigte* (Reconstituted) National Party the following year. The *verkrampte* HNP, led by former Cabinet Minister Albert Hertzog, failed to garner enough popular support to win seats in the House of Assembly in the 1970 and 1974 elections, but the most conservative Afrikaners gravitated toward the new party.

These divisions characterized white politics during the 1980s. Though Prime Minister P. W. Botha was known as someone willing to reform apartheid to save it, his NP government was still not reform minded enough to satisfy moderates within the NP, although it implemented too many reforms for those on the right. Botha concentrated political power within the government through organizational reforms in the late 1970s and government decision making became dominated by the military and the State Security Council. In 1982, another far-right group, the Conservative Party, emerged and took much of the HNP's support while also drawing from the NP. So despite political challenges from his right, Botha continued to reform apartheid even as he militarized the state, and in 1983 a new Constitution created separate parliamentary chambers for white, colored and Asian South Africans. The new arrangement, while allowing Asians and coloured South Africans limited representation for the first time, still did not allow the black majority the vote or to hold positions in the national government.

The new constitution sparked protest inside South Africa. The United Democratic Front (UDF), a coalition of religious, labor, and peace organizations formed in 1984, creating a powerful and well-organized umbrella for democratic activism. Also in 1984, the South African Defence Force was deployed, for the first time, in the black townships alongside the South African police to quell revolutionary activity. Later, as "unrest" intensified, the Botha government declared the first state of emergency in 1985. The states of emergency (partial July 1985 to March 1986; total June 1986 to December 1988) were essentially martial law: thousands were detained without trial, press reports were restricted, and both individuals and political organizations were banned (e.g. some 25 000 were detained from June 1986 to June 1987).[21]

The elite white opposition continued to be the right-wing Conservative Party. White liberals gravitated toward the Progressive Federal Party and later many of their members formed the Democratic Party in 1989. Within the National Party, more reform-minded members, who became known as the "New Nats," grew in numbers. F. W. de Klerk, the National Party leader of the Transvaal, rose to prominence as a voice for more reform, specifically suggesting some form of representation for black South Africans. De Klerk's hour came when P. W. Botha suffered a stroke in early 1989, and Botha was urged to step aside as party leader and then to stand aside in an election for president in September 1989. The NP campaigned for moderate reform: some representation for all under a system of jurisdiction for "own affairs." Over the 1980s, the NP drew smaller portions of the vote, going from 57 percent in 1981 to 48 percent in 1989: it lost support to both the left which campaigned for Western-style democracy and the right which argued for a return to strict apartheid. In the September 1989 election, the more-moderate de Klerk became president and in February 1990, de Klerk unbanned the ANC, PAC, Communist Party, and freed some political prisoners, including Nelson Mandela.

SANCTIONING SOUTH AFRICA

Outside South Africa a consensus slowly emerged that apartheid was wrong and ought to be eliminated; as Meg Voorhes, Nomazengele Mangaliso and David Black argue in this volume, the social movement and campaigns for sanctions helped increase the global awareness of apartheid and reinforced the pressures for greater sanctions. So, South Africa gradually became a pariah in the international community because of its policies of racial discrimination, political disenfranchisement, human rights abuses, and international aggression.[22] The first sanctions against South Africa, an embargo by India of exports to South Africa undertaken in July 1946, were followed by a range of economic, social, and political sanctions. A variety of actors – international organizations, states, corporations, universities, municipalities, unions, and individuals – gradually imposed sanctions, implementing a diverse range of voluntary and mandatory restrictions on relations with South Africa. By the late 1980s, there was a near consensus in the international community that at least some sanctions against apartheid South Africa were warranted and that the alternative was not partial reform, but truly democratic government.

Economic sanctions began to take shape slowly in the late 1940s, the first being India's comprehensive trade embargo against South Africa in 1946, which was followed by increasing diplomatic isolation in the 1950s and 1960s. At their height in the late 1980s, international sanctions touched nearly every facet of South African society from sport, to travel, to restrictions on technology transfer. Sanctions were not only undertaken by national governments and international organizations, but were also imposed by municipalities, small businesses, religious organizations, universities, international financial institutions, unions, and multinational corporations. The chronology at the end of this volume, compiled by the chapter authors, includes many key sanctions events.[23]

There were two principle policy aims of international sanctions against South Africa.[24] The primary policy goal was of course to force white South Africans to end apartheid. Mentioned much less frequently by sanctioners, the secondary goal, was to end South Africa's regional aggression, including its occupation of Namibia. In line with the primary goal, the conditions for lifting sanctions were actions by the South African government toward the easing of the harshest elements of apartheid and the initiation of negotiations for a new democratic dispensation. UN Security Council Resolution 182 of December 1963, which called for a voluntary arms embargo, called on South Africa to end discrimination and repression, release political prisoners and move toward a peaceful transformation. In Resolution 418 of November 1977, the Security Council recalled the South African government's aggression in the region and its "massive violence against and killings of the African people" and called on South Africa "urgently to end violence against the African people and to take urgent steps to eliminate apartheid and racial discrimination." In 1985, the Commonwealth Group called on the apartheid government to declare that the system of apartheid would be dismantled, end the state of emergency in South Africa, release those imprisoned or detained for their opposition to apartheid, lift the bans against political parties, and initiate "a process of dialogue . . . with a view to establishing a non-racial and representative government."[25] The US Comprehensive Anti-Apartheid Act, passed over President Reagan's veto in 1986, was "designed to bring about reforms in that system of government that will lead to the establishment of a nonracial democracy." The Act outlined six measures that it encouraged the government of South Africa to undertake:

(1) repeal the present state of emergency and respect the principle of equal justice under the law for citizens of all races;
(2) release Nelson Mandela, Govan Mbeki, Walter Sisulu, black trade union leaders, and all political prisoners;
(3) permit the free exercise by South Africans of all races of the right to form political parties, express political opinions, and otherwise participate in the political process;
(4) establish a timetable for the elimination of apartheid laws;
(5) negotiate with representatives of all racial groups in South Africa the future political system in South Africa; and
(6) end military and paramilitary activities aimed at neighboring states.[26]

The sanctions campaign against South Africa was, at its inception, a grass-roots and later an international effort that drew inspiration and direction from the anti-apartheid movement. To focus only on United Nations or individual government actions would miss much of the anti-apartheid activity. And in addition to sanctions, philanthropic foundations and many of the organizations that sanctioned South Africa provided financial and organizational assistance to the anti-apartheid movement. While the character of the South Africa sanctions campaign was *ad hoc*, it was part of a larger peace, justice, and democracy movement that mobilized millions all over the globe through the late 1970s to the early 1990s. The fact that the movement for sanctions against apartheid was linked to these other movements (e.g. European Nuclear Disarmament, Solidarity, Charter 77, Democracy in China, support for the Sandinistas, and the Nuclear Freeze) enabled organizers to reach broader audiences and allowed them to increase education and mobilization for further sanctions against South Africa.

The anti-apartheid sanctions regime was, in addition to being a patchwork of both voluntary and mandatory prohibitions undertaken by a multitude and variety of actors, extremely "leaky" – goods still found their way into and out of South Africa and many white South Africans were able to retain their individual contacts with the rest of the world. For example, though the US, Denmark, and France prohibited imports of South African coal in 1985, South Africa's coal exports grew overall and South Africa became the major supplier of coal imports to the European Economic Community in 1986.[27] This was also the case with regard to other commodities such as gold – while sanctioned by some, South Africa was sometimes able to find other buyers, though they were often forced to sell at an "apartheid discount." Overall, though South African trade fell dramatically with some trading partners (trade with Britain fell by 15 percent in 1986; trade with Germany fell 25 percent; 1987 trade with the US fell by 40 percent that same year) trade with others grew (trade with Japan increased 20 percent in 1987). And though some countries prohibited air travel with South Africa, many South Africans were able to fly via other countries. In addition, several important mineral commodities, considered strategic in the West, were never sanctioned to any significant degree. So, sanctions never completely isolated South Africa or white South Africans.

The end of sanctions was also gradual: some sanctions were relaxed after the release of Nelson Mandela in February 1990. The UN Security Council ended sanctions, including the arms embargo, only in May 1994 a month after the successful completion of all-race multi-party elections in South Africa. Because the South African government and political elites often had warning before sanctions were imposed – in some cases years of discussion preceded their imposition – they also had time to prepare for and react to any boycotts and restrictions. The length of time that sanctions were considered and imposed is one of the most important factors in understanding the consequences of sanctions in this case: the South African government and industries had time to reform their practices in response to sanctions and also to engage in resistance or sanctions busting.

THE CONTROVERSIAL ROLE OF SANCTIONS IN THE TRANSITION

When de Klerk freed Nelson Mandela and other political prisoners and unbanned political parties in 1990, the NP government continued a process of reform and secret negotiations that had begun under P. W. Botha. Over the next several years, negotiations among South Africans for a new Interim Constitution, the first democratic vote, and the procedures for transition, stopped and started, coinciding with continued government repression and the activities of a shadowy group of military and police attached to a "third force" of provocateurs. Even after the elections of April 1994 where all South Africans could vote for the first time, white resistance to democratization continued, and some parts of the government controlled by true believers in apartheid put up roadblocks to reform.

What explains the character of this long, and still incomplete transition? Why did the apartheid government begin along the road to reform and ultimately the handover of power via the vote? Given the massive violence that many expected, why was the transition relatively peaceful?[28] And, given the many forces for change at work in this complex situation, what role did sanctions play?

Taking the long view, Robert Price has argued that change is due to industrialization and a "trialectic": "the interaction of three elements – growing domestic opposition to racial rule, efforts of the state to preserve white minority control, and international pressure – gave rise to a process of debilitating economic crisis and intensifying political conflict that placed immense pressure on the South African state."[29] The engine of black politicization was, according to Price, industrialization:

Since the end of World War II, the South African system of white supremacy has been increasingly undermined by fundamental incompatibilities built into its system of racial rule. As the country's economic system became increasingly industrial, it came to depend on an ever larger and more urbanized black proletariat. In South Africa as in every other society, the social conditions of industrial production and urban life create a milieu conducive to collective organization and political activism. Thus everywhere that industrial modernization has ocurred, erstwhile peasants have shed their passivity and launched ever more effective demands for political inclusion.[30]

Herman Giliomee has argued that demographic factors did not favor continued white dominance in every sphere. Giliomee notes that throughout much of the twentieth century, until 1960, whites were about 20 percent of the total population of South Africa. By 1960 whites were in relative decline and by 1985 the white portion of the population had fallen to about 15 percent. "An acute shortage of white manpower began to develop in both public and private sectors. By the 1970s the shortage of whites increasingly forced employers in the private sector to breach the industrial colour bar to meet the need for skilled and semi-skilled manpower."[31]

Timothy Sisk argues that the negotiated transition occurred because the anti-apartheid movement was able to create the conditions for a "hurting stalemate." Moderates among the two sides were forced to cooperate because neither could win outright: the anti-apartheid movement and the NP had an interest in negotiations toward a more peaceful order. Sisk says the determinant of change was the recognition by all of their interdependence and the shift in power to relative parity between the black majority and the government.[32]

Others argue that change was only possible because reformist elites rose to prominence in the NP during the late 1980s: most could hardly imagine the hardliner "securocrats" who dominated the NP government until the late 1980s making a public opening toward the ANC, PAC, and Communist Party.[33] Jung and Shapiro note numerous reasons why reformers may become prominant in authoritarian governments: "A list would include sanctions and other external pressures, fissures within their own ranks (perhaps as the result of the collapse of their legitimating ideology), the growth of a normative commitment to democracy among members of the government, intractable economic problems, and civil unrest that threatens to spiral out of control."[34] South Africa was certainly subject to these forces. And as several scholars have noted, once authoritarian elites begin down the path of reform, it is often difficult to control the reform process.[35]

Finally, anti-apartheid activists emphasize their own role in winning democracy for South Africa. In their view, whites were forced to give up apartheid. Anti-apartheid activists stress the determined action of many groups over decades – not only the ANC but communists, the white feminists in the Black Sash, rent boycotters, trade unionists, and young lions in the townships engaged in mass action. The ANC saw sanctions as a tool of limited but important utility and sanctions thus became one of the four pillars of the ANC struggle against apartheid – a supplement to mass action, armed struggle, and diplomatic isolation.

While sanctions were underway, there were diverse interpretations of their potential and actual impact on South Africa's domestic and international behavior. Most in the anti-apartheid movement favored sanctions and endorsed the call by ANC President Albert Luthuli for sanctions in 1958. Despite the difficulties of polling a population on the question of sanctions in a context where advocating sanctions was sometimes a criminal offense, there were some studies of South African's attitudes toward sanctions. In general, surveys showed that black South Africans had qualified support for sanctions, though only a minority supported sanctions if they resulted in "serious" unemployment.[36]

By the late 1980s, most of the anti-apartheid movement regarded sanctions as crucial. The ANC office in London dedicated resources to coordinating and encouraging sanctions against South Africa, with the effort headed by important ANC officials.[37] ANC leader Oliver Tambo, in a communication to Nelson Mandela regarding his secret negotiations with P. W. Botha in the 1980s, told Mandela to go ahead with the talks. Tambo said, "Look, there is only one problem: don't manoeuvre yourself into a situation where we have to abandon sanctions. That's the key problem. We are very concerned that we should not get stripped of our weapons of struggle, and the most important of these is sanctions. That is the trump card with which we can mobilize international opinion and pull governments over to our side."[38] Of the anti-apartheid groups, only the Inkatha Freedom Party, founded in 1975, took a strong anti-sanctions position in the mid-1980s. Inkatha's leader, Mangosuthu Buthelezi argued: "Without a means for survival – because blacks in South Africa are cash-dependent – their grinding poverty and degradation will continue unabated. . . . Divestment will not help the struggle for liberation; it will hinder it."[39]

Some governments (including members of the OAU and the majority of the General Assembly) felt sanctions were essential and that they would probably be effective, and others (for instance the governments of the US and UK) felt that a policy of constructive engagement would bring about change. Andrew Young, US Ambassador to the UN under President Carter, argued that "Economic sanctions looked like an easy answer, but South Africa is one of the most self-sufficient nations in the world. It could get along without us. . . . If we cut off investments, we would lose jobs in this country and we wouldn't necessarily help Blacks in that country."[40]

Opinion about sanctions among white South Africans was also divided. In the late 1980s, a majority of white South Africans tended to see sanctions as a serious problem that would have a very harmful effect on the South African economy, though a somewhat smaller portion also tended to believe that South Africa could cope with sanctions.[41] Surveys of white South Africans in 1986, 1988, and 1990 showed that a majority thought the South African economy was not "strong enough" to prevent economic sanctions from hurting. In a survey of white South Africans in 1992, 92 percent of respondents said the South African economy had been hurt by sanctions.[42]

The apartheid power structure, and the intellectuals who supported it, discounted sanctions and in general tended to argue that sanctions would not work or would have a limited effect on South Africa, and they produced numerous studies to prove how sanctions would only impoverish black South Africans.[43] They argued that sanctions would jeopardize economic growth in South Africa and that "it is only continued industrial growth and the widening of black economic empowerment, that such growth involves, which will make the desired and needed political change possible at all."[44] Those whites who led the long negotiations with the ANC, and other groups who sought to end apartheid, have little reason to deviate from that position: to acknowledge the coercive effect of sanctions diminishes their claim to a benevolent and voluntary movement toward conciliation.

As Tshidiso Maloka shows in Chapter 9 below, estimates of the possible employment consequences of sanctions made inside South Africa during the sanctions era were highly politicized and predicted severe job losses, on the order of millions of workers. This was not an insignificant fear since overall unemployment was already growing throughout the 1970s and 1980s. In 1986 South Africa's Federated Chamber of Industries predicted that "medium intensity" sanctions would lead to increasing unemployment by over 200 000 in the first 18 months to two years and 685 000 over five years, while comprehensive sanctions could lead to increased unemployment of over 300 000 in the shorter term going up to 1 135 013 jobs lost over five years.[45] In 1987, Bethlehem argued that intensified sanctions in the late 1980s would lead to an increase of two million unemployed workers, mostly in the category of unskilled labor (since import substitution industries would create higher skilled jobs) by the year 2000.[46]

Studies of sanctions undertaken while apartheid was still in place suffered from both a scarcity of information and the biases induced by strong political and ethical commitments. Scholars also faced the problem of doing their analysis midstream – before the processes of change had come to conclusion.[47] Tom Lodge made one of the most interesting analyzes of the potential political effect of sanctions. He argued in 1989 that "total economic embargo would leave the vital decisions in the hands of armed bureaucrats on the one side and world statesmen on the other, and be a more costly and less beneficial measure than an attritional and cumulative process of partial though severe sanctions."[48] Partial sanctions, according to Lodge, held a better prospect of facilitating a peaceful and democratic political transition. Lodge's argument regarding "severe but partial sanctions" bears quoting at length:

> With continuing gold and mineral sales, South Africa would continue to have access to the foreign currency increasingly necessary to evade sanctions on vital imports. . . . South Africa would remain dependent on limited forms of foreign economic relationship. The fear of jeopardizing these might serve to dissuade the administration from instituting a complete clampdown on internal opponents, as well as curbing large-scale military interventions in the region, at least as far as Commonwealth states are concerned. Trade unions might also benefit in the short term from whatever employment is created by labour intensive import substitution, as well as maintaining the loyalties of their following through defensive struggles over conditions and job security. . . .
>
> Political divisions within the National Party's upper echelons could be important, in that a sanctions-induced import-substitution boom might enhance the political leverage of reformist business circles. Diplomats and financiers would continue to have a strategic importance in arresting, delaying or evading the application of further sanctions. All this could help check the development of a hegemony of soldiers and policemen. The radicalization of the National Party's white liberal opponents could gather momentum, and help to sustain the presence of a socially conciliatory local black leadership (however difficult it might be for it to control its mass constituency). . . .
>
> Sanctions will enhance the importance of external actors in the securing of black liberation. Many of these actors will direct their efforts at the promotion of compromise and negotiation.[49]

On the other hand, Merle Lipton argued that reform would be the result of internal political decisions and other domestic factors and she argued that "continued incremental sanctions seem unlikely to unseat the government, and more likely to impede rather than to accelerate reform (i.e. deracialization)."[50] Lipton believed sanctions could doom South Africa to increased polarization: "If sanctions have their intended effects, economic decline could erode those economic bonds that have drawn together the diverse people of (what has become) South Africa, and strengthen the fissiparous tendencies, thus making more possible partition, against a background of growing violence throughout the region."[51] Still others argued that sanctions were ineffective since the embargoes and boycotts of South Africa were not total.[52]

While passions have cooled and there is more information, evidence is still only partially available since many documents from the apartheid era have disappeared.[53] Academic assessments of sanctions following the transition to majority rule in South Africa in 1994 have generally been more favorable than Lipton's, though there is still disagreement on exactly how sanctions worked.[54]

The next chapter is a more detailed exploration of the *existing theories and models of sanctions* and offers a framework for analyzing sanctions. Neta Crawford and Audie Klotz argue for a framework that focuses on direct, indirect, and counterproductive effects of sanctions at the multiple sites of their potential impact. They widen the analytical perspective by looking beyond economic sanctions and consequences to social and strategic sanctions. Each of the subsequent chapters, making use of new evidence and interviews, examines a particular population or sector of the state, economy, or society targeted or affected by international sanctions against South Africa.

In Part II, three chapters examine the effects of *strategic sanctions* aimed at the vital military and economic capabilities of the target. Neta Crawford shows how the conventional arms embargo gradually hurt South Africa's war-making capacity even while resistance led to military industrialization. David Fig, in analyzing nuclear sanctions against South Africa, emphasizes how Pretoria managed to circumvent nuclear sanctions through their integration in the international nuclear industry. In the following chapter Crawford shows how despite its porousness, a leaky oil embargo became extremely expensive for South Africa.

In Part III, four chapters focus on *economic sanctions*. Meg

Voorhes surveys the US college and university divestment move-ment and its role in promoting even more biting sanctions. Mzamo Mangaliso compares disinvestment to the corporate codes of conduct adopted by a number of multinational corporations in the 1970s and 1980s. Xavier Carim, Audie Klotz, and Olivier Lebleu exam-ine financial sanctions, in particular looking at the sources and con-sequences of South Africa's debt crisis in the late 1980s. They show how financial restrictions undermined business confidence in South Africa and sharpened divisions among the white elite. Tshidiso Maloka assesses the impact of trade sanctions and disinvestment on black workers. He argues that though employment for black workers worsened in the 1980s, this cannot be attributed entirely to sanctions because the underlyng economic structure of apartheid accounted for black workers' vulnerability. Maloka also describes the debates over the number of jobs that might be lost due to sanctions and how arguments about black workers' vulnerability changed as the scope of sanctions increased.

In Part IV, three chapters examine *social sanctions*. Audie Klotz investigates South Africa's diplomatic isolation, showing how sanc-tions undermined apartheid and bolstered the legitimacy of the transnational anti-apartheid movement. David Black explores the impact of the sport boycott and Nomazengele Mangaliso examines the boycott of South African culture and academics. Black and Mangaliso emphasize the educational role that sanctions played inside and outside South Africa, and the fact that both sport and culture were points of Afrikaner pride and vulnerability.

In Part V, the last two chapters draw some broader implications. Gilbert Khadiagala explores the *vulnerability of the Southern Afri-can region* to sanctions against South Africa. He shows that econ-omic sanctions hurt the region but also prompted regional economic cooperation that has outlasted apartheid. In the concluding chap-ter Klotz synthesizes the evidence from the South African case and explores the *implications for other uses of sanctions*. She concludes that strategic, economic, and social sanctions may be a useful tool of international politics, though we cannot expect them to work in all contexts.

Notes

1. Audie Klotz made extensive comments as did the book's chapter authors and Tom Biersteker, Jacklyn Cock, Jendayi Frazer, Arlene Getz, Frene Ginwala, Willard Johnson, Norma Kriger, and Newell Stultz.
2. For literature reviews see D. A. Baldwin, *Economic Statecraft* (Princeton, NJ: Princeton University, 1985); G. C. Hufbauer, J. J. Schott, and K. A. Elliott, *Economic Sanctions Reconsidered: History and Current Policy,* 2d ed. (Washington, DC: Institute for International Economics, 1990); L. L. Martin, *Coercive Cooperation: Explaining Multilateral Economic Sanctions* (Princeton, NJ: Princeton University Press, 1992); W. H. Kaempfer and A. D. Lowenberg, *International Economic Sanctions: A Public Choice Perspective* (Boulder, CO: Westview, 1992); K. R. Nossal, *Rain Dancing: Sanctions in Canadian and Australian Foreign Policy* (Toronto: University of Toronto Press, 1994); A. Klotz, *Norms in International Relations: The Struggle against Apartheid* (Ithaca, NY: Cornell University Press, 1995); I. Eland, "Economic Sanctions as Tools of Foreign Policy," in D. Cortright and G. A. Lopez, eds., *Economic Sanctions: Panacea or Peacebuilding in a Post-Cold War World?* (Boulder, CO: Westview, 1995), pp. 29–42; M. Mastanduno, *Economic Containment: CoCom and the Politics of East-West Trade* (Ithaca, NY: Cornell University Press, 1992); E. S. Rogers, "Using Economic Sanctions to Control Regional Conflicts," *Security Studies* 4 (1996), pp. 43–72; R. A. Pape, "Why Economic Sanctions Do Not Work," *International Security* 22 (1997), pp. 90–136; J. Stremlau, "Sharpening International Sanctions: Toward a Stronger Role for the United Nations," Report to the Carnegie Commission on Preventing Deadly Conflict (New York: Carnegie, November 1996).
3. See Baldwin, *Economic Statecraft,* pp. 55–7.
4. Mobil Corporation, "Sanctions: The Last Resort," advertisement appearing on the Op-Ed page of the *New York Times*, 15 February 1996.
5. M. P. Doxey, *Economic Sanctions and International Enforcement* (London: Oxford University Press/Royal Institute for International Affairs, 1971), p. 57. However, Baldwin, *Economic Statecraft,* pp. 154–65, notes additional goals of the sanctions against Italy, leading him to a less critical overall assessment.
6. T. C. Morgan and V. L. Schwebach, "Fools Suffer Gladly: The Use of Economic Sanctions in International Crises," *International Studies Quarterly* 41 (1997), pp. 27–50: 28, 47.
7. Pape, "Why Economic Sanctions Do Not Work," pp. 106–7.
8. T. G. Weiss, D. Cortright, G. A. Lopez, and L. Minear, eds., *Political Gain and Civilian Pain: Humanitarian Impacts of Economic Sanctions* (Oxford: Rowman and Littlefield, 1997).
9. This is frequently the argument of policymakers who oppose sanctions (e.g. President Clinton's refrain about trading with China) but it is also used by multinational corporations with business interests in potential sanctions targets.
10. This connection between growth and liberalization has been challenged. See Leslie Elliott Armijo, "Mixed Blessing: Foreign Capital Flows and

Democracy in Emerging Markets," in L. E. Armijo, ed., *Financial Globalization and Emerging Markets* (Basingstoke, UK: Macmillan, 1999).

11. Pape, "Why Economic Sanctions Do Not Work." More rare is Jentleson's view that "optimally, sanctions may impose substantial economic costs and bring significant political influence. But they never have caused a nation-state to surrender. Conversely, while they may fall well short of their instrumental objectives, they rarely have absolutely no impact on the target state." B. Jentleson, *Pipeline Politics: The Complex Political Economy of East–West Energy Trade* (Ithaca, NY: Cornell University Press, 1986), p. 31.

12. For example, sanctions are "the deliberate, government-inspired withdrawal, or threat of withdrawal, of customary trade or financial relations" in Hufbauer, Schott, and Elliott, *Economic Sanctions Reconsidered*, p. 2. Alternatively, Doxey, *Economic Sanctions and International Enforcement*, p. 1, sees sanctions as primarily norm enforcement mechanisms – the means international organizations use to enforce multilateral standards. And sanctions have also been described as an aspect of a range of non-violent alternatives to military force (M. P. Doxey, *International Sanctions in Contemporary Perspective* [New York: St. Martin's, 1987], pp. 10–12).

13. Thus, sanctions only partially contrast with positive inducements – such as offers of military assistance, loans, participation in cultural and scientific communities, or technology transfers. Baldwin, in *Economic Statecraft*, takes the view that sanctions are one form of economic statecraft that includes economic warfare and foreign aid. See pp. 35–6 and 55. Also see tables 2 and 3 on pp. 41 and 42 of *Economic Statecraft* where Baldwin lists both positive and negative sanctions.

14. Sanctions may also be imposed to meet goals within the sanctioner and may "succeed in galvanizing public support for the sender government, either by inflaming patriotic fever . . . or by quenching the public thirst for action . . . ." Hufbauer, Schott, and Elliott, *Economic Sanctions Reconsidered*, p. 3. On the methodological difficulties of measuring the success of sanctions see Jentleson, *Pipeline Politics*, p. 31, and Baldwin *Economic Statecraft*.

15. Hufbauer, Schott, and Elliott in *Economic Sanctions Reconsidered* attempt to go beyond generalizations based on anecdote by quantifying the effects of sanctions in 116 cases of sanctions since World War I. The study has impressive breadth and their data has been widely used, notably by Martin, *Coercive Cooperation*. Concerns remain, however, about their methodology, especially the coding of cases. See Pape, "Why Economic Sanctions Do Not Work," who systematically disputes their coding and their statistical results, and Jentleson, *Pipeline Politics*.

16. The sanctions literature usually focuses on the "state." But one can obviously think of boycotts of goods and services provided by local governments, individual industries, multinational corporations, and retail outlets as sanctions.

17. The bulk of our attention is on the questions of how sanctions may or may not influence policy and on the unintended, sometimes counterproductive, consequences of sanctions. Though we occasionally touch

upon related issues such as the questions of when and why actors chose to adopt sanctions, how actors get other actors to join in isolating a target, and how to encourage and enforce international compliance with sanctions efforts. Several other works focus on the politics behind the adoption of sanctions, and the problem of enforcing compliance. See, for example: Baldwin, *Economic Statecraft*; Nossal, *Rain Dancing*; Klotz, *Norms in International Relations*, and Martin, *Coercive Cooperation*.

18. There are dozens of excellent histories. For short introductions see P. Maylam, *A History of the African People of South Africa: From the Early Iron Age to the 1970s* (London: Croom Helm, 1986); L. Thompson, *The Political Mythology of Apartheid* (New Haven: Yale University Press, 1985).

19. National Party governments were led by D. F. Malan (1948–54), J. G. Strijdom (1954–58), H. F. Verwoerd (1958–66), B. J. Vorster (1966–78), P. W. Botha (1978–89), and F. W. de Klerk (1989–94).

20. F. Wilson and M. Ramphele, *Uprooting Poverty: The South African Challenge* (Cape Town: David Philip, 1989), p. 4.

21. D. Webster and M. Friedman, "Repression and the State of Emergency: June 1987–March 1989," in *South African Review* 5 (Johannesburg: Raven Press, 1989), pp. 16–41.

22. See R. E. Bissell, *Apartheid and International Organizations* (Boulder, CO: Westview, 1977); Klotz, *Norms in International Relations*; United Nations, *The United Nations and Apartheid: 1948–1994* (New York: United Nations, 1994).

23. For discussion of early sanctions see D. G. Clarke, "Economic Sanctions on South Africa: Past Evidence and Future Potential," *Economic Sanctions Against South Africa* (Geneva: International University Exchange Fund: 1980). Other lists of sanctions are found in Hufbauer, Schott, and Elliott, *Economic Sanctions Reconsidered*, cases 62–2 and 85–1; T. U. Mozia, "Chronology of Arms Embargoes Against South Africa," in G. W. Shepard, Jr., ed., *Effective Sanctions On South Africa: The Cutting Edge of Economic Intervention* (New York: Praeger, 1991), pp. 97–108; S. Ferguson and P. Sluiter, "Existing Sanctions," in J. Hanlon, ed., *South Africa: The Sanctions Report Document and Statistics* (London: Commonwealth Secretariat, 1990), pp. 3–72; M. Lipton, *Sanctions and South Africa: The Dynamics of Economic Isolation* (London: Economist Intelligence Unit, 1988).

24. For the moment leaving aside the possibility that some sanctions were imposed simply to placate domestic constituencies.

25. "The Nassau Commonwealth Accord on Southern Africa, October 1985."

26. United States Public Law 99–440 "Comprehensive Anti-Apartheid Act of 1986," sec. 101.

27. J. Leger, "Coal Mining: Past Profits, Current Crisis?" in S. Gelb, ed., *South Africa's Economic Crisis* (Cape Town: David Philip, 1991), pp. 128–55: 128.

28. The transition was not entirely peaceful. Thousands died in violence between the African National Congress and the Inkatha Freedom Party. This "black on black" violence that was actually fueled by South Afri-

can military and police assistance to Inkatha. The Government also continued to use force against anti-apartheid activists and dragged its feet on the release of all political prisoners, while white right-wing groups escalated their own terrorist activities against both black South Africans and the white state.

29. R. M. Price, *The Apartheid State in Crisis: Political Transformation in South Africa, 1975–1990* (Oxford: Oxford University Press, 1991), p. 7.
30. Ibid., p. 5.
31. H. Giliomee, "South Africa's Democratic Surprise," *Global Forum Series Occasional Paper 96–01.1* (Duke University, April 1996), pp. 4–5.
32. T. Sisk, *Democratization in South Africa: The Elusive Social Contract* (Princeton, NJ: Princeton University Press, 1995).
33. Though it was the Botha government that initiated secret negotiations with Nelson Mandela while he was imprisoned. For discussions of this see N. Mandela, *Long Walk to Freedom* (New York: Random House, 1994), and A. Sparks, *Tomorrow is Another Country: The Inside Story of South Africa's Negotiated Revolution* (Sandton, South Africa: Struik, 1994).
34. C. Jung and I. Shapiro, "South Africa's Negotiated Transition: Democracy, Opposition, and the New Constitutional Order," *Politics & Society* 23 (1995), pp. 269–308: 278–9.
35. For example, S. P. Huntington, *The Third Wave: Democratization in the Late Twentieth Century* (Norman: University of Oklahoma Press, 1991).
36. See T. Maloka "Sanctions Hurt but Apartheid Kills: The Sanctions Campaign and Black Workers," in this volume. Also see M. Voorhes, *Black South Africans' Attitudes on Sanctions and Divestment* (Washington: Investor Responsibility Research Center, 1988); and M. Orkin, "Politics, Social Change, and Black Attitudes on Sanctions," in M. Orkin, ed., *Sanctions Against Apartheid* (Cape Town: David Philip, 1989), pp. 80–102.
37. Most notably, Frene Ginwala who later became the new South Africa's first Speaker of Parliament in 1994, coordinated the oil embargo effort from London.
38. Tambo quoted in Sparks, *Tomorrow is Another Country*, p. 65.
39. M. Buthelezi, "Discerning the Divestment Debate," in S. P. Sethi, ed., *The South African Quagmire: In Search of a Peaceful Path to Democratic Pluralism* (Cambridge, MA: Ballinger, 1987), pp. 165–69: 165.
40. Young quoted in the *Chicago Tribune*, 6 February 1978, p. 1, cited in M. S. Daoudi and M. S. Dajani, *Economic Sanctions: Ideas and Experience* (London: Routledge and Kegan Paul, 1983), p. 182. The Reagan administration coined the term "constructive engagement" and developed this policy in the early 1980s.
41. J. Hofmeyer, *The Impact of Sanctions on South Africa II. White's Political Attitudes* (Washington, DC: Investor Responsibility Research Center, 1990).
42. A. van Nieuwkerk and A. du Pisani, *What Do We Think? A Survey of White Opinion on Foreign Policy Issues*, no. 6 (Johannesburg: South African Institute of International Affairs, 1992), pp. 32–4.

43. For example, South African Institute of International Affairs, *South Africa and Sanctions: Genesis and Prospects* (Johannesburg: South African Institute of International Affairs, 1979); A. Spandau, *Economic Boycott Against South Africa: Normative and Factual Issues* (Cape Town: Juta, 1979); Sanlam, "Sanctions and the South African Economy," in *Sanlam's Economic Review* (February 1979), pp. 1–12.

44. R. Bethlehem, "South Africa's Imperative for Growth," in S. Magoba, J. Kane-Berman and R. Bethlehem, *Sanctions and the Alternatives* (Johannesburg: South African Institute of Race Relations, 1988), pp. 1–13: 2.

45. Federated Chamber of Industries, *The Effect of Sanctions on Unemployment and Production in South Africa* (Pretoria: FCI Information Services, 1986.), cited in C. Meth, "Sanctions and Unemployment," in Orkin, ed., *Sanctions Against Apartheid,* pp. 240–52: 250.

46. Bethlehem, "South Africa's Imperative for Growth," pp. 7–8.

47. One of most comprehensive yet concise studies of the economic impact of sanctions against South Africa was Lipton, *Sanctions and South Africa*. Other important studies undertaken while sanctions were in effect include Hanlon, ed., *South Africa: The Sanctions Report*; Orkin, ed., *Sanctions Against Apartheid*; R. Edgar, ed., *Sanctioning Apartheid* (Trenton, NJ: Africa World Press, 1990); Shepard, ed., *Effective Sanctions on South Africa*; Heider Ali Khan, *The Political Economy of Sanctions Against Apartheid* (London: Lynne Rienner, 1989); also Investor Responsibility Resource Center reports on South Africa.

48. Tom Lodge, "Sanctions and Black Political Organizations," in Orkin, ed., *Sanctions Against Apartheid*, pp. 34–51.

49. Ibid., passim, pp. 49–51.

50. Lipton, *Sanctions and South Africa*, p. 122.

51. Ibid.

52. S. Landgren, *Embargo Disimplemented: South Africa's Military Industry* (Oxford: Oxford University Press, 1989); A. J. Klinghoffer, *Oiling the Wheels of Apartheid: Exposing South Africa's Secret Oil Trade* (London: Lynne Rienner, 1989).

53. J. Pearce, "Search for Missing Cabinet Papers," *Weekly Mail and Guardian* 12, no. 21 (24 May 1996), p. 8.

54. For example, see J. Davis, "Sanctions and Apartheid: The Economic Challenge to Discrimination," in Cortright and Lopez, eds., *Economic Sanctions*, pp. 173–84.

2 How Sanctions Work: A Framework for Analysis
Neta C. Crawford and Audie Klotz

How do sanctions work, if they work at all? Do they convince actors to change their behavior and/or beliefs, or do they primarily alter the capabilities of states? Alternatively, when do restrictions of customary interactions provoke defensive isolation or retaliation? The conventional wisdom, mirroring the League of Nations concept of collective security, assumes that sanctions must be comprehensive to be successful. For collective security to work, a potential aggressor must believe that all or most other states will rally against it. Similarly, scholars of international trade highlight the financial incentives governments and corporations have to sell restricted commodities to embargoed states, evident in the long historical record of sanctions "busting". Does imposition and enforcement of sanctions have to be comprehensive, "watertight," to be effective, or can "leaky" sanctions influence the target? Which types of sanctions are best suited for particular purposes? Are there "smart" sanctions that can be focused on decision makers and have little adverse affect on non-target populations within the target state and neighboring countries?

Theories of sanctions pose divergent answers to these questions. Many limit their analysis to *negative* and *economic* consequences of sanctions on *states* narrowly conceived. Others suggest broad influence but do not show the precise mechanisms that produced those effects. In this chapter, therefore, we synthesize the existing sanctions literature in order to establish a framework for evaluating the consequences of sanctions. We cluster the arguments into two broad types. The first set consists of sometimes explicit, but more often implicit, theories of influence. The second set of arguments uses these theories of influence as background assumptions to develop hypotheses about the intended and unintended consequences of sanctions. Making the assumptions and arguments of this literature more transparent, we propose a framework for understanding the direct, indirect, and counterproductive consequences of sanctions.

25

THEORIES OF INFLUENCE

Theories of influence have different assumptions about actors, mechanisms of influence, the conditions that increase the likelihood of success, and the primary location of influence. Most theories assume a single mechanism, such as compelling the target to comply with the wishes of the sanctioner. But there have been attempts at multidimensional models. For example, Newell Stultz conceptualized three paths of change: under the "revolutionary" model, sanctions weaken a regime so that it may more easily be overthrown; in the "thumbscrew" approach, the costs of pursuing a policy are steadily increased to the point where targets have more to gain by change than by holding fast to the sanctioned policy; and in the process-oriented "evolutionary" model, a "combination of both carrots and sticks ... effect specific limited changes ... [that] work through the target's social and political systems" to gradually bring about the desired change.[1] Alternatively, Chien-pin Li, building on Herbert Kelman's work, identifies three possible processes: "compliance," where targets conform to gain rewards or avoid punishment; "identification," where targets want to be more closely associated with the initiator of sanctions; and "internalization," where targets accept the desired behavior because it is congruent with their own value system.[2] Li then adds two contextual variables – structural (degree of asymmetrical penetration) and the similarity of political ideology – to predict which model of sanctions linkage is more applicable.

We have reviewed the wealth of theories, hypotheses, and models of influence implicit in the sanctions literature and have distilled them into four models of influence. Table 2.1 summarizes the assumptions of these models which we call compellance, normative communication, resource denial, and political fracture.

The *compellance* model may be the most widely held view of how sanctions could work. Like the parallel literature in international security, this approach assumes that the locus of decision making and change resides within the self-interested, rational utility-maximizing decision making elite of the state who respond to actual or anticipated changes in the ratio of costs and risks to benefits. A rational decision making elite ought to re-evaluate the costs of pursuing its goals in light of the costs of actual or anticipated sanctions.[3] How elites assess the threat and costs of sanctions will depend on a number of factors, including bureaucratic politics, the psychology of key policymakers, and their perceptions and misper-

Table 2.1   Models of influence and their assumptions

	Actors	Mechanism of influence	Conditions for success	Primary site of influence
Compellance	decision making elite is rational	increase costs and/or decrease benefits	at least partial economic and military interdependence	elite decision makers
Normative Communication	decision making elite cares about norms	persuasion	elites clearly understand normative arguments	elite decision makers
Resource Denial	elites are stubborn: states need material capabilities	decrease target capabilities by limiting important resources	the behavior sanctioners seek to alter requires material resources; at least partial economic and military interdependence	institutional structures of the target government; economy
Political Fracture	government depends on elite and popular support	foster a legitimation crisis that leads to increased dissent or revolution	fragile elite; external ability to support groups that oppose the target government	elite decision makers and civil society

ception of the intentions and credibility of those who would impose sanctions.[4] For sanctions to work, they must threaten or actually impose higher costs than the benefits of pursuing a particular policy, and the threat and consequences of suffering must be credible and sustainable. In other words, sanctioners must be able to damage the target, the target must recognize this threat, and once sanctioned, target decision makers must experience damage.[5] If the target is autarkic in military and economic resources, and therefore relatively invulnerable, sanctions will not work.

The *normative communication* model, articulated more or less implicitly by many policymakers, suggests that elites and populations respond to moral arguments. Sanctioners working within this model seek to establish international norms by punishing a state for breaking global standards and multilateral rules – targets are punished for actions that are considered wrong.[6] Sanctioners aim to affect the worldviews of the target's elite decision makers and general population. Thus, for sanctions to work, decision makers must understand

and be persuaded by normative arguments. According to Li, actors "who share an ideological perspective will tend to agree on abstract principles, which facilitates mutual communication and cooperation."[7] Normative arguments may reframe issues in ways that delegitimize particular policies or actions, or they may change elite perceptions of self-interests and identities.[8] Sanctions work by making sure normative arguments are heard: they "send a clear signal" making it clear to targets that those who imposed the restrictions mean their normative arguments and are willing to pay the costs of imposing boycotts.[9] The act of sanctioning becomes more important than the costs to the target state or the effects of sanctions on a specific military or economic sector.[10]

The *resource denial* model assumes that elites and populations do not respond to compellance or normative communication. Rather, the behavior and policies of states change when declining capabilities prevent pursuit of objectionable policies; sanctions work by depriving the state of its ability to act. Yet some behaviors that the international community has sought to influence – for instance, the protection of human rights or the conduct of free elections – require relatively few material resources. Thus, for sanctions to succeed, the target's behavior must require resources that the sanctioner is able to withhold. Resource denial will not work if embargoes are porous or the target is self-sufficient.

The *political fracture* model also emphasizes the capacities of governments but stresses social and political capabilities – legitimacy and civil society – more than material capabilities. This model views the "state" as a collection of actors and institutions, suggesting that altering elite decisions is less important than manipulating the broader balance of political authority inside the target. Sanctions can produce a revolt or revolution within the target because state authority depends as much on internal support and voluntary submission as it does on repressive power. International pressure may produce or exacerbate a legitimation crisis by inflicting economic hardship that results in political "disintegration" or revolution. If the masses or powerful elites lose faith in the government, then they are likely to revolt, which in turn should bring about a policy change. Critics of this view, which Galtung calls the "naive theory" of sanctions, maintain that only the most economically vulnerable and politically unstable targets will suffer enough to change their policies, thus dramatically limiting the usefulness of sanctions.[11]

Kaempfer and Lowenberg articulate a more complex version of

the fracture model, arguing that "the effects of sanctions in the target country ... depends on interest group politics."[12] Sanctions and other shocks to the target may reduce the income of the advocates of objectionable policies. As a result, "Sanctions affect political processes in the target country not only through their income effects, but perhaps more significantly, through their impacts on each interest group's effectiveness in organizing the collective action of its members."[13] The economic and political consequences of sanctions and sanctions busting may be one of the sources of increasing political opportunities for social movements.[14] On the other hand, sanctions can also harm those in the opposition who seek to change target government policy. Thus, revolts and revolutions are possible but not inevitable if sanctions weaken potential domestic opponents of the target regime.

POTENTIAL CONSEQUENCES

These four models of influence still need to be more carefully grounded in an analysis of the possible consequences of sanctions. As noted in the previous chapter, theories of sanctions often treat the target as if it were a single entity and only examine economic effects of sanctions. Departing from the traditional approaches in international relations that consider states as unitary actors, these four models of influence suggest that there are at least five potential sites of influence that affect the likelihood of successful sanctions. The first site is the target government seen as a collection of decision making elites. Second, we view the target state as a collection of institutions that requires material resources. In both situations, the state is an agent that responds directly to international pressure. Shifting away from a focus on the elites and government institutions, a third view sees the state as vulnerable through its economy, regardless of whether it is comprised of state-owned or private enterprise (or a mix of the two). The fourth site, civil society, includes social groups, non-state political organizations, unions, and individuals within the target. Finally, there are often externalities and spillover effects of sanctions in regional and global contexts on non-target governments and populations, a consequence that is underemphasized in most studies.

In all five sites, denial of customary interaction may have direct, indirect, and counterproductive consequences. Of course, it is possible that there are no effects – sanctions may be inconsequential. Sanctioners may attempt to influence directly the capabilities and decision making of the target in hopes of altering the behavior, military and economic capabilities of the state, or the beliefs of the target's leaders and inhabitants. Economic conditions and social structures also mediate between sanctioners intentions and actual results, leading to desired change through indirect paths. However, leaders and populations that are the targets of sanctions might resist international pressure. Indirect consequences can result from attempts by the target to evade or diminish the direct impact of sanctions. Indirect effects alter the supporting political, economic, and social conditions in which political decisions are made – resistance may thus have the paradoxical effect of weakening the state. Counterproductive consequences, which may be both direct and indirect, are often unanticipated and certainly unintended.

All cases of sanctions may thus exhibit diverse and frequently contradictory effects. The task, therefore, is to identify the full range of consequences. Only then is it possible to assess whether, on balance, international influence succeeded – and at what cost. Disaggregating the potential consequences of sanctions into their direct, indirect, and counterproductive effects on elite decision makers, government structures, the target economy, and civil society along with any externalities or spillover (summarized in table 2.2), offers a framework for evaluating the consequences of sanctions.

Elite Decision Makers

In both the compellance and normative communication models, the target of sanctions is the decision making elite within government. This potential site of influence also includes those powerful elites who circulate among political office-holders and civil servants. Target elites often try to minimize the effects of sanctions or foster the appearance of normality, adding to the difficulty of assessing the impact of sanctions.

As discussed above, one way sanctions may succeed is by raising the symbolic and material costs of policies above a level that the state is willing to bear. Even when aggregate costs are relatively low, elites may choose to bargain with the sanctioners if the costs of complying with international demands are lower than those inflicted by sanctions. Further, the economic or military importance of a particular good may be less significant than the existence of a trading relationship.[15]

Table 2.2   Sites for potential consequences of sanctions

Site	Potential consequences		
	Direct	*Indirect*	*Counterproductive*
Elite Decision Makers	Elites change their assessment of costs and benefits or their normative beliefs	Relative bargaining power of elites within and outside the government shifts	Elites view and/or use isolation as legitimation for their "us" vs. "them" perspective; access to alternative ideas restricted
Government Structures	Threat or denial of resources leads to immediate or long-term decline in military capability and/or increased costs	Mobilization of human and physical resources	Target initates new alliances with other "outlaw" states and/or counter-sanctions
Economy	Threat or actual economic damage	Declining business confidence; expensive adjustments and opportunity costs; some growth in import substitution sectors	Import substitution fosters greater autonomy; some sectors benefit from sanctions
Civil Society	Global normative standards are communicated; identity formed and reformed; populations are moved to revolt	Some social and political actors become more legitimate, others less; changes in economic power increase political oppportunity structures for opposition	Domestic support for the status quo is bolstered; access to alternative ideas is restricted; the majority population is hurt, weakening their ability to oppose the target
Externalities: Regional or Global Spillover	Costs of implementing monitoring and enforcing sanctions; perceptions of non-targets/onlookers change; global awareness of the target grows, stimulating more sanctions	Conceptions of identity and interests are revised; innovative trade and cooperative arrangements develop; smuggling increases the wealth and political power of black markets; import-substitution industries benefit	Neighboring states and populations suffer; alliances and multilateral organizations fracture over whether to impose sanctions

Of course, target elites know that their bargaining position depends on the numerous factors that normally affect trading relationships within the global economic system. But the bargaining relationship between sanctioners and the target is not determined solely by their positions within global markets. Specifically, preexisting political relations, particularly the distinction between allies and adversaries, may have a substantial effect. If trade relationships are generally strongest among allies, connections between the sanctioners and the elites within the target state potentially increase leverage. Alternative suppliers will be harder to find, and the desire not to damage an alliance relationship in other issue areas might increase the target's willingness to compromise on its policies which have provoked sanctions.[16]

Such bargaining perspectives often presume rational decision makers, but this need not be the case. Individual beliefs and personalities may prove critical. Although most work in political psychology suggests that decision makers rarely change deeply held beliefs, sanctions could potentially be the kind of dramatic experience that directly affects elite views.[17] Sanctions, as a signal of international condemnation, may provoke a reassessment of fundamental assumptions about national interests and the legitimate means of pursuing them. Sanctions thus might function as a "teaching" method.[18] Target elites are also more likely to comply with what they consider legitimate demands of allies than what they reject as illegitimate pressures from adversaries.

While it is unlikely that all or most elite decision makers will revise their views, outside pressure may indirectly shift the relative balance of power among elite decison makers. For example, if sanctions and the resistance to them significantly stress the state or the economy, elites with ties to import-substitution industries or to newly valuable commodities may play an increasing role. International censure may also provide ammunition to elite reformers who are arguing for new policies.

On the other hand, Margaret Doxey and others have noted that "the target may be driven to adopt defiant and perhaps more extreme positions as a result of sanctions."[19] External pressure often inspires a sense of isolation and resentment at foreign interference which may provoke intransigence or may even take the aggressive form of economic or military retaliation. Sanctions may also bolster the credibility and legitimacy of decision makers that claim the outside world is hostile. If sanctions are perceived by the target as a prelude to war, the armed forces and militarists within the target state may assume a greater decision making role.

Government Structures

Because state bureaucracies require material resources, sanctions may undermine institutional capacities by directly contributing to declining material capabilities in the target or increasing the cost of acquiring necessary resources. Economic strength and war-making ability are deeply intertwined; states need natural, industrial, financial, and technological resources in order to maintain a strong military and police.[20] Hence sanctioners may selectively deprive the target of resources with the most military significance, such as armaments, advanced technologies, and oil. Sanctions that target these resources may "deny or delay improvements in the military capabilities of an adversary," regardless of the sanctions' economic impact.[21]

Frequently, targets react to the threat and imposition of sanctions by conserving and/or mobilizing human and material resources: "Typical advance action to reduce the effect of trade embargoes includes stockpiling; the development of alternative sources of supply; the stimulation and diversification of domestic production; control of strategic resources, and the development of industrial substitutes."[22] Resource mobilization may drive larger political and economic restructuring, which may, in turn, affect the relative balance of power among decision making elites. Stockpiling and the search for alternative supplies of embargoed material is expensive and usually underwritten by the state. Governments may also, for political reasons, expend resources protecting elite groups from feeling the pinch of sanctions.

The target may also seek to escape the costs of sanctions by forging new alliances, either in the region or globally, that may be counterproductive from the perspective of the sanctioner: "sanctions may prompt powerful or wealthy allies of the target country to assume the role of 'black knight,'" such as when Cuba turned to the Soviet Union in the face of isolation by the United States.[23] Alliances may decrease the target's political and economic vulnerability, thus reducing the influence of sanctioners. If isolated states work together, their capabilities may be enhanced. They may also be pulled in more extreme policy directions by their allies.[24] If commodities controlled by the target or its allies are particularly valuable, these pariahs may retaliate by depriving sanctioners of essential commodities. However these threats are not credible over the long run since a sanctioned economy will likely need the resources generated by the trade in these strategic commodities. In addition, the search for new allies or disseminating justifications for its policies may also require increased government expenditure.

Economy

Compellance and resource denial models of sanctions focus on the direct costs of sanctions on the target economy. Advocates of economic warfare assume that "the additional resources released by trade with an adversary are ultimately devoted, wholly or in part, to military pursuits, which results in a significant improvement in the adversary's military capabilities."[25] Consequently, "unless the target state trades foolishly, any commercial transactions will contribute, however marginally, to its economy and thus will release resources that could be put to military use."[26]

The magnitude of these costs (and opportunities) will vary depending on the conditions in the target economy and the types of sanctions imposed. For example, the elasticity of demand for products and the availability of substitute goods will affect whether the target can compensate for lost transactions. The most dire direct consequences of broad sanctions intended to cripple an entire economy may include immediate or long-term declining productivity, job losses, dampened domestic demand, and raising the costs of restricted goods.

There are also numerous and often interrelated indirect economic effects. Cutting access to global import and export markets may have substantial structural implications. For example, "When partial sanctions are imposed and the threat of more looms, business confidence by foreign investors and lenders, and even domestic business interests are chilled, causing substantial drag on the economic growth of the target nation."[27] Thus, the prospect and implementation of sanctions can lead to inflation, declining investment, capital flight, migration (brain drain) and declining government tax revenues as overall economic productivity declines. The loss of export markets may result in a decline in foreign exchange revenues, in turn potentially reducing imports and disturbing currency values. Declining productivity may set in motion a wave of disinvestment by multinationals.[28]

These economic effects may have direct and indirect political consequences. For example, under substantial pressure, business leaders who formerly supported government policies may defect. If they believe they are being badly hurt by sanctions they make take their businesses and resources elsewhere or champion alternative policies. The political fracture model also emphasizes that sanctions may cause so much economic pain, or call into question the government's ability to handle the economy, that populations rebel.

Even in the absence of sanctions, states and domestic economic actors frequently pursue import substitution as a response to changes in global supply and demand.[29] It is not surprising then that sanctioned economies may, usually with state assistance, pursue import substitution. At least in the short term, import substitution can work quite well and actually strengthen the state. Perhaps because of its focus on negative consequences, the sanctions literature has tended to emphasize inefficiencies and job losses due to sanctions but underplays the extent to which the number of jobs in some sectors may actually increase. Thus, it is unwise to presume that sanctions only produce negative economic effects.

But import substitution forced by sanctions may be inefficient if "resources could be better used elsewhere in the economy."[30] Advocates of market liberalism, stressing the benefits of comparative advantage, point out that developing "infant industries" raises welfare costs, since domestic producers and consumers are forced to pay higher prices for lower quality goods. In addition, shifting resources from industrial and consumer production to the military, in response to sanctions of strategic goods, increases aggregate welfare costs; the "multiplier effect" of military spending is arguably lower because weapons are not then used in new industrial and consumer production.

To the extent that sanctions prompt targets to develop economic self-reliance, the influence of outside actors potentially diminishes.[31] Import-substitution mobilization may also create new domestic economic interests that benefit from sanctions, leading them to actively discourage the state from complying with international demands.[32]

Civil Society

The normative communication and political fracture models emphasize that sanctions may succeed in directly communicating global normative standards to the target's populace. Sectors of civil society begin to redefine themselves as isolation calls previous norms, values or beliefs into question.[33] One consequence may be a widening political rift between leaders and the general population if most elites continue to hold on to their prior views.

Since political, economic and social conditions determine the strength of governments in relation to social forces, the consequence of sanctions will vary. The willingness of the target government and its population to accept an aggregate decline in welfare depends on the distribution of costs, as well as the nature of international demands. Although the "naive" theory may too quickly assume that the domestic population will rebel against the government, domestic opposition may nonetheless increase with the imposition of sanctions, contributing to new fractures in the ruling coalition and between the elites and the "masses" that, in turn, may undermine regime stability.

As an indirect consequence of sanctions, the relative bargaining power of elites both within and outside the state structure may change as the economic structure of the state changes to respond to sanctions. Specifically, Kaempfer and Lowenberg argue that those social groups and economic interests most affected are likely to pressure the government for policy changes.[34] In response, the target government may offer compensation to those sectors that are most damaged by sanctions and are most important to regime stability. Determining which groups are most important politically requires a case-by-case analysis, based on additional considerations such as the institutional structure of policymaking.

The influence of and balance between these domestic interests can also be significantly affected by the non-economic consequences of sanctions. For example, outside pressure promoting particular norms may benefit those domestic political actors who are advancing those ideas.[35] Although often described as a sort of contagion effect or as if populations were "waking up" to their subjugation, sanctioners may actually articulate arguments already being used by domestic actors as part of their domestic mobilization.[36] Further, sanctions signal international recognition of a particular problem, often resulting in increased media access for those who oppose the status quo. International actors may also give additional material support to activist groups within the target or offer compensation to domestic allies who suffer unduly from restrictions against the country as a whole. Non-governmental sanctioners, such as unions and solidarity groups, may also provide material and moral support to regime opponents.

As mentioned above, target economies that resist sanctions with a large-scale import substitution strategy may experience microbooms. Economic growth in some sectors can lead to increased educational opportunities among workers and create openings for union organizing. Yet growth will not necessarily lead to political consequences unless it occurs in a politicized context. In other words, economic opportunities created by sanctions, in the absence of a strong civil society and political organizing, will probably not open up political opportunity for domestic opponents of the target regime.

Sanctions may also have serious counterproductive consequences for the target's civil society. For example, even though one goal may be to disseminate new norms among elites and civil society, restricting interactions with the outside world may promote insularity and reduce the flow of the very ideas that sanctioners seek to promote. Denial of customary interaction may also limit the ability of outsiders to monitor changes within the target. Rather than spurring the dissent and division that sanctioners hoped, censure by outsiders can provide leaders in the target state a useful method for increasing their domestic support by creating an external threat. Or members of the population may spontaneously "rally around the flag" and thus increase the recalcitrance of both target elites and civil society.[37]

It is possible that those who suffer the most when sanctions hurt an economy are the ones that sanctioners most want to help. Women and children may bear a disproportionate share of this burden as they are generally in a weaker economic and political position in most societies.[38] This may undermine the ability of civil society to oppose the target government and calls into question the very notion of sanctions as a non-violent tool of statecraft.[39] Thus, any assessment of effects on civil society must include an accounting of import substitution, harm to the most vulnerable elements of the population, and increases in both dissent and popular support for the target regime.

Externalities and Spillover

Sanctions may have direct consequences on the instigators of sanctions, regional actors, and others. In addition to requiring resources to implement, monitor, and enforce compliance, complex embargoes and restrictions can be difficult to administer because many parties may seek to circumvent these measures. Further, sanctioners could and sometimes do provide compensation to neighboring states to defray the unintended impact of sanctions, adding to the costs of implementing the policy. Yet these direct costs may be beneficial if the expense signals resolve. As Baldwin argues: "Costs are widely regarded as a standard indicator of the intensity of one's resolve."[40] Other potential norm violators may also think twice about committing violations in the future if they know that members of the international community are likely to impose credible sanctions. Thus, short-term costs to sanctioners may have substantial long-term benefit.

Boycotts of the target's exports may also indirectly affect import substitution industries within sanctioning and non-sanctioning countries.[41] Multinational corporations, private black-market merchants, commodity intermediaries, and non-embargoing states often profit from supplying resources and expertise. Sanctions may even generate new economic opportunities if, for example, a corporation leaves the target and relocates in a neighboring state.

The imposition of sanctions may also serve as a focal point for redefining interests and identities outside the target. The nature of regional alliances may be particularly important for enforcement of restrictions. New alliances or trading arrangements can help to implement sanctions or to mitigate any adverse consequences of dependence on or proximity to the target. Conversely, existing alliances may be strained.

Furthermore, neighbors may implement balancing or bandwagoning behavior at the regional level which reflects global political divisions. Alliances may serve to bring a greater sense of common identity to their members, helping to create a community.[42] Collective regional identity, in turn, may pull on inhabitants and decision makers within the target state in ways that encourage capitulation to international demands, because isolation entails social costs that are not measurable in economic terms.[43] Finally, the process of initiating sanctions may serve to educate people about the target state and their links to it. This could further mobilize political actors who then push for even more stringent restrictions.

But sanctions may be counterproductive for sanctioners and bystanders. The civilian populations of neighbors with disproportionate economic dependence on the target may be hurt by a weakened target economy. Multinational corporations may lose investment and revenue. And sanctioners and their allies may be countersanctioned by the target in retaliation for their role in imposing sanctions. All these counterproductive consequences may weaken the resolve of sanctioners and lead to a disintegration of the sanctioning effort.

SUMMARY

Academics and policymakers rest their claims about sanctions on quite complex, though often unstated, assumptions and models of influence. We have tried to make those sometimes contradictory premises and arguments more explicit and to organize them into a framework. We also advocate an analysis of how sanctions work that is broader than the usual focus on negative and economic effects of sanctions on states conceived as unitary actors. We argue for a comprehensive accounting of direct, indirect, and counter-productive effects on the target and other actors. By pointing out the interconnections between conditions at different sites of potential influence, we have tried to capture the complexity of sanctions as a policy instrument and their sometimes paradoxical and contradictory effects. The following chapters apply this disaggregated view of the effects of strategic, economic, and social sanctions to the South African case.

Notes

We thank the book's chapter authors and Tom Biersteker, Jendayi Frazer, Arlene Getz, Willard Johnson, Norma Kriger, Kim Richard Nossal, and Newell Stultz for extensive comments.

1. N. M. Stultz, "Sanctions, Models of Change, and South Africa," *South Africa International* 13 (1982), pp. 121–9.
2. Chien-pin Li, "The Effectiveness of Sanction Linkages: Issues and Actors, *International Studies Quarterly* 3 (1993), pp. 349–70: 353.
3. D. A. Baldwin, *Economic Statecraft* (Princeton, NJ: Princeton University Press, 1985), pp. 118–30. Baldwin argues that decision makers ought to consider costs, risks, and benefits but rarely do so in a precise manner. Also see B. Jentleson, *Pipeline Politics: The Complex Political Economy of East–West Energy Trade* (Ithaca, NY: Cornell University Press, 1986), p. 29; A. Hirschman, *National Power and the Structure of Foreign Trade* (Berkeley: University of California Press, 1945); E. M. Crumm, "The Value of Economic Incentives in International Politics," *Journal of Peace Research* 32 (1995), pp. 313–30.
4. See G. Allison, *Essence of Decision* (Boston: Little Brown, 1971); A. L. George and R. Smoke, *Deterrence and American Foreign Policy: Theory and Practice* (New York: Columbia University Press, 1974); R. Jervis, *Perception and Misperception in International Politics* (Princeton, NJ: Princeton University Press, 1976).
5. See Baldwin, *Economic Statecraft*, pp. 96–114. Sanctioners may increase

the credibility of their threat through institutionalized cooperation. Several argue that multilateral measures strengthen the sanctioners' commitment to collective policy implementation and offer leaders in the sanctioning effort increased opportunities to persuade or offer incentives to more reluctant allies. See M. P. Doxey, *Economic Sanctions and International Enforcement* (London: Oxford University Press/ Royal Institute for International Affairs, 1971); L. L. Martin, *Coercive Cooperation: Explaining Multilateral Economic Sanctions* (Princeton, NJ: Princeton University Press, 1992), pp. 37–9; Jentleson, *Pipeline Politics*, p. 36.

6. Doxey, *Economic Sanctions and International Enforcement*; A. Klotz, *Norms in International Relations: The Struggle against Apartheid* (Ithaca, NY: Cornell University Press, 1995); K. R. Nossal, *Rain Dancing: Sanctions in Canadian and Australian Foreign Policy* (Toronto: University of Toronto Press, 1994).

7. Li, "The Effectiveness of Sanctions Linkages," p. 355. This parallels the view in the literature on epistemic policy communities that actors agree on a scientific framework, understand the evidence, and are persuaded by good evidence. See P. Haas, ed., "Knowledge, Power, and International Policy Coordination," *International Organization*, special issue 46 (1992), pp. 1–35.

8. See N. C. Crawford, "The Making of World Politics" (manuscript).

9. C. Joyner, "Sanctions and International Law," in D. Cortright and G. A. Lopez, eds., *Economic Sanctions: Panacea or Peacebuilding in a Post–Cold War World?* (Boulder, CO: Westview, 1995), pp. 73–87: 74.

10. Nossal, in *Rain Dancing*, stresses punishment as a goal of sanctions. In this view, sanctions are successful simply if they are implemented, independent of the reaction of the target.

11. J. Galtung, "On the Effects of International Economic Sanctions: With Examples from the Case of Rhodesia," *World Politics* 19 (1967), pp. 378–416, esp. 388–9. Also see G. C. Hufbauer, J. J. Schott, and K. A. Elliott, *Economic Sanctions Reconsidered: History and Current Policy*, 2d ed. (Washington, DC: Institute for International Economics, 1990), pp. 38–9, and W. H. Kaempfer and A. D. Lowenberg, *International Economic Sanctions: A Public Choice Perspective* (Boulder, CO: Westview, 1992). The skeptical view is articulated by Baldwin, *Economic Statecraft*.

12. W. H. Kaempfer and A. D. Lowenberg, "The Problems and Promise of Sanctions," in Cortright and Lopez, *Economic Sanctions*, pp. 61–71: 65.

13. Ibid., p. 67.

14. Though not usually connected, the revolutionary fracture model could usefully be linked with a focus on political opportunity for social movements. While not explaining why people mobilize, increased opportunities may accelerate the growth and effectiveness of movements. See S. Tarrow, *Power in Movement* (Cambridge: Cambridge University Press, 1994); D. McAdam, J. D. McCarthy, M. N. Zald, eds., *Comparative Perspectives on Social Movements: Political Opportunity, Mobilizing Structures, and Cultural Framings* (Cambridge: Cambridge University Press, 1996).

15. Baldwin, *Economic Statecraft*, pp. 96–114; M. Mastanduno, *Economic Containment: CoCom and the Politics of East–West Trade* (Ithaca, NY: Cornell University Press, 1992), pp. 52–7.
16. See J. Odell, *U.S. International Monetary Policy: Markets, Power, and Ideas as Sources of Change* (Princeton, NJ: Princeton University Press, 1982); J. Gowa, *Allies, Adversaries and International Trade* (Princeton, NJ: Princeton University Press); Hufbauer, Schott, and Elliott, *Economic Sanctions Reconsidered*, pp. 12 and 99; Li, "The Effectiveness of Sanction Linkages."
17. See Y. Y. I. Vertzberger, *The World in their Minds: Information Processing, Cognition, and Perception in Foreign Policy Decision Making* (Stanford: Stanford University Press, 1990).
18. M. Finnemore, "International Organizations as Teachers of Norms: The United Nations Educational, Scientific, and Cultural Organization and Science Policy," *International Organization* 47 (1993), pp. 565–97.
19. M. P. Doxey, *International Sanctions in Contemporary Perspective* (New York: St. Martin's, 1987), p. 146.
20. See, for instance, P. Kennedy, *The Rise and Fall of the Great Powers* (New York: Random House, 1988).
21. Mastanduno, *Economic Containment*, p. 47.
22. Doxey, *International Sanctions in Contemporary Perspective*, p. 111.
23. Hufbauer, Schott, and Elliott, *Economic Sanctions Reconsidered*, p. 12.
24. See D. Geldenhuys, *Isolated States: A Comparative Analysis* (Cambridge: Cambridge University Press, 1990).
25. Mastanduno, *Economic Containment*, p. 42.
26. Ibid., p. 44; Bans on East–West trade during the Cold War exemplify this perspective. See Hirschman, *National Power and the Structure of Foreign Trade*, and Jentleson, *Pipeline Politics*.
27. Eland, "Economic Sanctions as Tools of Foreign Policy," in Cortright and Lopez, eds., *Economic Sanctions*, p. 38.
28. See K. A. Rodman, "Public and Private Sanctions Against South Africa," *Political Science Quarterly* 109 (1994), pp. 313–34.
29. For example, S. Haggard, *Pathways from the Periphery* (Ithaca, NY: Cornell University Press, 1991).
30. Eland, "Economic Sanctions as Tools of Foreign Policy," p. 38.
31. Mastanduno, *Economic Containment,* p. 42.
32. Galtung, "On the Effects of International Economic Sanctions."
33. On identity see Klotz, *Norms in International Relations*; D. Campbell, *Writing Security: United States Foreign Policy and the Politics of Identity* (Minneapolis: University of Minnesota Press, 1992); C. Weber, *Simulating Sovereignty: Intervention, the State, and Symbolic Exchange* (Cambridge: Cambridge University Press, 1995).
34. Kaempfer and Lowenberg, *International Economic Sanctions*.
35. Klotz, *Norms in International Relations*.
36. See N. C. Crawford, "Decolonization as an International Norm: The Evolution of Practices, Arguments and Beliefs," in L. W. Reed and C. Kaysen, eds., *Emerging Norms of Justified Intervention* (Cambridge: American Academy of Arts and Sciences, 1993), pp. 37–61: 46; Klotz, *Norms in International Relations*.

37. Galtung, "On the Effects of International Economic Sanctions," p. 389.
38. L. Buck, N. Gallant, and K. R. Nossal, "Sanctions as a Gendered Instrument of Statecraft: The Iraqi Case," *Review of International Studies* 24 (1998), pp. 69–84.
39. Nossal, *Rain Dancing*, pp. 262–5. Lori Fisler Damrosch argues that economic sanctions should be implemented so that they differentiate their effects between the "perpetrators of wrongdoing" and non-perpetrators (L. F. Damrosch, "The Civilian Impact of Economic Sanctions," in L. F. Damrosch, ed., *Enforcing Restraint: Collective Intervention in Internal Conflicts* [New York: Council on Foreign Relations, 1993], pp. 274–315: 279). Also see T. G. Weiss, D. Cortright, G. A. Lopez and L. Minear, eds., *Political Gain and Civilian Pain: Humanitarian Impacts of Economic Sanctions* (Oxford: Rowman and Littlefield, 1997).
40. Baldwin, *Economic Statecraft*, p. 107; also see pp. 17–18, 24.
41. Kaempfer and Lowenberg, "The Problems and Promise of Sanctions," p. 63.
42. See Martin, *Coercive Cooperation*.
43. See Klotz, *Norms in International Relations*.

Part II

Strategic Sanctions

3 How Arms Embargoes Work[1]

Neta C. Crawford

> However Utopian this may be, in the visible future the dynamic
> equilibrium of politics will work in favor of civilianism to the
> extent that people – that is large populations, including the lower
> classes – continue to be positively valued for military purposes.
> Hitherto the dependence of arms production upon a huge labor
> force has been a factor making for a degree of democratization.
>
> (Harold Lasswell)[2]

Apartheid South Africa was the object of a long-term international
embargo of armaments and other military equipment. These were
actually voluntary and mandatory, multilateral and unilateral,
embargoes that began in 1963 and were in force until mid-1994.
Initially intended to halt weapons and technology flows that the
minority government could use for internal repression against the
majority population, sanctions were also later intended to decrease
South Africa's ability to threaten its neighbors, and to undermine
South Africa's ability to continue its illegal occupation of South
West Africa/Namibia. What impact did the arms embargo have on
South Africa?

UN and individual nations' embargoes never completely halted
the flow of weapons and military technology to South Africa; in
fact, quite a bit of both got through.[3] Nor is it likely that the arms
embargo changed any minds inside South Africa's ruling elite. If
anything, the embargo contributed to Afrikaners' feelings of encir-
clement, and was used by the government to mobilize white South
African society for war and repression.[4] Nevertheless, the international arms embargo did have several important consequences.

First, the embargo had little *immediate* impact in terms of decreased military capability: during the early part of South Africa's
war with Angola and its regional destabilization, making little difference to the hundreds of thousands who died or were injured in
Angola, Mozambique, and Namibia at the hands of the South African military, and to the thousands who suffered and died within

South Africa. However, after the embargo had been in place for many years, South Africa's military capability *vis-à-vis* its neighbors declined. By the late 1980s, South Africa's shortages of spare parts, and the difficulty they had fielding more advanced equipment, was increasingly felt on the battlefield. Second, South Africa's resistance to the embargo – clandestine arms purchases and the development of a large import substitution industry – was expensive and that expense must be seen as an opportunity cost. The South African government devoted resources to evading the embargo that it could have spent directly on repression. Third, development of an indigenous arms industry had ripple effects in the politics, economy, and society of apartheid South Africa that were probably largely unanticipated by those who imposed the embargoes. South Africa's arms import substitution strategy actually helped alter, and over the long run weaken, the social, political, and economic structures of apartheid. Finally, a long-term effect of the embargo was that South Africa grew to have one of the world's largest armament industries and the economy became partially dependent on the arms as a leading sector. The clandestine and illegal culture of the arms export sector, in particular the pursuit of exports to any market, also survived apartheid's demise.

ARMS EMBARGOES IN THEORY

Arms embargoes are intended to decrease the military effectiveness of the target state by denying the target material and technological resources crucial for waging war. Arms embargoes ought to, if kept in place over a long period of time, lead to declining military capabilities *vis-à-vis* non-embargoed states. Still, it is usually the case that not all parties will implement an embargo. Transnational corporations, individual arms merchants, and other pariah states often circumvent embargoes although the target of the embargo will usually pay a premium for purchasing weapons covertly. Thus it seems that the effectiveness of an arms embargo should be measured by whether or not the embargo completely denies military resources for the targeted state.

But understanding the effects of arms embargoes and evaluating their "success" is more complicated than looking at whether arms were completely denied to the target. Specifically, arms embargoes stimulate resistance by a stubborn target states, who mobilize their productive capacities for import substitution, or seek alternative sources of military equipment on the international market. Resistance may be more or less successful at replacing the arms embargoed. Such resistance is practically guaranteed if targets of arms embargoes are engaged in war or large-scale domestic repression, and in this context the demand for arms and military equipment will be relatively inelastic.

An embargo may not actually have to be implemented to produce resistance: merely the threat or anticipation of an embargo may start the target state's leaders along the path to military import-substitution industrialization. Ironically, arms embargoes that spark military industrialization may decrease the direct leverage of the embargoers over time, as the state that is embargoed becomes more self-sufficient in weapons manufacture.

But that does not mean that arms embargoes lose their punch over time and are inneffectual – rather, the lever of influence shifts from denial to political economy. This is because developing an indigenous arms industry usually occurs in stages that alter the target's political economy. Military industrialization begins with making repair, overhaul, and maintenance for imported weapons a local process. Then local manufacturers purchase a license for local production. The new producer gets help from the licenser "in the organization of the necessary infrastructure, actual production facilities, training and education."[5] Getting to the stage of developing a capacity for indigenously produced designs, may take years:

> First, samples of the weapon are delivered in complete form; a second batch is locally assembled from imported complete sub-assemblies; at a third stage components are imported to make up locally constructed sub-assemblies; fourth, certain raw materials are imported to enable local construction of components. Theoretically, the ideal of this model would be the local construction of the weapon from components from locally produced raw materials, and finally, to be able to procede with local research and development of the next generation of the weapon system.[6]

Military industrialization is more difficult under sanctions if weapons production licenses are revoked and new licenses are not granted to the target of sanctions. If the target has already received the blueprints and know-how, then revoking preexisting licenses may have little effect and production will likely go ahead. Still, even without new licenses, incremental modifications and some moderni- zation will be possible as the scientific, technical, and production resources of the target are mobilized. Thus, targets of arms em- bargoes may be able to maintain the flow of weapons based on imported designs for quite some time, although the developing of an arms industry that is able to match or excede the innovations of an adversary's arms industry may not occur quickly enough to meet battlefield needs.

The speed and success of military industrialization depends on the status of the embargoed economy at the time the import sub- stitution effort begins because the requirements for developing military industries are not unlike those for starting other high-tech- nology industries. Requirements "include the overall level of in- dustrialization, the existance of an adequate economic infrastructure, the supply of skilled labour, the existence of backward and for- ward linkages with other industries (for the supply of raw materi- als, subcontracting, and the marketing of spin-off products), the level of state support and protection, and the existence of a mar- ket for the goods."[7] But not only does military industrialization *require* certain factor endowments and inputs, rapid military indus- trialization alters an economy as those inputs are mobilized, and as the industry grows. Thus, sanctions that prompt military indus- trialization may promote change in larger economic and political spheres (as some theorists of modernization predict). The quality and quantity of these effects depends on the target's level of in- dustrialization at the beginning of their resistance to an embargo.

If the target is not very industrialized, import substitution may involve rapid, large-scale industrialization, with all the social and political consequences that entails – adding the wrinkle that this growth is occurring in a context of war or repression.[8] And if an economy at a relatively low level of industrialization acquires a significant arms manufacturing sector, the economic health of the state may become significantly dependent on the arms industry beyond the embargo era. This is especially likely if the arms industry becomes a leading economic sector that holds a large concentration of the economy's scientific, technological, and manufacturing expertise.

If the target economy is already fairly industrialized, mobiliza- tion for domestic arms production may, more simply, be a matter of shifting production assets, for example, from automobiles to armored personnel carriers, or from commercial aircraft to transport aircraft. Still, as the requirements for increasing specialization and sophistication of weapons grows, more research and development (R&D), and more capital and technology intensive production capacities, are required to manufacture high technology weapons. Thus, even in already industrialized societies, the desire for sophisticated weapons can have important social and political effects. These changes could occur with military industrialization regardless of whether it occurred under an arms embargo, but sanctions complicate and frustrate military industrialization and technical innovation. Embargoes also tend to increase costs and delay or deny the acquisition of war material and designs. In the case of more comprehensive embargoes, sanctions impede acquisition of scientific knowledge and technical expertise.

Analysis of arms embargoes must also take into account several additional considerations. First, weapons and military equipment are ambiguous categories in several respects: military technology and civilian/commercial technologies are frequently interchangeable. For example, an embargo on spare parts for military aircraft may be circumvented by purchasing spare parts for civilian aircraft. "All items in international trade, even ostensibly 'peaceful' goods, can conceivably serve military purposes. . . . Trucks can carry troops to war or produce to market. And the same computers useful in weather forecasting may be valuable in the design of nuclear weapons. In short, virtually every material, product, or technology can be defined as having a 'dual use,' that is, both military and civilian applications."[9] Embargoes of military equipment that select the weapon embargoed by offensive or defensive purpose are difficult to define and enforce because in many weapons categories the differences between offensive and defensive technologies are marginal.[10] Bans on "offensive" weapons may be circumvented by modifying the technology of defensive weapons and/or the training of military personnel to make "defensive" weapons suitable for offensive purposes. Moreover, non-weapons technologies are also necessary for military operations, or for efficient and successful import substitution. Arms embargoes that do not take dual use and vital supporting technologies into account are necessarily porous. Thus arms embargoes will probably always be leaky, to a certain extent, unless the target state is completely quarantined.

Second, peacetime arms embargoes have different effects than wartime sanctions. In war, rates of consumption and the level of equipment loss are difficult to predict consistently. Embargoes may thus affect the ambitiousness of military operations, or their range and duration, as ammunition, spare parts, and equipment become more scarce. On the other hand, target states may succeed with import substitution or clandestine trade, but acquire much more of a commodity, such as ammunition, than they finally use. Such an investment is costly: the target may have paid a premium to acquire embargoed military equipment, and that commodity may have little or no use in peacetime.[11]

Third, with long arms embargoes or long wars, military-technical innovation occurs. Over the long run, weapons must not only be replaced, they must be improved (modernized) in a way that at least keeps pace with an adversary's weapons and technology, since the target may face a country or coalition whose arms have been modernized. Modernization may only become a significant concern after several years, as new "generations" of weapons and weapons platforms are put on the battlefield. So, to be effective, import substitution must also include investment in R&D to promote military-technical innovation. Military innovation is slow regardless of whether a state is embargoed, and military-technical modernization typically occurs over several years as weapons move from R&D, design, and prototype phases, to production and deployment. Sanctions that take into account the level and quality of the target's military industrialization and scientific capacities may be more successful at frustrating the modernization process over the long term.[12]

Fourth, arms embargoes may also, paradoxically, increase regional and global insecurity. Embargoed states may, not unreasonably, feel encircled and under assault. The isolated regime's sense of being subject to international assault may bolster domestic arguments for preemptive mobilization and even external aggression. Further, sanctions can heighten regional security dilemma dynamics as the embargoed state's preemptive mobilization and military industrialization makes neighbors feel less secure. Moreover, like other states with military industries, embargoed states that develop an arms industry often feel pressure to export their weapons both to recoup some of the expense of rapid military industrialization and to decrease the per-unit costs of weapons. Arms exports may also be used to cement alliances and secure collaboration with other "pariah" states.

Fifth, arms embargoes tend to act as a form of protectionism, sheilding infant military industries in the target from external competition. This "protection" may lead to inefficient industries that are not competitive once the embargo is lifted. The end of an embargo may thus cause economic disruption if the military industries that are not competitive must either convert to non-military production, or workers are laidoff.

Finally, arms embargoes that lead to import substitution are likely to prompt changes in the relations between the "state" and "capital" and perhaps democratization. As the primary entity that organizes and conducts wars, the state is the primary client for high-technology weapons; it is also usually the only entity powerful enough to mobilize the resources necessary for rapidly developing truly innovative military industries. States both demand rapid military industrialization and their resources are required for industrialization's success. But industrialists are also required. Thus, governments promoting military industrialization become more involved in industrial policy, and the importance of certain industrialists grows. Tighter relationships between the state and industry will likely persist beyond the embargo and military industrialization era. Further, as Tilly and others have argued for different contexts, the "mounting of a major arms export industry will have the paradoxical effect of reducing the autonomy of... generals, and thus speeding a kind of democracy through the accretion of civilian bureaucracies, vested interests, and bargains with the civilian population. . . ."[13]

THE ARMS EMBARGOES

Apartheid South Africa depended on military force to survive at home and to promote its regional policies. South Africa occupied Namibia with military force until 1990, and was until 1990 persistently engaged in several military conflicts with its neighbors, including Angola, Botswana, Mozambique, and Zimbabwe. South Africa invaded Angola several times after 1975 and occupied portions of southern Angola until 1989. South Africa provided weapons and military equipment to its ally Rhodesia, which was itself under embargo until 1980, and to contra-like armies in Angola and Mozambique through the 1980s. Moreover, besides its police force, South Africa used the army and military equipment inside the country for repression, and in the 1980s, the military increasingly occupied black townships.

In response to South Africa's behavior, the United Nations and individual states gradually restricted the arms trade with South Africa. The UN Security Council adopted a voluntary arms embargo against South Africa in August 1963. Resolution 181 referred to South Africa's apartheid policies, noting the "recent arms build-up" and that South Africa "is seriously disturbing international peace and security." It called upon all states to "cease forthwith the sale and shipment of arms, ammunition of all types and military vehicles to South Africa."[14] Resolution 181 was followed a few months later by the more strongly worded Resolution 182. Both resolutions called upon South Africa to release all those imprisoned or interned because of their opposition to apartheid.[15]

In 1977, UN Security Council Resolution 418 condemned South Africa for its "acts of repression" and "attacks" on its neighbors and made the embargo mandatory: "the military build-up by South Africa and its persistent acts of aggression against the neighboring states seriously disturb the security of those states." It declared that the "acquisition by South Africa of arms and related *matériel* constitutes a threat to the maintenance of international peace and security."[16] The mandatory embargo prohibited exports to South Africa of weapons, ammunition, military vehicles and equipment, paramilitary and police equipment, and spare parts, while also prohibiting granting licensing arrangements to manufacture military equipment in South Africa. In 1982 the UN urged an embargo on purchasing South African armaments. The South African Defence Force moved into the townships in the mid-1980s and regional military aggression increased. UN Security Council Resolution 558, in December 1984, requested all states to refrain from importing South African produced arms, ammunition, and military vehicles; and in November 1986 the UN expanded the scope of items embargoed from export to South Africa to spare parts and police equipment.[17]

These UN resolutions never included a precise and exhaustive definition of military equipment, nor a list of items to be embargoed. Individual nations were left to decide just which equipment and technology contributed to conventional or nuclear capabilities. National legislation was often more precise. In some cases, such as the United States, unilateral restrictions included procedures for certifying that exports to South Africa were not for military purposes. But South Africa was still able to maintain, through much of the embargo era, significant ties to British and French military industries.[18] The UN Security Council lifted the import and export arms embargoes on 25 May 1994 and unilateral restrictions were eased at varying points, with the US finally ending its embargo in late February 1998.[19]

SOUTH AFRICAN RESISTANCE

Though South Africa produced military equipment for Western allies during World War II, including tanks, aircraft, and ammunition, arms production essentially halted at the end of the war. By the 1950s the only military production – run by the government – was for small arms and ammunition.[20] Thus the SADF in the early 1960s was almost entirely dependent on imports for weapons and military equipment, much of it supplied by the United Kingdom.[21] While UN resolutions declared South African behavior a threat to international security, South African officials described the arms embargo as part of the "total onslaught" they more generally perceived as being directed at them by the "enemies of the Republic of South Africa," the international community.[22] South Africa's resistance to weapons sanctions was multifaceted, consisting primarily of import-substitution industrialization but also of clandestine arms purchases.

Import Substitution

Import substitution began years before the United Nations' 1963 call for a voluntary arms embargo. During the early 1960s, South Africa was successful in acquiring licenses for the production of military equipment and armaments and in 1961 acquired 127 such licenses.[23] South Africa moved to develop an indigenous military production base, establishing an Armaments Production Board in 1964 under the Armaments Act later reorganized and renamed the Armaments Development and Production Corporation of South Africa (Armscor). Armscor was actually several companies owned by the state, and a large number of partially state-owned and private companies, all coordinated by Armscor to ensure that the weapons needed by the SADF were produced by South African industries or procured from abroad. In addition, Armscor made clandestine deals to purchase military equipment, technical expertise, and component upgrades for existing weapons systems. In the mid-1970s, South Africa increased its procurement schedule in anticipation of the mandatory UN armaments embargo. The 1977 Defence White Paper declared: "The RSA must, as far as practicable, be self-sufficient in the provision of arms and ensure their continued production."[24] In addition, after 1978, Armscor ran South Africa's nuclear weapons program – which itself cost as much as R700-800 million.[25] By the late 1980s, South Africa was able to cut its dependence on imports by more than half.[26]

Armscor consisted of research, development, and test facilities as well as of companies directly owned and operated by the government, known as subsidiaries, which engaged in final assembly of military equipment. Table 3.1 lists the South African government-owned-and-run subsidiaries of Armscor existing in 1990 and describes their role in the production of South Africa's military equipment.

To promote self-sufficiency, by the late 1970s nearly all weapons research, in addition to production and acquisition, in South Africa was controlled by Armscor. The government increased the resources put into military research, which since the 1950s had been coordinated by the Council for Scientific and Industrial Research (CSIR), and its National Institute for Defence Research. Armscor figures indicate that in 1983, 14.5 percent of total spending on research and development was for military research, accounting for 28.7 percent of engineering R&D. By 1989, military-related research and development accounted for over 32 percent of all R&D spending by the government and accounted for 64.4 percent of spending on engineering R&D.[27]

Armscor was integrated into South Africa's private sector. The government made an effort to put an increasing share of the money it invested in arms into South Africa's private sector, with 50 percent in 1973 going to private companies and 80 percent directed to the private sector in 1990.[28] By 1973 the Armaments Board was working with "approximately 200 contractors (and subcontractors) in the RSA, who in turn make use of several hundred of subcontractors."[29] By the mid-1980s Armscor worked with over 2000 private contractors and subcontractors inside South Africa who were wholly or in part dependent on government contracts, in the mid-1980s "at least 400 of these [contractors] being unable to survive without defense contracts."[30] By 1990, in addition to state-owned companies, 975 private South African contractors were directly engaged by Armscor.[31] Further, thousands of companies serving as subcontractors fed components to contractors and Armscor sub-

Table 3.1   Armscor subsidiaries

Subsidiary	Established	Type of weapon/component
Atlas	1964	airplanes and helicopters retrofit and redesign, e.g. Impala; assembly of French Mirage, Cheetah engines
Kentron	1978	guided weapons, e.g. Kukri air-to-air missile
Eloptro	1974	electro-optical laser and night vision
Naschem	1800s	large-caliber ammunition, bombs, grenades, landmines; e.g. 155 mm shells for the G-5 and G-6 guns
LEW (Lyttleton Engineering Works)		small arms, artillery, e.g. Uzi production, G-5 and G-6 guns
Somchem	1962	rockets, explosives, propellants
Infoplan		data processing
Swartklip		ammunition, grenades, demolition charges
PMP (Pretoria Metal Processing)		small-caliber ammunition
Musgrave		commercial rifles and ammunition distribution
Houwteq		missiles and related systems

Sources: RSA, *Briefing on the Organization and Functions of the South African Defence Force and the Armaments Corporation of South Africa, Limited 1990* (Pretoria: Ministry of Defence, 1990), p. 69; S. Landgren, *Embargo Disimplemented: South Africa's Military Industry* (New York: Oxford University Press, 1989), passim; G. Begg, "SAAF and the Arms Industry," *Ad Astra*, 10, no. 2, pp. 11–14.

sidiaries. Armscor acquisitions policy was that "only those items which, for technological reasons, cannot be manufactured in the Republic of South Africa at this stage or which should not be manufactured in the Republic of South Africa for economical reasons" were imported.[32]

Despite South Africa's huge R&D investment, much of its engineering and technical knowledge, as well as important equipment, was still derived from abroad through contacts with the hundreds of foreign engineering firms with offices in South Africa, foreign equipment purchases, and study abroad by South African scientists.[33]

Table 3.2   Official expenditures for arms acquisition

Year ending	Millions of rand
1967	23
1969	52
1971	68
1973	102
1975	296
1977	689
1979	921
1980	1 178
1981	1 235
1982	1 450
1983	1 591
1984	1 571
1985	1 865
1986	2 463
1987	2 300
1988	2 743
1989	4 845

Source: RSA, *Briefing*, p. 66.

South Africa also depended on foreign supplies of machine tools since they were unable to develop their own suppliers.[34] For example, the CSIR sent a team of scientists to France in 1964 to learn about air-to-air missile guidance.[35] After the embargo tightened, new weapon designs were often based on knowledge procured clandestinely from foreign producers, or by copying the weapons South Africa purchased or captured on the battlefield.

Table 3.2 shows South Africa's official account of Armscor acquisitions. It is unlikely that the clandestine purchases of armaments are included in these official figures, and the budget was also supplemented by the resale of weapons South Africa acquired on the black market. Thus, the figures should be seen as illustrative of South Africa's domestic procurement, not definitive, for the period of 1967–89. The share of the military budget spent on procurement grew from under 15 percent in 1961 to about 65 percent in the years just prior to the embargo, and hovered at just over 40 percent during the early 1980s. By the late 1980s the share of the military budget spent on procurement was back up to nearly 60 percent.[36] Table 3.2 illustrates the growth in expenditures as reported by the government.[37]

CONSEQUENCES OF MILITARY INDUSTRIALIZATION

Growing from almost nothing in the late 1940s, by the 1980s the scale of Armscor in relation to South Africa's industrial economy was enormous. Despite the UN embargo on purchasing South African produced weapons, by 1987 Armscor was South Africa's single largest exporter of manufactured goods, valued at $900 million in that year.[38] The ripple effects of developing a large arms industry were substantial and contributed to developments that both undermined strict apartheid, brought different, in some cases, more liberal, white business people from private industry into contact with the government, and facilitated black organizing, especially in trade unions.[39]

While South Africa was already industrialized before sanctions, manufacturing grew during the embargo era. In 1961 agriculture and mining together accounted for just over 25 percent of South Africa's GDP and manufacturing was just over 19 percent; in 1988 agriculture and mining accounted for under 18 percent of GDP and manufacturing was responsible for 24.5 percent of GDP.[40] Military industry, and the industries that fed components to Armscor subsidiaries, were probably the leading sector of industrial growth in South Africa as resistance to the embargoes proceeded.[41] Perhaps in part to justify the expense, the South African government stressed the effects of the arms industry on the local economy. For instance, in 1973, the Defence White Paper stated: "A considerable fund of know-how and skill has been built up locally, and, in a material sense, the economic growth of the RSA has been stimulated by the local manufacture of armaments."[42] In 1986 the South African government argued that military spending, especially on the arms industry, was "one of the primary driving forces of the economy."[43] Indeed, the 1986 Defence White Paper devoted a "model" and several pages of discussion to the benefits of arms production to the South African economy which it estimated at 5.42 percent of GDP in 1982.[44] Armscor trained thousands of workers each year.[45] The White Paper also refered to manpower training and "a leakage of personnel to other sectors as a result of personnel turnover."[46]

Arms industry employment grew dramatically; in fact, armament employment grew while overall manufacturing employment declined 1 percent from 1980 to 1985, while the entire South African economy suffered a recession.[47] The 1986 White Paper estimated that "Armscor

Table 3.3　Armscor and total arms industry employment

Year	Armscor employment	Estimated total employed in arms manufacture	Estimated percent of all manufacturing jobs in arms manufacture
1975	7 390	36 950	2.83
1976	7 919	39 595	2.92
1977	10 590	52 950	4.02
1978	16 870	84 350	6.43
1979	22 540	112 700	8.46
1980	24 560	122 800	8.64
1981	25 890	129 450	8.58
1982	24 960	124 800	8.09
1983	23 180	115 900	7.91
1984	25 340	126 700	8.57
1985	23 310	116 550	8.16
1986	25 190	125 950	8.23
1987	27 610	138 050	9.02
1988	30 930	154 650	10.14
1989	31 150	155 750	10.17
1990	23 630	118 150	7.75
1991	18 280	91 400	6.16
1992	15 700	78 500	5.46
1993	15 200	76 000	5.41
1994	15 000	75 000	
1995	14 000	70 000	

Sources: P. Batchelor, "History and Overview of the South African Arms Industry" (unpublished), presented to the Group for Environmental Monitoring Workshop on the Future of the South African Arms Industry, Johannesburg, 7–8 February 1996; Financial Mail, "Public Sector Corporations," Financial Mail Special Survey: Top Corporations (Johannesburg), 30 June 1995, pp. 248–52: 251.

and its main contractors provided work for an average of 34 700 people annually for the past five years" the majority of whom were skilled workers.[48] By the late 1980s, Armscor, its subsidiaries, and various contractors and subcontractors probably employed about 160 000 people, though the output of subcontractors was certainly not entirely devoted to military production.[49] While government reports of jobs directly associated with Armscor are disputable, defense economist Peter Batchelor has compiled some figures based on official Armscor documents and interviews for the period of most intense armaments production. Batchelor estimates that "as a rule of thumb, 1 job in ARMSCOR supports approximately 5 jobs in the private sector defence industry. Therefore in the late 1980s about 150 000 people [were] employed in the defence industry."[50] Table 3.3 shows the growing importance of arms manufacturing for the economy.[51]

Economic reforms were crucial for rapidly developing an arms industry large enough to support South Africa's use of force in Angola and Namibia. With white workers comprising a relatively small portion of potential workers in South Africa, apartheid barriers to black worker education and employment had to be relaxed. In the late 1970s, P. W. Botha moved to incorporate the business sector more fully into the total national strategy by meeting with important English and Afrikaner business leaders in South Africa and forming a Defence Advisory Board of leading businessmen.[52] Prime Minister Botha urged private industry to continue to help implementing the total strategy at the late 1979 Carlton Conference of 250 leading South African businessmen. Thus government had to strike a delicate balance: maintaining apartheid while reforming and reorganizing apartheid labor relations and public policy:

What was required was a means of containing black resistance to white domination *and* policies that would permit the more effective use of the black work force. To reinforce measures to this effect the reformist wing of the NP proposed the recognition of black trade unions, some form of political representation for blacks living outside the homelands, the establishment of homelands as viable economic and political units, the eroding of job reservation, the promotion of methods for training black workers, and the creation of a stable urban black population.[53]

Military industrialization increased pressure to relax apartheid. To facilitate the labor of "non-whites" in white areas, laws about the number and location of Africans in urban areas, "influx control" had to be abandoned in the early 1980s.[54] This was particularly ironic because part of the original impetus behind the apartheid legislation of the late 1940s and early 1950s was to halt and reverse the flow of Africans to urban areas that resulted from the industrialization spurred by World War II. In the late 1970s, even as demand for African workers grew in the urban areas, the government articulated a strong commitment to influx control and increased enforcement, but by the mid-1980s increased white emigration and the growth of industrial capacity meant that even more "non-white" workers were necessary to fill skilled labor positions.[55] Urban "gray areas" where people of all races could live together were increasingly tolerated until influx control was finally abandoned in 1986. Armscor had an incentive to treat all race groups well: "the greatest threat to this sensitive industry is an inefficient and/or disloyal employee corps." Thus, "Armscor's personnel policy is structured to offer good and similar working situations and conditions of employment to all its employees, irrespective of race or sex. . . ."[56]

So, military industrialization "meant blacks had to be trained for these skilled jobs, which in turn, meant upgrading their education and admitting them to previously whites-only technical institutes and universities."[57] From 1980 to 1988 there was a nearly 435 percent increase in the number of black students in technical colleges and technikons, while for the same period white enrollment grew less than 1 percent. Moreover, there was a 240 percent increase in the number of black students in teacher training and universities from 1980 to 1988 while during the same period there was a 30 percent increase in the number of whites in universities and teacher training.[58]

Unfortunately, there is no publicly available breakdown of the composition of employment in arms manufacturing by race and gender, nor a breakdown of wages and salaries for the arms industry in comparison to other manufacturing industries. General manufacturing statistics suggest that white employment was consistently between 20 and 24 percent between 1975 and 1993. While white workers' wages remained roughly constant, and always much higher than workers from other population groups, wages for black workers in the manufacturing sector nearly doubled during this period.[59] If employment patterns in the arms industry were similar to those of the South African military, where women, Asian, colored, and black personnel began to play an increasing role over the last decades of apartheid, then it is likely that the arms industry became increasingly integrated.[60]

Further, military industrialization increased spending on research and development, with military research accounting for "more than 30 percent of government's total research spending."[61] Investment into R&D for military technology benefited various sectors of the economy. "A burgeoning new sub-division of the engineering industry involved the manufacture and repair of various types of weapons and military equipment: aircraft, armoured vehicles, tanks, personnel carriers, field guns, rifles, bombs, missiles, ammunition, etc. . . . These developments, in turn, helped to stimulate the local electronics industry, which had been in its infancy in 1960."[62] Though it probably would have been more efficient to stimulate these industries directly, they did grow under the arms embargo.

In sum, the South African government's import substitution boosted the overall level of industrialization. While mining remained an important part of the South African economy and South Africa continued to be a primary product exporter (e.g. of gold, diamonds, coal, uranium, and platinum), manufacturing grew: in 1949 slightly more people were employed in the mining than manufacturing sectors, but by 1990 there were over twice as many employed in manufacturing.[63] Moreover, military industrialization stimulated overall industrialization. To make military industrialization work, more liberal industrialists were brought closer to the state, and South Africa's apartheid business practices were modified to facilitate the efficient use of black labor. Even if whites took the most skilled and highest paying jobs in the military industries, skilled black workers still had to fill in the skilled jobs abandoned by white workers employed in other sectors, and skilled black workers were also needed to work in the industries created to feed military industries. Increased education and employment opportunities stimulated by military industrialization, along with black unionization, helped sustain the anti-apartheid movement inside South Africa.

The Clandestine Arms Trade

Notwithstanding a large investment in import substitution, South Africa was never able to achieve self-sufficiency in armament production. So, while embargoed, South Africa secretly purchased military designs and equipment from abroad. And even after the 1982 UN embargo on purchasing South African-made weapons South Africa nevertheless managed to sell arms to about 30 countries. So, at its peak in the 1980s South Africa was the seventh or eighth largest arms producer in the world; on the eve of the 1994 elections the South African arms industry was still the world's tenth largest weapons producer.[64]

Many of the details of the apartheid government's clandestine arms trade may never be known.[65] Managed by Armscor, the import trade included contact with black market arms merchants and about 140 front companies South Africa set up all over the world.[66] South Africa's covert purchases of military equipment were costly at a mark-up of between 20 and 100 percent.[67] Stockholm International Peace Research Institute estimates of South African spending on military imports show an overall decline; but, despite a nearly fivefold decrease, South Africa continued to spend large sums importing weapons, averaging $452 million per year from 1973 to 1977 and $92 million from 1978 to 1992.[68] Much of this money was spent acquiring upgrades and designs for weapons the South African military industry found expensive or impossible to design and/or produce (such as the Israeli modification of the British Centurion tank which enabled South Africa to field a main battle tank, the Olifant). Armscor subsidiaries, contractors, and subcontractors, made extensive use of the technology and knowledge they acquired from transnational corporations outside and based in South Africa.[69]

A flavor of the clandestine trade was revealed in 1994 and 1995 when the new South African government investigated the clandestine weapons trade undertaken by Armscor after the new government came to power.[70] Exposure of an attempted arms shipment to Yemen – despite the pledge by President Mandela and Armscor head Tielman de Waal that weapons would not be shipped to countries in the midst of war[71] – led the ANC government to open an official inquiry, headed by Judge Edwin Cameron, into Armscor dealings which exposed even greater past and present illegalities and questionable dealings.[72] The Cameron Commission "exposed a world of freewheeling and idiosyncratic characters; of intrigue, deception and subterfuge; of lucrative and often extravagant commissions and of high living. . . ." which it said had roots in the embargo era.[73] Primarily restricted to the post-apartheid arms exports, the Cameron Commission nevertheless shed light on apartheid era arms import transactions. For example, P. C. Smith, Armscor's general manager for import and export, produced a written report to the Commission detailing purchases of 3 500 AK47 rifles from 1976 to around 1986 from Yugoslavia, Poland, Hungary, Romania, and Bulgaria at an average cost of between R200 and R300 via arms dealers and agents. South Africa purchased 20 000 G3 rifles from Portugal for R70 to R80 each from 1978 to 1980. From 1985 to 1989, Armscor purchased an additional 35 000 AK47 rifles from the People's Republic of China at an average price of approximately R100. Smith reported that "The G3s were purchased on behalf of SAAF [the air force] as Armscor could not deliver sufficient quantities of R1 rifles due to production limitations."[74]

MILITARY CONSEQUENCES

Military consequences of arms embargoes should be a gradual decline in relative military capabilities of the embargoed state if its adversaries are not embargoed. This decline ought to be most marked in those arms or military components where it is difficult to develop an indigenous capacity for innovation and production, and where innovation by adversaries is comparatively quick and difficult to counter by changing military organization or operations. The arms embargo against South African illustrates this effect and two other significant military consequences of arms sanctions. First, to the extent that material, financial, and human resources were devoted to arms manufacture and the purchase of weapons on the black market at embargo-inflated prices, these resources were not available to be used directly in South Africa's wars in Angola and South West Africa. Second, the South Africans were less flexible in their ability to acquire and deploy weapons and resources. This was clear by the mid-1980s and mentioned in official discourse. "Due to the changing nature of the threat, there has been a sharp decline in the demand for certain arms during the past 3 years and an increased need for others. . . . Where there were sudden massive increases in demand, it was important to satisfy the needs without investing additional capital in greater production capacities, capacities which perhaps could be underutilized again later on."[75]

Despite the best efforts of Armscor, South African weapons gradually became obsolete. This is most clearly illustrated with regard to combat aircraft, probably the sector of conventional (non-nuclear) armaments that requires the most sophisticated primary and secondary production capacities including advanced electronics, engines, and weapons. Combat aircraft, in addition to providing the ability to deliver bombs to distant areas, also protect one's own troops by keeping other aircraft away from them or by providing fire in support of ground operations. Thus aircaft are versatile in many offensive military roles, in addition to their ability to provide reconnaissance information and assist in the transport of equipment and troops. South African inventories of all types of aircraft suffered after the embargo went into force.[76] Perhaps most significant in the context of South Africa's war in Angola was the fact that, after 1977, South Africa was unable to continue licensed production of its most modern ground-attack aircraft, the French Mirage, and found it difficult to produce new platforms.

The embargo thus increasingly limited South Africa's ability to wage war in Angola as the Angolan military acquired more advanced military equipment, including more sophisticated anti-aircraft systems, from the Soviet Union and Cuba. As Soviet weapons were delivered to Angola, particularly air-defense radars that enabled Angolan forces (supplemented increasingly in the mid-1980s by Cuban forces) to shoot down South African fighters, the South African government recognized that their investment in indigenous production was inadequate. "A major problem is that some of the most reliable main armaments are obsolescent. More modern armaments available to our enemies contributed toward this process of obsolescence."[77] So, despite an ability to acquire some designs from abroad, and an enormous investment in military R&D, South Africa was still not able to produce an attack helicopter, nor a new advanced fighter, nor ground-attack aircraft. South Africa was almost entirely limited to retrofitting existing airframes and modifying the designs of aircraft they had acquired before the embargo.

The embargo also made it difficult to acquire some spare parts and this also affected the ability to keep existing aircraft flying. Of the few (less than 70) sophisticated French Mirage aircraft in the South African arsenal, in the late 1980s more than half of the aircraft were grounded due to the lack of spare parts.[78] South African Air Force (SAAF) Colonel Willcock argues that they became quick and innovative with repairs for most contingencies but "it was the smallest, strangest" things that the repair crews were sometimes unable to fix and that led to longer groundings.[79]

These three factors – limited spare parts, difficulty innovating or getting more advanced equipment, and the adversary's military upgrades – gradually changed the air superiority equation (the ability to operate aircraft without much challenge over a combat area). In the early years of the war with Angola, South Africa had air superiority. Still, in June 1980 South Africa lost four Impala aircraft to surface-to-air missile and ground fire in Angola.[80] By the mid-1980s, South Africa had lost its ability to overfly Angola with impunity and had even begun to suffer the loss of more difficult-to-replace aircraft. During Operation Askari of December 1983, South Africa lost five or six Mirage aircraft in Angola.[81]

Declining air superiority and reduced aircraft inventory was evident in the 1988 battle for Cuito Cuanavale in Angola when the SADF attempted to take an Angolan miltary stronghold. While their pilots were able to bail out, South Africa lost domestically produced Impala aircraft in southern Angola as the war progressed.

Accounts of the activities of the SAAF in Angola indicate that the South Africans primarily relied on the Mirage ground-attack aircraft for difficult offensive action.[82] The SADF never had more than 20 Mirage FIAZ ground-attack and Buccaneer bombers deployed in southern Angola in early 1988, and of these there were probably no more than 12 Mirages deployed in any one mission. The SAAF was apparently at times "pinned down" by Angola's use of Soviet-made fighters and ground-attack aircraft – by late 1987 the Angolans had deployed 18 MiG-23 fighters and 13 MiG-21 ground-attack aircraft to the area.[83] South Africa lost at least 2 Mirage fighters during the efforts to take Cuito Cuanavale – one shot down, and another apparently lost due to equipment failure in February and March, in addition to the Mirage piloted by the then Captain Arthur Piercy, shot by MiG-23s in September 1987.[84]

Declining air superiority forced operational changes. For example, the SAAF aircraft were moved further back from the fighting. The SAAF also developed a stand-off bombing capacity of 20 km and flew longer-range aircraft, Buccaneer and Canberra bombers, from South Africa. In addition, South African Mirage pilots moved toward quicker raids, timing their runs so that they were out of range before Angolan and Cuban pilots could scramble. Loss of air superiority also altered the conduct of major ground operations and perhaps helped push South Africa to begin negotiating seriously for an end to the war with Angola:

> By January 1988, South Africa began to lose air superiority. An SADF analysis made then argued that it was possible to take Cuito, but that it would entail the loss of up to 300 white troops, along with some 2 000 SWATF [black South West African Territorial Force] and an unspecified but large number of Unita troops.
>
> The substantial losses were deemed unavoidable by the SADF strategists, since the massive land assault required to take Cuito Cuanavale would not enjoy much aircover from the SAAF as a result of the introduction of advanced anti-aircraft missiles, radars and MiG-23/Su-22 fighters for the defence of the town.
>
> The plan to take Cuito through infantry assault was shelved. Instead Pretoria opted for a drawn out artillery battle....[85]

In sum, since South Africa was unwilling to use its six nuclear weapons, declining conventional military capabilities were significant. Ultimately, the arms embargo meant that South Africa was far enough behind in military technology to help turn the balance in Angola's favor. This shift in military capabilities was also only possible because Soviet weapons and thousands of Cuban military forces were pumped into Angola at the request of the Angolan government. Thus, it was the combination of South Africa's relative military isolation and the increase in quality of Angolan equipment that led to the shift in the balance of forces. If South Africa had been able to modernize, more Cuban and Soviet aid might have been sent, further escalating international involvement.

WINDING DOWN

Arms industries persist after embargoes, and the incentive for arms exports grows as domestic demand falls and competition with other suppliers provides increased incentive for a reduction in unit costs. At the same time, with the protection of the embargo ended, local arms industries may be less robust and competitive than other weapons manufacturers, potentially leading to substantial job losses. Further, the tight relationship between the state and arms industry may persist, perhaps prompting continued government subsidy of arms industries. Events followed this scenario in South Africa.

In April 1992 Armscor was reorganized into a procurement agency, and the original Armscor divisions were subsumed under a quasi-commercial structure known as Denel (Den for Dentron or 23 divisions and el for electronics) under control of the Ministry of Public Enterprises. With assets of R3.84 billion in March 1994, Denel's net income grew after the lifting arms embargo, while Armscor's net income declined 87 percent between June 1994 and June 1995 from R40.2 million to R5 million.[86] In 1993 and 1994 Denel's net income was R335 million and R239 million respectively, and R260 million in 1995. The most profitable elements of the armaments industry were thus privatized by the de Klerk government.

Armscor executives aimed to double or perhaps quadruple South Africa's arms export business and worked to increase exports.[87] Anticipating the end of the embargo, Armscor began showing its military equipment at international arms shows.[88] After the UN lifted the embargo against purchasing South African made weapons in May 1994, South Africa moved immediately to capture a larger share of the international market in which it had already made over $225 million a year.[89] Still, after it made peace with

Angola and ended its occupation in Namibia, South Africa's weapons demands decreased and employment in the arms industry fell, as did the number of companies involved in military production. Armscor's Executive General Manager Tielman De Waal said that 70 000 people were employed by Armscor (80 percent in the private sector) in 1994 and that about 20 000 more jobs were expected after the UN arms embargo lifted.[90] But, despite these optimistic projections, downsizing continued in the arms industry as South African spending on weapons procurement fell; despite a jump in exports, and manufacturing (Denel) employed 15 000 people in 1994, but this fell to 14 000 in 1995.[91] And in 1996 there were about 700 companies engaged in military production – down by over 200 companies since 1990.[92]

CONCLUSIONS

Direct military effects of the arms embargo against South Africa – denial of weapons and spare parts and declining military capability *vis-à-vis* adversaries – were not felt until years after its imposition. South Africa's military-industrialization effort managed to put significant weapons and ammunition in the hands of the SADF, the clandestine arms trade was partially successful, and military innovation by adversaries can take many years. But South Africa did eventually face a problem on the battlefield as its weapons stocks diminished or technology became obsolete.

The indirect effects of the arms embargoes were perhaps more immediate, substantial, and long lasting. Import substitution imposed opportunity costs, taking resources that the state could have spent directly on repression or on promoting economic growth. Military industrialization also, paradoxically, promoted growth, and because it became the leading manufacturing sector in South Africa, it stimulated the incorporation of black workers into the skilled-labor portion of the economy.

Would industrialization have occurred at a faster pace without sanctions? This is difficult to know. But, given the structure of the domestic economy under apartheid – with the majority impoverished and the much richer white population comprising less than 15 percent of the population – it is likely that there would have been little demand for massive import substitution since the majority population lacked the purchasing power to fuel such an

expansion. Moreover, though there would have been some industrialization, South Africa could have remained extractively oriented
and postponed integration. The desire to produce military equipment to arm the SADF provided an immediate demand for import-substitution industries (along with the demand to replace oil
imports). In addition, until the reforms instituted to promote industrialization for military and other industries, the education policies
of the apartheid government were the opposite of those of a government interested in promoting the skilled workforce necessary
for producing the capital goods necessary to fuel industrialization.[93]

The long-term consequences of the arms embargoes are mixed.
South Africa now has a high-tech arms industry that its government and society are ambivalent about and whose place in foreign
policy is ambiguous.[94] While arms manufacture provides high technology, foreign exchange, and much-needed jobs, there is an intense debate inside South Africa about whether non-military
industries would do better at providing these benefits. And the
relationship between the state and military-industrial capital remained
close after the transition to democracy. At the same time, through
the Cameron Commission the new government grappled with the
problem that the weapons it sells may decrease regional security.[95]

In sum, from the perspective of sanctioners, the tighter an arms
embargo obviously the better. But, even if they are leaky, embargoes can "work" through their indirect effects. Arms embargoes do
not work quickly and it is probably unreasonable to expect immediate results in either military or economic spheres. Sanctions can
decrease military capabilities; they also tend to increase the share
of military spending that goes toward procurement (an opportunity cost), and they tend to provoke import substitution and clandestine trade. Military industrialization will likely be frustrated by
a carefully constructed embargo, and embargoed producers may
be unable, even with a significant black-market arms trade, to keep
pace with the military-technical innovations of non-embargoed states.
Sanctioners wishing to further complicate import-substitution industrialization ought to focus on halting high technology and machine-
tool transfers. Further, military industrialization has wide implications
for the economy, politics, and social relations of the target state,
tending to promote either minor or major economic restructuring
depending on the preexisting level of industrialization; this may in
turn help anti-government forces within the target to resist the state.
Over the long run, military industrialization alters relations between

the state and capital, and increases incentives for the embargoed state to export its weapons. The end of an arms embargo, because it halts externally imposed protectionism, will likely lead to job losses in military industries.

Notes

1. Amy Nash provided research assistance. Peter Batchelor and Jacklyn Cock gave generous intellectual support. I also learned from David Fig, Norma Kriger, Kim Nossal, and Meg Voorhes. Navy Captain Derek Christian, Captain Robert (Rusty) Higgs, and Air Force Colonels P. B. Willcock and Brian Wilford and Air Force Major Arthur Piercy (retired) of the South African National Defence Force spoke candidly about military operations and the effects of sanctions.
2. "The Garrison-State Hypothesis Today," in S. Huntington, ed., *Changing Patterns of Military Politics* (New York: Free Press, 1961), pp. 51–70: 65.
3. Throughout, I focus on the UN embargo, with less discussion of bilateral sanctions.
4. I do not take up two elements of the arms embargo – how and why multilateral embargo implementation is successful or unsuccessful, and political uses of isolation to bolster the target regime. On this, see L. L. Martin, *Coercive Cooperation: Explaining Multilateral Economic Sanctions* (Princeton, NJ: Princeton University Press, 1992); M. Mastanduno, *Economic Containment: CoCom and the Politics of East–West Trade* (Ithaca, NY: Cornell University Press, 1992); M. P. Doxey, *Economic Sanctions and International Enforcement* (London: Oxford University Press, 1971). I also do not discuss nuclear sanctions; see D. Fig, "Sanctions and the Nuclear Industry" Chapter 4 in this volume.
5. S. Landgren, *Embargo Disimplemented: South Africa's Military Industry* (New York: Oxford University Press, 1989), p. 14.
6. Landgren, *Embargo Disimplemented*, p. 14.
7. K. Krause, *Arms and the State: Patterns of Military Production and Trade* (Cambridge: Cambridge University Press, 1992), p. 13.
8. War and rapid industrialization often go together – something historians and sociologists have often remarked upon, but one that is little explored by political scientists. For an exception, see W. D. Coleman, and K. R. Nossal, "The State, War and Business in Canada, 1939–1945," in W. Grant, J. Nekkers and F. Van Waarden, eds., *Organizing Business for War: Corporatist Economic Organisation during the Second World War* (Providence: Berg, 1991), pp. 41–73.
9. Mastanduno, *Economic Containment*, p. 48.
10. The difference between offensive and defensive weapons is not dichotomous; offensiveness depends more on the use of weapons than "inherent" characteristics.
11. Demand does not depend on price in two senses: in hot and cold wars weapons may be seen to be essential regardless of price, and the

demand for weapons may suddenly decline because of political and military factors other than price.

12. In addition to slowing or halting innovation, embargoes may affect the types of weapons produced: isolated military industries may produce weapons that are less "baroque," or more streamlined in their designs and easier to produce and maintain.

13. C. Tilly, *Coercion, Capital, and European States, AD 990–1992* (Oxford: Blackwell, 1992), p. 223.

14. UN Security Council (SC) Resolution 181, 7 August 1963.

15. UN SC Resolution 182, 4 December 1963.

16. UN SC Resolution 418, 4 November 1977.

17. See Landgren, *Embargo Disimplemented*; T. U. Mozia, "Chronology of Arms Embargoes Against South Africa," in G. W. Shepard, Jr., ed., *Effective Sanctions On South Africa: The Cutting Edge of Economic Intervention* (New York: Praeger, 1991), pp. 97–108.

18. See Landgren, *Embargo Disimplemented*, pp. 194–228; N. Chandler, "French Role in SA Defence Industry Revealed," *The Star*, 29 April 1996.

19. UN SC Resolution 919, 25 May 1994. T. Weiner, "U.S., After 35 years, Lifts Arms Embargo Against South Africa," *New York Times*, 28 February 1998.

20. See M. Brzoska, "South Africa: Evading the Embargo," in M. Brozska and T. Ohlson, *Arms Production in the Third World* (London: Taylor and Francis, 1986), pp. 193–214: 194–5; R. Matthews, "The Development of the South African Military Industrial Complex," *Defense Analysis* 4 (1988), pp. 7–24: 7–9.

21. Landgren, *Embargo Disimplemented*, p. 9. Also see W. Cobbett, "Apartheid's Army and the Arms Embargo," in J. Cock and L. Nathan, eds., *Society at War: The Militarization of South Africa* (New York: St. Martin's, 1989), pp. 232–43.

22. Republic of South Africa (RSA), *Briefing on the Organization and Functions of the South African Defence Force and the Armaments Corporation of South Africa, Limited 1990*, hereafter cited as RSA, *Briefing* (Pretoria: Ministry of Defence, 1990), p. 63.

23. Landgren, *Embargo Disimplemented*, p. 41. Also see G. Simpson, "The Politics and Economics of the Armaments Industry in South Africa," in Cock and Nathan, eds., *Society at War*, pp. 217–31: 221.

24. RSA, *White Paper on Defence 1977* (Pretoria, 1977), p. 9.

25. J. W. de Villiers, R. Jardine and M. Reiss, "Why South Africa Gave Up the Bomb," *Foreign Affairs* 72 (1993), pp. 98–109: 102, 105; Fig, "Sanctions and the Nuclear Industry."

26. P. Batchelor, "South Africa's Military Industry: History and Overview" (Cape Town: Centre for Conflict Resolution, 1996), unpublished photocopy, table 5.

27. Ibid., table 9.

28. RSA, *White Paper on Defence and Armament Production, 1973* (Pretoria, 1973), p. 17; and RSA, *Briefing*, p. 66.

29. RSA, *White Paper on Defence and Armament Production, 1973*, p. 17.

30. Matthews, "The Development of the South African Military Industrial Complex," p. 10.

31. RSA, *Briefing*, p. 66.
32. Ibid.
33. Chandler, "French Role in SA Defence Industry Revealed."
34. Matthews, "The Development of the South African Military Industrial Complex," pp. 17, 19 and 23.
35. Begg, "SAAF and the Arms Industry," *Ad Astra*, 10 (1989), pp. 11–14.
36. Batchelor, "South Africa's Military Industry," table 2.
37. Not in constant rand.
38. *Washington Report on Africa*, 6, no. 3 (1 March 1988), p. 11.
39. On other effects of the "total strategy," see N. Crawford, "The Domestic Sources and Consequences of Aggressive Foreign Policies: The Folly of South Africa's 'Total Strategy,'" working paper no. 41 of the *Southern African Perspectives* series (Bellville, South Africa: University of the Western Cape, 1995).
40. S. Jones and A. Mullen, *The South African Economy, 1910–1990* (New York: St. Martin's, 1992), p. 231.
41. Simpson, "The Politics and Economics of the Armaments Industry in South Africa," p. 223.
42. RSA, *White Paper on Defence and Armament Production, 1973*, p. 17.
43. RSA, *White Paper on Defence and Armament Supply, 1986* (Pretoria, 1986), p. 38.
44. Ibid., p. 36.
45. Matthews, "The Development of the South African Military Industrial Complex," p. 24.
46. RSA, *White Paper on Defence and Armament Supply, 1986*, p. 35.
47. A. Black, "Manufacturing Development and Economic Crisis: A Reversion to Primary Production?" in S. Gelb, ed., *South Africa's Economic Crisis* (Cape Town: David Phillip, 1991), pp. 156–74.
48. RSA, *White Paper on Defence and Armament Supply, 1986*, p. 35.
49. "Survival of the Fittest," *Financial Mail* 138 (20 October 1995), pp. 30, 34: 34.
50. Peter Batchelor, personal communication, 26 February 1996.
51. Figures for percent of all manufacturing jobs devoted to full- and part-time arms manufacture are calculated from employment figures in Central Statistical Service (CSS), *South African Statistics 1994* (Pretoria: Government Printing Office, 1994), p. 7.11.
52. S. Metz, "Pretoria's 'Total Strategy' and Low-Intensity Warfare in Southern Africa," *Comparative Strategy* 6, no. 4 (1987), pp. 437–69: 446–7. J. Barber and J. Barratt, *South Africa's Foreign Policy: The Search for Status and Security* (Cambridge: Cambridge University Press, 1990), pp. 257–8. One important meeting between the business sector and the state in 1977 was opened by General Magnus Malan, co-chaired by Major-General Neil Webster, and the chair of Standard Bank.
53. G. Huston, "Capital Accumulation, Influx Control, and the State in South Africa, 1970–1982," *Journal of Contemporary African Studies* 7 (1988), pp. 111–31: 125. These measures were implemented more or less successfully over the next several years.
54. "The modifications [of influx control] introduced were intended to improve the productivity of labour or comparable economic functions on the one hand, and to reduce the levels of opposition to the state

on the other." A. Stadler, *The Political Economy of Modern South Africa* (New York: St. Martin's, 1987), pp. 96–101: 97.

55. Between 1975 and 1990, emigration among professional and production workers was generally higher than for other categories of labor in South Africa. This brain- and skilled-worker drain was partially redressed domestically though there were certainly immigrants classified as professional and production workers. CSS, *South African Statistics 1994*, pp. 2.10–2.12.

56. RSA, *Briefing*, p. 69.

57. A. Sparks, *The Mind of South Africa* (New York: Alfred A. Knopf, 1990), p. 314.

58. Calculated from statistics given in RSA, *South Africa 1989–1990, The Official Yearbook of the Republic of South Africa, Fifteenth Edition* (Pretoria: RSA, 1990), p. 778.

59. Based on figures in CSS, *South African Statistics 1994*, p. 7.11.

60. By 1986, SADF personnel was 24 percent Asian, Black and colored and women played an increasing role in the forces. Racial integration of the SADF is discussed in RSA, *White Paper on Defence and Armaments Supply 1986*, pp. 17–20.

61. *Financial Mail* 138, "Survival of the Fittest," p. 30.

62. Jones and Mullen, *The South African Economy, 1910–1990*, pp. 283–4.

63. CSS, *South African Statistics 1994*, p. 7.4.

64. J. Cock, "Rocks, Snakes and South Africa's Arms Industry," *Mayibuye* (February 1993), pp. 20–1: 20. There is a great disparity among the top international weapons producer's market share and the share held by smaller exporters. South Africa's share of the market was well under one percent in 1996, down from previous years (K. Naidoo, remarks on "Defence Industries" at the conference "Defensive Restructuring of the Armed Forces in Southern Africa," Johannesburg, South Africa, 4 March 1996).

65. For example, there were some links between South African arms exports to Middle Eastern countries and oil sanctions busting.

66. Naidoo, "Defence Industries."

67. *Washington Post*, 24 February 1985, p. A26. Cited in G. C. Hufbauer, J. J. Schott, and K. E. Elliot, *Economic Sanctions Reconsidered: History and Current Policy*, 2nd ed. (Washingto, DC: Institute for International Economics, 1990) Supplemental Case Histories, p. 232.

68. Figures reported in J. Cohen and A. Peach, *World Combat Aircraft Holdings, Production, and Trade* (Cambridge: Institute for Defense and Disarmament Studies, 1994), pp. 114–5.

69. R. Vayrynen, "The Role of Transnational Corporations in the Military Sector of South Africa," *Journal of Southern African Studies* 5, (1981).

70. Under apartheid, South Africa widely marketed G3 and AK47 automatic weapons within Africa and abroad. Indeed, after the transition to democracy, the G3 and AK47s were offered to both UNITA and the MPLA (after UNITA was unable to make payment), apparently without the full knowledge of the new government. By offering to sell arms to UNITA, South Africa's arms merchants violated a 1993 United

Nations arms embargo against UNITA. The effort to sell the G3s and AK47s in Angola were unsuccessful, and when a buyer was finally found, the arms were shipped to Yemen, also apparently without full South African government knowledge.
71. B. Keller, "Apartheid's Arms-Maker Finds Respectability," *New York Times*, 26 August 1994.
72. Armscor's sales of millions of dollars of weapons, including grenades and rifles, to Rwanda between 1992 and 1993, were already admitted. New revelations included the exposure of illegal apartheid era arms sales to other African nations, to countries in the Middle East (including to both sides of the Iran–Iraq war) and to the former Yugoslavia. There were admissions that over 4 500 AK47s previously under SANDF possession had recently disappeared, and that between 1991 and 1993 Armscor had sold $3.4 million in anti-personnel mines as well as Milan anti-tank rockets and rocket launchers to the Christian militias in Lebanon.
73. Cameron Commission, "Commission of Inquiry into Alleged Arms Transactions between Armscor and One Eli Wazan and Related Matters," (Johannesburg: Republic of South Africa, 15 June 1995), pp. 23 and 107. Hereafter cited as Cameron Commission Report, part 1.
74. P. C. Smith, "The Smith Report," p. 5, reprinted as appendix 6 of the Cameron Commission Report, part 1.
75. RSA, *White Paper on Defence and Armament Supply, 1986*, p. 33.
76. South Africa had difficulty modernizing electronic countermeasures and electronic warfare equipment, and maintaining its aging fleet of transport and surveillance aircraft. T. Ohlson, "The Cuito Cuanavale Syndrome: Revealing SADF Vulnerabilities," *South African Review* 5 (Braamfontein: Ravan, 1989), pp. 181–90: 186. Also see G. Crown, "Success of the Arms Embargo," in J. Hanlon, ed., *South Africa: The Sanctions Report Documents and Statistics* (London: James Currey, 1990), pp. 168–74. Similarly, because it was difficult to get replacements, South Africa kept its Harvard trainers in service for decades, retiring them only in 1995, well beyond what would have been their natural service life.
77. RSA, *White Paper on Defence 1984*, p. 22.
78. Coker, *South Africa's Security Dilemmas*, (New York: Praeger, 1987, Washington papers no. 126), pp. 33–4.
79. Interview, SANDF Headquarters, 5 March 1996.
80. Coker, *South Africa's Security Dilemmas*, p. 35.
81. Ibid., p. 33. Colonel Willcock believes South Africa lost air superiority in 1986. Interview, 5 March 1996.
82. Buccaneer bombers, introduced to South Africa in the 1960s, were also used in ground-attack missions, but the Mirage FIAZs were apparently used most frequently in combat sorties. For a detailed account, from a South African perspective, of the war's later phases see H.-R. Heitman, *War in Angola: The Final South African Phase* (Gilbraltar: Ashanti, 1990). Also see W. Steenkamp, *South Africa's Border War: 1966–1989* (Gilbraltar: Ashanti, 1989).
83. Heitman, *War in Angola*, p. 181.

84. Ibid., pp. 243, 272, 285. J. Geldenhuys, *A General's Story: From an Era of War and Peace* (Johannesburg: Jonathan Ball, 1995), p. 222. Telephone interview with Major Arthur Piercy, 18 March 1995, Pretoria, South Africa.
85. Ohlson, "The Cuito Cuanavale Syndrome," p. 182.
86. *Financial Mail*, "Public Sector Corporations," p. 251.
87. S. Willett, *Open Arms for the Prodigal Son: The Future of South Africa's Arms Trade Policies* (London: British-American Security Information Council, 1994), p. 6; F. Smyth, "Arms and Mandela," *The Washington Post*, 22 May 1994.
88. Armscor made relatively less baroque military equipment, better suited to regional conditions, helping it gain a niche in the international arms market for the kinds of low-maintenance, relatively inexpensive and high-quality weapons it developed and produced under the embargo. For example, the *Rooivalk* attack helicopter developed by Atlas Aviation to fight in Angola and Namibia, but never used in those conflicts, became attractive because of its ability to operate at low altitude (between 15 to 50 feet) to avoid detection, advanced munitions, and the relative ease of maintaining it in the field. South Africa also developed expertise in retrofitting old weapons platforms with new systems. Willett, *Open Arms for the Prodigal Son*, p. 7; L. Birns, "Chopper on the Block," *South Africa: The Journal of Trade, Industry and Development* (February/March 1995) 26–30.
89. Associated Press, "South Africa Pitches Firepower," *Clarinet News*, 8 September 1994.
90. T. Deen, "Pretoria Arms Policy Upsets UN," *InterPress Service*, 3 June 1994.
91. D. Silverberg, "The New Armscor," *Armed Forces Journal International* (May 1994), pp. 45–8. *Financial Mail*, "Public Sector Corporations," p. 251; "Survival of the Fittest," p. 30.
92. Naidoo, "Defence Industries."
93. These observations raise an important question often posed by advocates of constructive engagement: If industrialization promotes growth and political change, why not forgo sanctions and let the target industrialize more naturally? The answers are simple. First, the pressure of sanctions increases opportunity costs, forcing targets to make increasingly difficult choices. Second, military capabilities gradually decline under embargoes.
94. On early post-apartheid foreign and military policy, see N. C. Crawford, "South Africa's New Foreign and Military Policy: Opportunities and Constraints," *Africa Today* 42 (1995), pp. 88–121.
95. Volume 2 of the Cameron Commission Report dealt exclusively with the problem of developing an arms export policy.

4 Sanctions and the Nuclear Industry
David Fig

When South African president F. W. de Klerk announced to a joint session of parliament on 24 March 1993 that the country had developed "nuclear devices," he confirmed what many suspected. From 1974, South Africa had secretly become a nuclear weapons power, devoting immense resources – between R700 million (the officially confessed figure) and ten times that amount (which experts calculate is more likely) – to manufacturing nuclear weapons. The apartheid state later claimed it would never have exploded the devices: it hoped that in any apocalyptic conflict with its foes, that the revelation of South Africa's nuclear weapons status would act as a sufficient deterrent, a *deus ex machina* saviour of apartheid.

How was it possible for a country as isolated as South Africa became during the height of sanctions, to acquire sufficient technology to manufacture nuclear bombs? President de Klerk asserted that "at no time did South Africa acquire nuclear weapons technology or materials from another country."[1] Documentation of the weapons manufacturing process has, we are told, been destroyed,[2] and brand names were filed off machinery which survived the decommissioning of the weapons.[3] These acts conceal the precise extent to which international nuclear trade sanctions were defied, as well as the identities of sanctions busters. Whether one believes that South African weapons were entirely home grown or not, their existence transcended sanctions. It is important to examine how various stages of the nuclear fuel cycle were put in place despite growing sanctions. Were international measures against nuclear collaboration effective in restricting the scope of the South African nuclear program, or were they merely an incentive for the apartheid regime to develop a viable domestic nuclear capability?

I argue that, despite official assertions to the contrary, South Africa was not in any position to have manufactured nuclear weapons without imported ideas and equipment. The South African nuclear industry was, from its earliest days, a transnational enterprise encouraged by Western countries in exchange for supplies of uranium.

In return for South African uranium, Western nuclear weapons states made it possible for South Africa to establish a viable domestic nuclear research establishment, capable of developing a number of the stages of the nuclear fuel cycle. Sanctions were only intensified once it was clear that the apartheid government had developed the capacity to proliferate nuclear weapons. With the mandatory arms embargo in 1977 nuclear sanctions affected development of a civil nuclear power industry and a nuclear weapons capability. By this time, sanctions might appear to have been futile. Yet sanctions contributed to a climate of paranoia, tied up resources, and did manage to slow South Africa's technical progress in nuclear weapons design.

INTEGRATION INTO THE GLOBAL NUCLEAR INDUSTRY, 1945–77

Uranium Supply

South Africa's integration into the nuclear weapons production process began during World War II. Until the mid-1960s, the United States and Britain almost exclusively depended on South African uranium supplies for their nuclear weapons programs.

As part of their wartime collaboration, US President Franklin Roosevelt, Canadian Prime Minister Mackenzie King, and British Prime Minister Winston Churchill, negotiated the Quebec Agreement in August 1943. This led to a Combined Development Policy Committee, established to exchange information and resources on constructing the nuclear bomb. The Quebec Agreement also led to a joint US–British–Canadian organization for the procurement of uranium, the Combined Development Trust, that was to search for and purchase uranium from areas of the world outside the control of the three partners. The worldwide scan for uranium and other fissile materials first examined sources in North America, Portugal, India, and the then Belgian Congo.

Uranium supplied by the Belgian Congo was used in the first Manhattan Project bombs. However this was not a large source and the search for uranium broadened. The British government informed South Africa's prime minister Jan Smuts of the Manhattan Project in 1944, requesting him to launch an investigation into reported deposits of radioactive minerals in South Africa and South

African-controlled South West Africa (now independent Namibia). Most of the key deposits were found in the Witwatersrand, a gold-bearing reef, located in the area surrounding Johannesburg. At the height of its production in the late 1980s, South Africa controlled the second-largest uranium reserves in the capitalist world economy (300 000 tons or 17 percent) and accounted for 13 percent of non-communist world production (including its South West African/Namibian reserves, which at that time were still under its control).

Fear that the Soviet Union might develop its own weapons fuelled US–British haste to build their stocks of weapons. With adequate finance, South African uranium mining would secure the US and British nuclear weapons arsenal. Realizing the importance of these substantial deposits, Smuts took a keen personal interest in the development of uranium mining. He liaised with the British government, with the South African gold mining industry, and with South African scientists, setting up a Uranium Research Committee answerable to the prime minister's department. Collaboration on uranium extraction was likely to give South Africa some leverage with Britain and the US. After 1945, exclusively white-ruled South Africa came under attack for its racial policies from the Afro-Asian and Soviet blocs within the recently established United Nations. Smuts's strategic ties with Britain and the US, two powerful permanent members of the Security Council, became important to South Africa as a powerful counterbalancing device at the UN.

The sluggish postwar mining industry in South Africa also stood to benefit from new investment, as did the closely connected heavy engineering sector. Pessimism about the price of gold could be offset against the lucrative new commodity, uranium, and financial support offered to the uranium mining industry by Britain and the US could be used to subsidize the development of the Orange Free State goldfields; it was therefore crucial that South Africa collaborate closely with both countries. The Witwatersrand finds proved so rich that Smuts told British Secretary of State for Air, Philip Noel-Baker, that these deposits would replace the Canadian mines as the richest source of atomic fuel.[4]

As a Commonwealth member, South Africa fell outside the purview of the Combined Development Trust; a separate new body had to be formed. This time, the Canadians were excluded, because they had no intention of creating an atomic weapons program. The existence of the new Combined Development Agency (CDA) was kept secret, for at least five years at first, even from Smuts.[5]

Originally the British and Americans, acting together as the CDA, put up the money for 4 extraction plants on 4 Witwatersrand gold mines. This later expanded to a total of 17 plants servicing 27 mines.

Smuts drew up plans to broaden the Uranium Research Committee into an organization with control over atomic research and development in South Africa as well as the production and trade of all radioactive substances on behalf of the state as owner. His idea was a body resembling the US Atomic Energy Commission or the British Atomic Energy Authority. To avoid confusion, the South African version was to be known as the Atomic Energy Board (AEB).

In May 1948, before the relevant legislation could be passed, Smuts lost not only his seat, but his party lost control of parliament to the purified National Party in the general election for a whites-only parliament. Under the new prime minister, Dr. D. F. Malan, who had campaigned on the slogan of apartheid, it became the task of Malan's Minister of Mines, Dr. A. van Rhijn, to steer the atomic legislation through parliament. The Atomic Energy Act No 35, of 1948, allowed for the formal establishment of the AEB on 1 January 1949. Secretly the CDA signed an agreement with the AEB to buy up all the uranium produced from each mine for the first ten years of the life of each plant.

Although the CDA made the deal with the government's AEB, mining companies made the profits. Because contracts were long term, and the South African government was anxious to be of strategic help to the new North Atlantic Treaty Organization, profits were limited to a cost-plus fixed ratio. Nevertheless, profit taking was substantial, rising from £1.8m in 1953 to £37.75m in 1958.[6] The CDA also helped unplug bottlenecks in the industries, transport and steelmaking, which were vital to the production of uranium. Mining finance houses also gained a new inflow of hard currency which – along with windfall profits from diamond mining and the British currency devaluation – assisted in the capitalization of the new gold mines in the Orange Free State. Thus South Africa reported to the First International Conference on Peaceful Uses of Atomic Energy that "It can safely be said that no major industry in the history of South Africa has been developed as rapidly as the uranium industry."[7] Equally, the huge uranium reserves served as the basis for the development of South Africa's nuclear technological capacity.

Britain and the US had great difficulty criticizing apartheid. One of the reasons for this must certainly have been their need for

uranium from 1950–64.[8] From 1950, for as long as they were obliged
to honor their agreements with the mining industry, the US and
British weapons (and possibly commercial energy) programs relied
extensively on South African uranium. In turn, South Africa obtained an injection of foreign exchange, whose investment in the
mining and engineering industries was able to help fuel the postwar industrial boom. There were other strategic considerations, such
as the 1955 Anglo–South African Simon's Town Agreement, guaran-
teeing South African naval facilities to the Royal Navy in times of
war, which persisted through to 1975, when it was cancelled by
Britain's Labour government.[9] The arms embargo advocated by the
UN General Assembly in 1963, was taken seriously by the US, but
never seriously applied by the Europeans: nuclear material continued to flow in both directions. By 1964, the US and Britain had
found alternative sources and the agreements began to be phased
out. South African and Namibian uranium continued to be exported
to a variety of countries after the mines were released from giving
first preference to the US and Britain.

US Technology Transfer

To avert nuclear proliferation the US began to emphasize nuclear
controls. President Eisenhower addressed the UN General Assembly regarding "Atoms for Peace" on 8 December 1953, advocating
a joint US–UK–USSR reduction of weapons-grade uranium stockpiles and the establishment of an international control agency.
Nuclear materials, information and expertise would be allowed on
condition that recipients use them exclusively for "peaceful" purposes such as power generation, medical procedures and civil engineering.[10] The proposal was received enthusiastically in the infant
South African nuclear industry. By June 1958, under the leadership of its President Dr. A. J. A. "Ampie" Roux, the AEB formulated a nuclear research program including "research on a power
reactor concept appropriate to South Africa."[11] Cabinet approval
of this policy was formally announced by Senator Jan de Klerk,
then minister of mines, chairman of the AEB, and father of the
future president, on 5 September 1959.

The research program had three prongs, focusing on uranium and
other fissile materials, radio-isotopes and radiation, and establishing
a nuclear power reactor. To house its research, the AEB needed a
venue more suitable than its suite in a Pretoria office block and it

secretly purchased farmland to the south of Hartebeespoort Dam. Known as Pelindaba ("the talking is over"), the South African National Nuclear Research Centre's first buildings were occupied in 1963.

One building was designed to house a research reactor. At first the AEB went shopping for a British reactor, but American offers were more attractive.[12] Under "Atoms for Peace," the US agreed to supply a 20 MW capacity reactor running on the highly enriched weapons-grade uranium (HEU) available. The US was also willing to supply enriched uranium on condition that South Africa signed a safeguards agreement allowing for international inspection of the facility. South Africa accepted these conditions and the US prepared to provide weapons-grade uranium under safeguard for at least the next ten years, not deeming it to fall under the ambit of an arms embargo. The South African Fundamental Atomic Research Reactor, SAFARI-1, was commissioned on 18 March 1965.[13]

The "Atoms for Peace" initiative included a secret treaty, the US–South African Agreement for Co-operation Concerning Civil Uses of Atomic Energy, that enabled training in reactor physics for a cadre of South African scientists at Argonne National Laboratories outside Chicago, Oak Ridge National Laboratory in Tennessee, and at other US venues.[14] On returning to South Africa, this cadre formed the nucleus of an increasingly powerful nuclear bureaucracy. Some of these scientists became the research division heads at Pelindaba. One of them, Dr. Wynand de Villiers, rose to become the second president of the AEB. By the mid-60s, South African universities were running their own nuclear research departments. The AEB was able to recruit 75 scientists to staff Pelindaba. Thus, with intensive US collaboration, South Africa's nuclear research effort reached critical mass. Twenty years later, Dr. Roux paid homage to the decisive support offered by the United States to South Africa's fledgling nuclear industry:

We can ascribe our degree of advancement today in large measure to the training and assistance so willingly provided by the USA during the early years of our nuclear program; [South Africa's research reactor] is of American design, [and] much of the nuclear equipment installed at Pelindaba is of American origin, while even our nuclear philosophy, although unmistakeably our own, owes much to the thinking of [American] nuclear scientists.[15]

In his speech of 24 March 1993, president de Klerk claimed that the nuclear weapons program was initiated in 1974. Yet there could be no question of a nuclear weapons program without South Africa having stockpiles of HEU enriched to a content of 90 percent of U_{235}. The SAFARI-1 experimental reactor runs on exactly the same level of enriched uranium, but because of the strict safeguards insisted upon by the US in providing the enriched uranium for SAFARI-1, there was little chance of South Africa diverting a significant amount toward weapons manufacture. Given the unlikelihood of being able to import unsafeguarded HEU in secret, South Africa was left with no choice but to develop its own capability to enrich uranium.

Even if one were to discount the military rationale, South Africa's nuclear bureaucracy made a decision very early on to develop an enrichment capability. From 1961, when senior nuclear scientists returned from their training abroad, they were bent on developing an enrichment facility. They calculated that it would be more cost effective for future power reactors to run on enriched rather than on natural uranium. Having secured political support from Prime Minister Verwoerd for the development of the enrichment technology, Dr. Roux turned his attention to evaluating appropriate methods of isotope separation. The AEB's plans were carefully explained to Verwoerd, who visited the future site of Pelindaba in 1961 soon after construction began. In one of the construction huts the AEB Division heads outlined their proposals for developing an enrichment facility. They were impressed by Verwoerd's ready acceptance of their views on the need to develop enrichment technology and secured his full support in its financing and promotion.[16]

West German Technology

The only workable method of commercial enrichment available in the 1960s was the United States' gaseous diffusion process. This demanded massive capital investment, which had been feasible when enrichment programs were developed for military purposes. South Africa did not have the financial strength to embark on this route. Attention turned to the gas centrifuge method, pioneered in a joint venture between West Germany, Britain, and the Netherlands, but the technology had extremely demanding technical requirements which, on its own, South African scientists would have difficulty resolving. Roux therefore embarked on a course which he would later claim was "an entirely new principle. . . . We have thought it out and worked it out ourselves – every calculation and every little step in the process. . . . It is all the work of South Africans."[17] This claim was later contested by many critics, including the ANC and the World Campaign against Nuclear and Military Collaboration with Apartheid, who claimed that the South African enrichment process was developed in close collaboration with the West German nuclear industry.

The enrichment research program began in a quiet warehouse on Du Toit street, central Pretoria, prior to the completion of the Pelindaba facility under the leadership of Dr. Wally Grant.[18] He designed and perfected the method whereby uranium hexafluoride ("hex") gas was introduced in a vortex to a stationary-walled centrifuge, enabling separation of the isotopes. Hex is notoriously corrosive, toxic and difficult to process.

It was not until 1967 that the AEB felt it had demonstrated the feasibility of the enrichment process on an experimental scale. In April 1968, a special three-member, government-appointed panel, chaired by Dr. H. J. van Eck (head of the state-owned Industrial Development Corporation), endorsed Roux's plan for constructing a pilot enrichment plant. They persuaded the cabinet in February 1969, then headed by Verwoerd's successor, B. J. Vorster, to vote the funds for the program, and the AEB obtained land adjacent to Pelindaba for the pilot plant. The new site was called Valindaba, "the talking has ceased."

Despite the South African nuclear bureaucracy's own optimism about its ability to develop an enrichment process, critics felt that South Africa lacked the capital, manufacturing capacity, and human skills to go it alone. Yet open international nuclear research collaboration was becoming more difficult because of growing and potential sanctions. One exception was West Germany, which had developed a significant nuclear industry, but which was not permitted to manufacture its own nuclear weapons. West Germany had already shown a practical interest in supporting the initiatives of Brazil and Iran to develop their own nuclear fuel chains.

A flurry of West Germans visited Pelindaba, including the ultraconservative Bavarian politician Franz Josef Strauss, who had served as federal minister of science, and thus headed the federal nuclear program. A staunch friend of the apartheid regime, Strauss made numerous visits to Pretoria. Clandestine visits by top-ranking West German military leaders to South Africa were also a feature of this period. Many of the interactions were facilitated by Donald Sole, Vorster's ambassador to Bonn, who had previously been a governor of the International Atomic Energy Agency (IAEA) in Vienna, and was intensely interested in South African collaboration with West Germany in the nuclear sphere. During 1969–70, the Nuclear Research Center (GfK) at Karlsruhe offered special training to four South African nuclear scientists. Among them was Dr. Waldo Stumpf, destined to become chief executive officer of the Atomic Energy Corporation (AEC, the AEB's successor) in 1990. The GfK also hosted Dr. Wally Grant in November 1969. South African scientists were keen to gain a full understanding of the jet-nozzle enrichment process designed by German scientist Dr. E. W. Becker. Grant also claimed experience in jet-nozzle experimentation. The similarities between the Becker method and the final enrichment technique adopted by South Africa led to substantial speculation about the close levels of collaboration.

As the pilot plant began to take shape at Valindaba, it became clear that the intense secrecy around the enrichment program could not be maintained. Since an official statement would be preferable to accidental discovery of Valindaba's purpose, on 20 July 1970, Vorster revealed information about South Africa's enrichment plans in the House of Assembly. As a major uranium exporter, he argued, South Africa could derive more foreign exchange exporting uranium in its enriched form. A further motive was the immense cost of importing enriched uranium to fuel South Africa's nuclear power program, envisaged as having a capacity of 20 000 MW by the year 2000.[19] At no stage was there any mention of a military application of uranium enrichment. Vorster emphasized the peaceful intention of the program three times during his speech, and offered to collaborate with any non-communist countries in the exploitation of the process. Vorster also set in train the creation of a separate parastatal entity charged with the enrichment of uranium. Within a month of his speech, the legislation had been signed creating the Uranium Enrichment Corporation of South Africa Limited (UCOR).[20]

UCOR attempted to use the West German connection to create an international partnership in which its activities would be adequately financed and its product marketed globally. For six years UCOR conducted discussions and negotiations with potential West German partners, with a view to securing a joint venture. The German company STEAG, which the GfK had entrusted with the licensing of the jet-nozzle process, actually signed a memorandum of understanding with UCOR in August 1973. STEAG aimed to make UCOR a sublicensee of the jet-nozzle process. However, there was no unanimity in the West German cabinet, which had to approve the deal, and STEAG withdrew its formal application for federal government approval. Although the official deal fell through, collaboration continued in the form of a "feasibility study" comparing South African and German enrichment processes. Many saw this study as a smokescreen for continued collaboration.

Early Sanctions and Enrichment

Since Pretoria failed to accede to the Nuclear Non-Proliferation Treaty (NPT) which had entered into force in 1970, the US increasingly obstructed the South African nuclear program, embargoing the provision of South Africa with further highly enriched uranium from 1976. Passage of the Nuclear Non-Proliferation Act by the US Congress in 1978 halted transfers of US nuclear technologies to non-signatories of the NPT, and meant that the South African process would have to generate more HEU than it had planned.[21]

These factors constrained the output of HEU, acting in turn as a brake on South African development of nuclear weapons. Whilst transfers of Western nuclear technology and know-how had undoubtedly occurred, it proved impossible for South Africa to acquire a turnkey enrichment process from the West. Was this due to economic constraints, as the South African industry argued, or was it necessary to develop a dedicated local technology in the face of potential sanctions?

The timing of the establishment of the pilot enrichment plant may be key in answering some of these questions. By 1967 the technological choice had been made to promote the locally developed process. By 1969 this had gained full cabinet approval in the form of a five-year research and development budget. It took until 1974 before the pilot enrichment plant began production, and only in January 1978 did it begin to produce HEU.

Located in the Y-plant at Valindaba, the pilot plant had to overcome a number of serious mechanical and chemical problems.[22] This included a period, from August 1979 to July 1981, during which there was a complete halt in production. The plant was reopened in 1981. Since South Africa was not a party to the NPT, there was never any international inspection of the plant, which remained unsafeguarded.

Vorster had provided parliament with the rationale that the process would add value to South African uranium oxide, and that the power program would not have to depend on foreign enrichment programs. But this was patently false with respect to the pilot plant. It was never in a position to manufacture the 3.5 percent enriched uranium to meet the anticipated needs of South Africa's nuclear energy program. Ostensibly it was meant to be producing some of the HEU required by SAFARI-1, because of the United States embargo. However, almost from the beginning, the Y-Plant was dedicated to enriching uranium for the weapons program. It provided HEU for the six nuclear weapons which President de Klerk admitted were manufactured between 1978 and 1990. South Africa was only working on a seventh gun-type device, when orders came in 1990 to cease production. It is no surprise that the Y-plant was decommissioned in 1990, in view of South Africa's prospective adherence to the NPT.

Sanctions, and the threat of their intensification, also led South Africa to establish a plant to manufacture enriched uranium for reactor fuel. This was only fully commissioned in 1988 and it took a further three years to reach optimal output. Known as the Z-plant, it was also located at Valindaba, and two-thirds of its full output of 300 000 Separative Work Units were destined for use in the Koeberg reactors, leaving one-third of its output available for export. However, the international slump in contracts for enriched uranium made it extremely difficult for the AEC to find customers. Although the Electricity Supply Commission (Eskom), which operates the Koeberg reactors, was originally committed to purchase AEC low-enriched uranium, it was not obliged to buy all its fuel from the AEC, and turned to cheaper sources for some of its requirements.

The AEC enrichment process proved to be highly energy intensive. Even though Eskom gave the AEC a preferential rate, the Z-plant utilised close to 250 MW of electricity (equivalent to 1 percent of Eskom's total output, or 13 percent of Koeberg's installed capacity). Thus, the Z-plant was doomed to run at a perpetual loss. Dr. Stumpf openly referred to it as the industry's "problem child,"[23] and losses were so great that AEC plans to close down the plant between 1996–98 were accelerated to ensure final closure in March 1995. Ultimately, the South African enrichment process was a commercial disaster.

It is clear from the foregoing evidence that from 1945 onwards, South Africa was integrated into the international nuclear industrial system established by the US and Britain. Uranium was supplied for the weapons programs of these countries, who looked favorably upon the need to spread technology and know-how to the South African nuclear bureaucracy. The arms embargoes implemented from 1963, including the voluntary embargo instituted by the UN in response to the Sharpeville massacre and subsequent repression in South Africa, failed to deal with nuclear materials. Until 1964, the US and British weapons programs relied heavily on South African uranium. There was no attempt in these years to restrict transfers of "peaceful" nuclear technology; in fact, Britain and the US were rival bidders to supply South Africa with its first experimental reactor. The arms embargo had no impact on the training and exchange visits of South African nuclear scientists to the laboratories of the uranium importing countries.

As South Africa's arrangement with the CDA came to an end in 1964, the uranium mining industry sought to avoid having to deal with a depressed international price for uranium. The market for nuclear reactors was still underdeveloped, and the US instituted measures which ensured that all uranium destined for its reactors had to be of US origin after 1966. In the early 1970s, South Africa secretly became involved in a market-sharing arrangement with other uranium producing countries (Australia, Canada, and France) to ensure high uranium prices on the world market. The cartel, which met regularly in Paris or Johannesburg, saw the spot market price of uranium oxide rise from US$8/lb in March 1974 to US$39/lb two years later. The mining industry was very influential in the determination of South African nuclear policy.[24] Although associated more with international capital, the mining industry also began to diversify its interests to encompass almost all other sectors of the economy, establishing strong subsidiaries within the manufacturing sector, and maintaining its rapport with the Afrikaner nationalist government.

Through the mid-1970s, the Cold War was the principal factor in the relationship between South Africa and uranium-consuming countries. Apartheid's increasingly brutal measures were officially overlooked, and conciliatory policies were adopted by the West. Britain and the US exercised their UN Security Council vetoes to prevent anything more than a rhetorical condemnation of apartheid. Being one of the world's most significant gold suppliers – gold underpinned the value of the US dollar, and hence of other hard currencies, until August 1971 – also helped insulate South Africa from Western disapproval of its domestic policies. This lasted until mandatory arms sanctions were imposed by the UN in 1977 in the wake of the Soweto massacres of the previous year.

INTENSIFIED SANCTIONS, 1977–95

Prior to 1977, certain nations had imposed voluntary embargoes. However, in November 1977, the UN Security Council passed Resolution 418 imposing a mandatory arms embargo on South Africa. Arguing under Chapter VII, Article 39, that South Africa's continued commitment to a policy of racial discrimination constituted a threat to peace, the resolution provided that "all states shall cease forthwith" supplying military equipment or the means to manufacture it.[25] A further blow to South Africa's nuclear establishment was its removal from the Board of Governors of the IAEA during 1977.[26] South Africa was also subsequently excluded (at the IAEA General Conference in New Delhi in 1979) from the deliberations of the Agency. South Africa lost its seat on the Board to Egypt, the next most developed nuclear state in Africa. South Africa chose to avoid attending further general sessions of the IAEA. And as noted above, significant nuclear collaboration with the US tailed off under the Ford and Carter administrations.[27]

The end of Portuguese rule in Southern Africa also increased the South African government's isolation and paranoia. As a result, it intensified its efforts to increase its capacity to manufacture nuclear weapons. The climate of secrecy and sanctions meant that it was vital to retain links with at least one state with an advanced nuclear research capability. South Africa's strategy was simply to turn away from the cosy "Atoms for Peace" relationship with the US and to substitute it with collaboration with the West Germans. The US refused to continue supplying HEU to South Africa for the SAFARI-1 reactor, on the grounds that South Africa persisted in not signing the NPT. Carter had also responded to Brezhnev's alert that a South African test site had been prepared in the Kalahari desert, insisting on its dismantling.[28] The US suspected that the continued refusal to place Valindaba under IAEA safeguards meant that South Africa was capable of producing nuclear weapons, which caused the US to end all nuclear fuel and reactor exports under the 1978 Nuclear Non-Proliferation Act.

The Reagan administration tried to soften US policy towards Pretoria. Under "constructive engagement" Reagan authorized the renewal of all nuclear exports not mentioned in the Nuclear Non-Proliferation Act. This included technical assistance to Koeberg, licences for dual-use commodities, and brokering of sales of enriched uranium from Europe.[29] Reagan reputedly accepted the advice of Kenneth Adelman, then Director of the US Arms Control and Disarmament Agency, that the US should support the security needs of South Africa in order to reduce the incentive of nuclear proliferation and to gain vital military intelligence in Southern Africa.[30]

Yet domestic pressure grew on the Reagan administration to opt for stronger economic sanctions against South Africa. Attempting to head off Congressional sanctions legislation during 1985, Reagan issued an executive order on 9 September, which included a ban on most transfers of nuclear technology. Not sufficient to placate the anti-apartheid movement, the US Congress passed the Comprehensive Anti-Apartheid Act on 2 October 1986 over Reagan's veto. This effectively banned purchases of South African uranium, further provision of enriched uranium to South Africa, and what the law called "special nuclear material or sensitive nuclear technology."[31]

The US and UN embargoes were difficult to monitor, especially on the question of dual-use equipment for the nuclear industry. Mindful that its resolution 418 had not specifically referred to nuclear collaboration, the UN Security Council passed resolution 569 (1985), which "urges (the) prohibition of all new contacts in the nuclear field." However, this was not regarded as binding on member states, since it had not been preceded by a finding under article 39 of the UN Charter.[32] The European Community Council of Ministers enacted what were subsequently called "positive measures" to end apartheid. On 10 September 1985, the European Community agreed to a prohibition of all new nuclear collaboration. This, and a further package of sanctions the following September, banned the exports of sensitive equipment to the South African Defence Force, though EC measures did not apply to Namibia, which at the time was still under illegal occupation by South Africa.[33] The 1985 Commonwealth Heads of Government summit in the Bahamas issued the Nassau Declaration on 20 October, which included a "ban on new contracts for the sale and export of nuclear goods, materials and technology" to South Africa.[34] Although these sanctions were the most significant, other states, such as Australia, France, Japan, New Zealand, and the Scandinavian countries also instituted nuclear-related sanctions against South Africa.

It may be argued that many of these sanctions lacked efficacy because they were often implemented by governments that were more reluctant to apply them than the legislators and anti-apartheid campaigners for sanctions. Sanctions came very late in the overall picture of international collaboration and only had limited or partial effect. Further, it is likely that dual-use equipment escaped the net of sanctions. Lathes, computers, and other items necessary for weapons manufacture could have been imported for other purposes, without the real end-use being made known. South Africa clearly also possessed sufficient engineering skills to copy certain necessary equipment. Hanlon and Omond cite other reasons for the porousness of nuclear sanctions: the fact that Israel remained in full collaboration with South Africa, the dependence of certain countries on South African and Namibian uranium contracts, and the uncertainty about the extent of any weapons research or manufacture. They also point to the fact that many of the sanctions implemented in the mid-1980s only addressed "new" collaboration, permitting historic contracts and support to continue.[35] Thus, the weakness of sanctions, coupled with South Africa's development of a domestic nuclear power industry, enabled South Africa to become a nuclear weapons state.

THE NUCLEAR POWER INDUSTRY

For the weapons program to be insulated from sanctions, a domestic enrichment capacity needed to be put in place: on the one hand, the apartheid state wished to insulate the fuel cycle from prospective trade sanctions; on the other hand, from 1974 the state wanted maximum control of the front end of the fuel cycle in order to manufacture nuclear weapons. To justify enrichment without acknowledging their weapons program, a nuclear power industry was necessary, although in a country with ample coal reserves, there was no proven need for developing nuclear power. South Africa justified acquisition of nuclear power on economic grounds.

The nuclear bureaucracy, although at times divided, was broadly in favor of South Africa developing a nuclear power industry. One key argument was that the Western Cape was too distant from the coal seams to warrant coal-fired power stations. Nuclear reactors also gave nuclear scientists gainful employment. Further, a power industry would justify domestic attempts to enrich uranium and manufacture nuclear fuel. The Chamber of Mines and the Anglo American Corporation of South Africa, which had a major stake in the uranium market, were also a major exponent of a nuclear power station for the Cape. Their logic was revealed in a paper presented to the South African Institute of Mining and Metallurgy in April 1957, by an executive of the Anglo American Corporation:

> I hope that the Electricity Supply Commission will take the lead in recommending the use of atomic power at the Cape at the earliest available date. The justification for this, apart from the competitive cost, would be that, as large sellers of uranium, we should be setting an example. Our prestige is at stake. We want an atomic station also because we want to offer employment to the young men who would otherwise seek employment overseas after their qualification as atomic technicians.[36]

Note that there was little stress placed in these comments on the special interests of the uranium producers. The industry detected that with demand for South African uranium falling in the US (the main CDA partner) it was unlikely that the contracts for South African uranium would be extended beyond the fixed date of 1964. Having developed production to a level of 5 000 tons per year, specifically to meet CDA military needs, the South African industry would be faced with a marketing problem. One of the ways round this would be to press for a local power industry in order to create a captive domestic outlet for the spare uranium.

A Commission of Enquiry was established to look into the matter, but in its report of April 1961, it pointed to changes in the economy which refuted some of the original assumptions of those promoting the establishment of a nuclear power station in the Western Cape. The Commission concluded that no economic advantage would result from the introduction of nuclear power in South Africa.[37] The impact of the report meant scotching proposals for constructing nuclear power stations. But the plans were only placed in abeyance. From the 1960s it was the AEB's nuclear research program under Dr. Roux which kept the plan alive. The cadre of scientists who had been trained at Argonne all returned with the idea that South Africa needed nuclear power stations.

By 1965, SAFARI-1 was in place. In addition, a significant part of the AEB's research initiative was devoted to the development of a second reactor, called Pelinduna. Pelinduna, an attempt to build a domestic reactor based on home-grown know-how, utilized a design since abandoned by the US, which required natural (unenriched) uranium as the fuel, heavy water (deuterium) as the moderator, and sodium as a coolant.[38] The government could not stretch the AEB's research budget to develop both Pelinduna and an enrichment capacity, and the former was dropped. It seemed illogical to go simultaneously in the direction of enrichment and also to build a reactor based on the use of natural uranium. The AEB calculated that, in the long run, reactors fuelled with enriched uranium would be more cost efficient.

By May 1971, Eskom put aside its long-held misgivings about going nuclear, and purchased the farm Duynefontein, 28 km north of Cape Town. But it was not until the oil crisis broke, that Eskom could justify the costs of nuclear power. The Arab oil boycott of South Africa had been instituted during the Yom Kippur war of October 1973 and Eskom argued that its coal reserves were needed to feed the existing and planned Sasol oil-from-coal complexes, as well as the local power and export markets.[39] The escalation of energy prices made nuclear power relatively more competitive.

Tenders were invited for two identical pressurized water reactors to be located on the Duynefontein site, renamed Koeberg after a nearby landmark. The first unit of Koeberg was required to be on stream by September 1982, and the second a year later. Three shortlisted consortia vied for the contract, a South African/West German group (Kraftwerk Unie with Murray and Roberts Construction), a Dutch/Swiss combine, and a French-led consortium. Initially Eskom awarded the contract to the second of these, the Dutch/Swiss combine of Getsco-Brown-Boveri-Benucom, with the US General Electric Company contracted to provide the nuclear fuel assemblies, conditional on the governments of the contracting companies giving full permission for export of relevant materials.

No problems were envisaged, since neither the Netherlands nor Switzerland required export permits for the nuclear engineering industry. However, because of the level of expenditure involved, the contract had to be approved by the Dutch parliament. A fierce and divisive debate ensued in the lower house, which would not endorse the contract on the grounds that South Africa had not signed the NPT. There were also interministerial battles in the ruling coalition. In early May 1976 the South African government, through a diplomatic note, sought assurances that the Dutch, Swiss, and US governments would not stand in the way of the contract. The

Table 4.1   The Franco-Belgian consortium charged with building Koeberg

---

Framatome

51 percent owned by Creusot-Loire (Franco-Belgian Schneider-Empaign group)

15 percent owned by Westinghouse, a US company which is the world's largest constructor of nuclear reactors and whose reactor design would be used for Koeberg

30 percent owned by French nuclear parastatal Commissariat a l'Énergie Atomique. Until 1975 this share of Framatome was also owned by Westinghouse, who sold it in exchange for long-term uranium contracts with France

Spie-Batignolles
A construction company 51 percent owned by Schneider SA

Alsthom
A subsidiary of French electric concern Compagnie Générale d'Electricité

Source: UN Special Committee against Apartheid, *Collaboration by Member-states of the United Nations in Developing South Africa's Nuclear Weapons Capability* (Report of the Sub-committee on the Implementation of UN Resolutions and Collaboration with South Africa), June 1978.

Dutch cabinet split on the issue, which stalled the contract beyond its deadline. Effectively the sanctions lobby in the Netherlands, including the left political parties, had sabotaged the contract. More conservative parties were also uncertain, mindful of US Secretary of State Henry Kissinger's recent speech opposing a nuclear capability for South Africa.[40]

Eskom used this snag to award the contract to the French-led consortium, bending some of the rules to enable it to accept the South African conditions. Eskom calculated that the anti-apartheid movement was much weaker in France than in the US and the Netherlands, so there was a stronger chance for the French contract to go ahead unchallenged. The consortium consisted of Framatome (40 percent), which was to supply the reactors; Spie-Batignolles (40 percent), which would do the civil engineering; and Alsthom (20 percent), which would provide the turbo-generators. Contracts for the provision of fuel in the initial years of operation went to a US company, and the Franco-Belgian concern Eurofuel. The latter would also be responsible for all reprocessing. South African subcontractors were to receive approximately 30 percent of the work.

The Koeberg contract was signed in Johannesburg and Paris in August 1976, followed by a bilateral agreement between France and South Africa in October. A trilateral agreement with the IAEA on safeguards for the reactors entered into force on 5 January 1977. South Africa was comfortable with the French deal. France offered good credit: 82 percent of the finance for Koeberg was provided by a group of French banks led by state-owned Credit Lyonnais and the Banque de l'Indochine et de Suez (now Banque Indosuez which absorbed the French Bank of Southern Africa). And France offered training facilities for over a hundred reactor staff. Finally, ignoring UN boycotts, France had been sympathetic to the South African regime's defence needs, providing submarines, Crotale missiles and Mirage jets.

The two Koeberg reactors were eventually commissioned in 1984 and 1986 respectively. Nuclear electricity, which, at conservative official estimates, costs more than twice as much as coal-fired power to produce, has never been economically viable.[41] Their joint installed capacity is 1930 MW, but they seldom reached the total sent-out rating of 1840 MW. Each reactor has to be closed for partial refuelling on an annual basis though the cycle was extended more recently to 18 months to reduce down time. Nevertheless, Koeberg's record was not a good one. Prior to 1988, power was only available from Koeberg on average 41.8 percent of the time. In 1988, Eskom announced that this had risen to 71.2 percent, an indication of severe teething troubles in the reactors.[42] Nuclear electricity output amounted to under 6 percent of South Africa's total electricity output in 1992. The electricity industry's excess capacity caused it to mothball several conventional plants.

Despite growing sanctions, South Africa was able to play off prospective tenders, and in the end opted for the transfer of technology from France. In effect the French turnkey pressurized water reactor was based on a US model perfected by the Westinghouse corporation. France agreed to reprocess the spent fuel from Koeberg. It also had no scruples in training South Africans in reactor operation and maintenance, and provided a pair of turnkey nuclear reactors. Although under IAEA safeguards, the reactors provided South Africa with new nuclear know-how, and a justification for the operation of the Z-plant and of BEVA, a unit at Pelindaba charged with the manufacture of enriched uranium into nuclear fuel pellets destined for the fuel rods at Koeberg.

The dilemma faced by the Western countries was their desire to curb proliferation but also to stimulate nuclear equipment sales. Compromises, like guarantees of adhering to safeguards, helped ease the dilemma, and took the pressure off having to institute strong sanctions against the building of nuclear reactors. Whilst the US vacillated during the 1970s and 1980s about how much to engage with the South African nuclear program, in the end, its sanctions led South Africa to turn to Western Europe and China for supplies of start-up, low-enriched uranium for the reactors.

THE NUCLEAR WEAPONS PROGRAM

The decision to build nuclear weapons was taken by Prime Minister Vorster in 1974, the year of the fall of the Portuguese dictatorship in Lisbon; the frontline had suddenly reached South Africa's borders. In Pretoria, paranoia about the communist threat to the white South African power structure intensified. South Africa decided to invade Angola. Withdrawal of direct US support for this invasion deepened Vorster's suspicion of perfidious Western powers. With growing calls for mandatory arms sanctions, South Africa would have to fend for itself. Military solutions replaced Vorster's earlier foreign policy of "dialogue" and "*détente*." In such a political climate the bomb-construction program seemed a logical step: South African strategists argued that bombs were not for launching but for gaining political leverage. In a doomsday situation, the regime could gain time if challenged by its neighbors, the Soviet Union or even the NATO countries.

Armscor, the South African government arms procurement agency, and the AEC claimed that South African nuclear devices were "of the so-called cannon type, a very old technological concept," and have refrained from any claim that the design was a local one, although they vigorously rejected suggestions that any technology or support was received from abroad.[43] The cannon or gun-type device dates back to the earliest weapon produced by the Manhattan Project. Consisting of two sections, each containing a subcritical mass of nuclear material, the design required the one section to be propelled to impact on the other, resulting in the two subcritical uranium bodies going critical, triggering a nuclear explosion. Once the design was acquired, it was initially evaluated by AEC scientists and engineers at Pelindaba.

The AEC was not only involved in testing the design of the bombs. It was also involved in the development of their fuel. From 1974, the budget of the AEC reflected a sudden massive increase, coinciding with the drive to deliver weapons-grade enriched uranium for the bombs. We saw earlier that the first production of highly enriched weapons-grade uranium by the pilot Y-plant took place in January 1978. The AEC's chief executive officer at the time, Dr. Wynand de Villiers, later admitted that the pilot enrichment plant had been dedicated to the production of weapons-grade uranium.[44] Once the problems of the Y-plant had been sorted out, the weapons program could rely on local supply of the nuclear material needed in the bombs.

Even intensified sanctions, therefore, were ineffective in halting the program. Nuclear scientists justified their work in terms of sanctions-busting and chauvinist ideology. "The cameraderie was amazing," a former technician was later to admit, "We were proud that our efforts were beating the sanctions. We did something here that has amazed the world. It made us one of the top seven nations."[45] However, sanctions might have played an important part in limiting the program to the manufacture of a small number of rather crude devices. It is unclear whether the plans to develop more advanced implosion-type devices were very advanced. Armscor has claimed that "no implosion tests were done up to the time that the program was terminated and no prototypes were constructed."[46] Whether this was due to financial, technological, or skill-related constraints is difficult to know. If we accept the Armscor view, it suggests that sanctions must have significantly constrained the nuclear program.

During 1977 the first gun-type device was completed by the AEC, and later tested in Building 5000 at Pelindaba. It did not contain the fissile component, since the Y-plant was not fully on-stream to provide sufficient HEU. A second device, also not loaded with fissile material, and nicknamed "Melba" was built by the AEC in 1978, and kept for the duration of the program as a demonstration model. Thereafter, between 1981 and 1989, Armscor took over manufacture and assembly; the role of the AEC was reduced to providing the weapons-grade uranium.[47] Over the following eight years four more bombs were manufactured in the small Circle factory at Advena to the east of Pretoria. By 1989 the pilot enrichment plant at Valindaba had manufactured sufficient HEU for a seventh bomb.[48]

In 1989, two months after F. W. de Klerk became president of the Republic of South Africa, Wynand de Villiers (due for retirement as chief executive officer of the AEC), underwent a crisis of conscience about the nuclear bombs. "As the world situation changed in 1989," de Villiers later revealed, "I became convinced that South Africa did not need such a terrible weapon. If we had ever used it in anger, it would have been the end for this country. I knew we would never use it and many others were agreeing with me."[49] Wynand de Villiers's next move – on 13 November 1989 – was to approach the newly appointed minister of mineral and energy affairs, Dr. Dawie de Villiers, who was charged with conveying the AEC's views to the president.

It is not known whether the alluring prospect of South Africa normalizing its international nuclear standing convinced de Klerk to dismantle South Africa's nuclear bombs or whether the nuclear bureaucracy feared a future ANC government with access to nuclear weapons. Whichever the case, de Klerk issued orders to have the weapons destroyed on 26 February 1990. The first move was to close down the R210 million pilot enrichment plant – the so-called Y-plant. Although nuclear material for the seventh bomb had been produced, it was never built. Throughout the Gulf War, dozens of nuclear scientists and engineers worked at Armscor's Advena warehouse to dismantle the nuclear weapons and decontaminate the buildings. Afterwards, de Klerk attended a celebration party at Advena. "He was grateful," commented one scientist: "In our hearts we all knew it was the right decision. These bombs are not things that can be used."[50]

In July 1991, South Africa became a signatory to the NPT. Under the Treaty, there is no obligation to reveal details of its past proliferation. By the time the safeguards agreement entered into force in September, the remaining HEU had been returned from Advena to Pelindaba. In November, IAEA inspectors were shown around Pelindaba and Valindaba, and expressed some suspicions about what might have occurred in Building 5000. It was only after de Klerk's announcement to parliament in March 1993 that South Africa had made nuclear weapons, that the IAEA insisted on inspecting the Circle and other buildings in the Advena complex.

AEC and Armscor officials maintained that the weapons program was completely indigenous. Only South African-born nationals were employed. However, in their efforts to develop a new generation of more sophisticated thermonuclear weapons, it subsequently came to light that they had managed to import 30 grams of tritium from Israel, "enough to manufacture explosive devices for twelve atomic bombs."[51] Although the AEC claimed that it never utilized the tritium and allowed its useful life to expire, it remains an indication that at least one other nation had given deliberate assistance to South Africa's nuclear weapon research and development efforts. The destruction of the documentation relating to the program raises questions of other types of support, including provision of dual-use equipment.

CONCLUSIONS

South Africa's nuclear establishment continues to claim that nuclear technology was entirely home grown. Despite international sanctions, South Africa's nuclear industry managed to put in place a number of the links in the front end of the nuclear chain. In the immediate postwar period, Britain and the United States saw South Africa as a major source of uranium destined for their weapons programs. They offered financial support to the mining industry and for infrastructural improvements, amounting to tens of millions of pounds. This ensured that the capital-hungry mining industry could overcome many of the difficulties it then faced, and to develop the rich goldfields of the Orange Free State. Under the "Atoms for Peace" proposals, the US furnished South Africa with a research reactor, highly enriched uranium, and training for a cadre of nuclear scientists during the 1960s. This cadre went on to develop its own research program within its own well-resourced institutions. Their program included plans for civilian power reactors, and by 1974, plans for military applications. This was followed by collaboration with the then West German nuclear industrial complex; similarities have been noted between the German Becker process and the final enrichment technology developed for the South African industry. It is clear that significant transfers of technology for nuclear power reactors took place with the support of the French-led consortium, Framatome. The pressurized water reactor model utilized by Framatome followed that of the US-based Westinghouse corporation.

There was, in addition, a more secretive relationship with Israel. The supply of tritium has been mentioned, and speculation persists about the double-flash over the South Atlantic detected by

Vela satellites in 1979. One version is that South Africa was assisting the Israelis to test a nuclear device. The relationship between the two embattled states, both with secret weapons programs, transcended purely nuclear transactions, since South Africa was certainly testing Israeli missiles at the Overberg test range in the Western Cape. The dimensions of the nuclear relationship with Israel is not yet fully known.

Thus, acquisition of "front end" nuclear technologies was dependent on a great deal of international collaboration. The South African nuclear industry, due to many years of international collaboration, had matured by the mid-1980s to the point where sanctions had only limited impact. Shrouded in secrecy, it was an industry whose very existence aimed at resisting and bypassing external measures to restrain it. It is this collaboration which made it possible for South Africa to develop its nuclear technologies to the point where, by 1987, J. D. L. Moore could declare that "South Africa is now almost totally independent of outside assistance for the 'front end' of the fuel cycle – from uranium mine to reactor."[52]

Whilst sanctions came too late to prevent South African proliferation, they were not entirely futile. They raised the financial and technological costs of the enrichment process. They blocked the import of certain equipment and materials and created a capacity to substitute certain imports with more costly local goods. Sanctions also drew attention to South Africa's nuclear industry. They were important in pressuring the regime in general, and, together with other forms of political pressure, particularly from the Clinton administration, contributed towards the decision made by the de Klerk government that proliferation was no longer politically viable. These pressures ultimately caused the dying apartheid regime to dismantle the apartheid bomb and adhere to the NPT before surrendering power to a new democratic project. Dismantling its nuclear weapons and adherence to the NPT also laid the foundation for South Africa's re-entry into international nuclear politics. South Africa played a role in the Review and Extension Conference of the NPT in New York in April–May 1995. It was also a significant supporter of the African nuclear-weapons-free zone, the Treaty of Pelindaba. South Africa resumed its activities in the IAEA and the US renewed its treaty allowing for trade in nuclear materials and for extending nuclear cooperation.

Notes

1. F. W. de Klerk, parliamentary speech, 24 March 1993, *Press Release*, p. 5.
2. Ibid., p. 4. The observer of the destruction process, Professor Wynand Mouton later admitted, "I did have a bit of a doubt whether it was really necessary to destroy them (the 12 000 documents). The IAEA would have been happier if we had not." See P. Hounam and S. McQuillan, *The Mininuke Conspiracy: Mandela's Nuclear Nightmare* (London: Faber and Faber, 1995), p. 49.
3. Personal observation on visiting Advena's Circle building, 31 March 1993.
4. *Daily Express*, London, 7 February 1947. Noel-Baker originally met Smuts as far back as the 1919 Versailles Conference (personal communication, 11 June 1976). Although he served in various Labour cabinets after 1945, and had some responsibility for defense policy, Noel-Baker, awarded a Nobel Peace Prize, subsequently became a firm advocate of nuclear disarmament.
5. Ironically, the Soviet Union knew about it; Donald Maclean, the secretary of the Trust, worked in the British Embassy in Washington. He later fled to Moscow when his spying activities in the same ring as Philby, Burgess, and Blunt were uncovered.
6. "Between 1952–70, uranium sales amounted to R1 billion," according to M. Lipton, *Capitalism and Apartheid* (Cape Town: David Philip, 1986), p. 116.
7. C. S. McLean and T. K. Prentice, "The South African uranium industry," report of the South African delegation to the First International Conference on the Peaceful Uses of Atomic Energy in Geneva in 1956, mimeographed.
8. Michael Dutfield, in *A Marriage of Convenience: the Persecution of Ruth and Seretse Khama* (London: Unwin Hyman, 1990), pp. 103–4, argues that South Africa's uranium sales influenced Britain's refusal to allow Sir Seretse Khama to take up the Bamangwato chieftainship in Bechuanaland (now Botswana) on the grounds that his marriage to an Englishwoman would cause offence to the South African government, whom the British thought might then seek to incorporate Bechuanaland into South Africa, as allowed for under the South Africa Act of 1909.
9. The British by then had abandoned their pretentions to strategic policing of the Indian Ocean "east of Suez." The 20 years duration of the agreement enabled the SA Navy to expand considerably: "accomplished through the purchase from Britain ... of ten coastal minesweepers, four frigates, four seaward defence boats, and Buccaneer, Albatross and Wasp naval aircraft and helicopters. Regular exercises continued to be held with the Royal Navy." G. Cawthra, *Brutal Force: the Apartheid War Machine* (London: International Defence and Aid Fund, 1986), p. 115.
10. See S. Ambrose, *Eisenhower the President, 1952–59* (London: George Allen and Unwin, 1984), pp. 147–51.
11. A. R. Newby-Fraser, *Chain Reaction: Twenty Years of Nuclear Research*

and Development in South Africa (Pretoria: AEB, 1979), p. 40.

12. United Kingdom, Public Records office, Document EG1/2OO/E75A, November 1959.
13. Due to be completed late in 1963, the reactor vessel slipped from its rigging as it was being moved after construction. The damage took a further year to be repaired before it could be shippped to Pelindaba. Within eight hours of being in operation, the reactor began to release abnormal levels of radioactivity. Alarm bells sounded, and the reactor team shut SAFARI-1 down. South Africa's first nuclear accident occurred during the country's first self-sustaining nuclear chain reaction.
14. Severed under President Carter in 1976, the agreement resumed on 25 August 1995 when President Clinton's Secretary for Energy, Hazel O'Leary, visited Pretoria.
15. *Washington Post*, 16 February 1977.
16. See Newby-Fraser, *Chain Reaction*, pp. 97–8.
17. RSA Department of Mines, *Minerals: a Report for the Republic of South Africa* (Pretoria: Government Printer, 1970).
18. Grant was a mechanical engineer who had worked under Frank Whittle on the development of the jet engine in wartime Britain. On his return to South Africa, he had been a subordinate to Roux in the Council for Scientific and Industrial Research, before both of them were transferred to the AEB.
19. More than 20 Koeberg-sized reactors.
20. On UCOR's establishment in November 1970, Dr. Roux became chairperson of its board, while Dr. Grant became its general manager.
21. United States Public Law 95–242.
22. This was "due to a massive catalytic in process gas reaction between the UF_6, and the hydrogen carrier gas, a mixture that is thermodynamically unstable, and, when contaminated by certain impurities, can react to form uranium tetrafluoride (UF_4) plus hydrofluoric acid. . . . the 1979 incident . . . resulted in a massive gas loss," W. Stumpf, "South Africa's Nuclear Weapons Program: from Deterrence to Development," *Arms Control Today* 25 (December 1995/January 1996), pp. 3–8.
23. Presentation to Macro Economic Research Group, Pelindaba, 31 March 1993.
24. The cartel collapsed only after Westinghouse, tied into long-term contracts, discovered how the price had risen, and sued the cartel members in US courts. M. Radetzki, *Uranium: a Strategic Source of Energy* (London: Croom Helm, 1981), p. 117.
25. See N. C. Crawford, "How Arms Embargoes Work," in this volume, and J. Dugard, "Sanctions against South Africa: an international law perspective," in M. Orkin, ed., *Sanctions against Apartheid* (Cape Town: David Philip, 1989), p. 117.
26. See P. Bossew et. al, *The International Atomic Energy Agency: a Critical Documentation of the Agency's Policy* (Vienna: AAI, 1993).
27. Outlined in G. Houser, "United States Policy and Nuclear Collaboration with South Africa," *Nuclear Collaboration with South Africa: Report of United Nations Seminar, London, 24–25 February 1979* (Oslo: World Campaign against Military and Nuclear Collaboration with South

Africa, 1979), pp. 9–10. Also see L. S. Spector and J. R. Smith, *Nuclear Ambitions: the Spread of Nuclear Weapons, 1989–90* (Boulder, CO: Westview, 1990), pp. 270–7.

28. R. W. Walters, "U.S. Policy and Nuclear Proliferation in South Africa," Western Massachusetts Association of Concerned African Scholars, *U.S. Military Involvement in Southern Africa* (Boston: South End Press, 1978), pp. 172–96.

29. Spector and Smith, *Nuclear Ambitions*, p. 274.

30. K. Adelman, *Impact upon US Security of a South African Nuclear Weapons Capability* (Arlington, VA: SRI International, 1981), pp. 68–76. Also see his "Can South Africa Go Nuclear?" *Orbis* 23 (1979), pp. 633–47.

31. US Public Law 99–440, the Comprehensive Anti-Apartheid Act of 1986. K. Danaher, "The US Struggle over Sanctions against South Africa," in Orkin, ed., *Sanctions against Apartheid*, pp. 136–8.

32. Dugard, "Sanctions against South Africa," p. 117. As permanent members of the Security Council, Britain and the United States vetoed any subsequent attempts by the Security Council to implement mandatory sanctions.

33. J. Hanlon and R. Omond, *The Sanctions Handbook* (Harmondsworth, UK: Penguin, 1987), p. 200.

34. Ibid., p. 310.

35. Ibid.

36. R. B. Hagart, "National Aspects of the Uranium Industry," *Journal of the South African Institute of Mining and Metallurgy* 57 (1957), p. 578.

37. The commission reasoned that the postwar economic boom, and the bottlenecks experienced by the railways, had abated, and the railways predicted spare freight capacity over the following eight years. Coal transported to Cape Town was only 7 percent of the route's freight, and thus a marginal cost. Existing power sources in the Cape would suffice until the end of the 1960s. It was too early to estimate the capital and operating costs of a South African nuclear power station, but they were thought to be at least double the cost of a new conventional station. See South Africa, *Report of the Commission of Enquiry into the Application of Nuclear Power in South Africa* (the Forsythe Commission), April 1961.

38. "Pelinduna" after the first syllables of Pelindaba, PELIN, combined with the chemical symbols for the deuterium, uranium and sodium, D + U + Na.

39. See N. C. Crawford, "Oil Sanctions Against Apartheid," the next chapter in this volume.

40. M. S. D. Ho, "Crucial Underwriting Decisions in Dutch Public Export Credit Insurance" (paper presented at the International Studies Association's 37th Annual Convention, San Diego, 16–20 April 1996), pp. 21–3, 25.

41. Nuclear costs are 5.2 cents as opposed to 1.89 cents per kilowatt-hour for coal, *Hansard*, 26 March 1986. Eskom more recently argued that the "primary energy costs of coal and nuclear are very competitive in terms of rands per megawatt hour sent out." See S. Murray, *Koeberg: Eskom's Nuclear Success Story* (Cape Town: Churchill Murray, 1995), p. 111; see S. Thomas, *The Operating Performance of the Koeberg Nuclear*

Power Plant (Cape Town: Energy & Development Research Centre, March 1996), pp. 1–10.

42. Eskom, _Annual Report_ (Megawatt Park: Eskom, 1988), p. 22.
43. "Media statement jointly issued by the Atomic Energy Corporation and Armscor," Pretoria, 26 March 1993, para. B1. Hounam and McQuillan claim, on the basis of many interviews, that full information about the South African program had not been disclosed by de Klerk, who only revealed the facts about an earlier phase of gun-type devices, allegedly completed in 1981, eight years earlier than admitted. They assert that the Advena plant was totally devoted to producing tactical and strategic warheads. See their _The Mininuke Conspiracy_, p. 148.
44. _The Sunday Star_, Johannesburg, 28 March 1993. This link was confirmed in the "Media Statement jointly issued by the Atomic Energy Corporation and Armscor," Pretoria (26 March 1993), paragraph A1.
45. _The Sunday Star_, Johannesburg, 28 March 1993.
46. D. Albright, "South Africa's Secret Nuclear Weapons," _ISIS Report_ 1, no. 4 (May 1994), p. 15.
47. Ibid., pp. 6–9.
48. A. Buys, "The Conversion of South Africa's Nuclear Weapon Facilities," presented to Conference on International Co-operation to Promote Conversion from Military to Civilian Industry, Hong Kong, 7–10 July 1993.
49. _The Sunday Star_, 28 March 1993.
50. Ibid.
51. D. Blow, "Nuke Bombshell," _City Press_, Johannesburg, 2 April 1993. Also see David Albright's analysis in "Israeli Friends," _ISIS Report_ 1, no. 4 (May 1994), p. 5.
52. J. D. L. Moore, _South Africa and Nuclear Proliferation: South Africa's Nuclear Capabilities and Intentions in the Context of International Non-Proliferation Policies_ (London: Macmillan, 1987), pp. 103–4.

5 Oil Sanctions Against Apartheid[1]

Neta C. Crawford

> There were times when it was reported to me that we had enough oil for only a week.
>
> (P. W. Botha, president of South Africa in April 1986)

Anti-apartheid activists thought oil sanctions would work against the apartheid government because South Africa had no known oil reserves and depended on imports for the fuel that it used to police the townships, run the economy, occupy Namibia, and wage war against Angola. Though discussion of oil supply issues was illegal and the embargo rarely mentioned in official sources, some white elites apparently shared the anti-apartheid movement's view that South Africa was vulnerable to an effective oil embargo.[2] In 1979 the Afrikaner-dominated business group Sanlam economic report on sanctions said that "Without a doubt the Republic's Achilles' heel is *oil.*"[3] And an effective oil embargo – one where oil imports to South Africa were cut off voluntarily, or as a result of mandatory UN Security Council action – would likely have had the effects that the apartheid power structure feared and that the anti-apartheid movement hoped for: the crippling of South Africa's economy.

But sanctions never totally cut South Africa off from the international oil market. Some, like Arthur Jay Klinghoffer, argued that, because of incomplete implementation, the oil sanctions against South Africa had negligible effects: "Embargoes habitually fail to achieve their political aims because disunity usually prevails among those applying sanctions and considerable laxity characterizes their implementation. Target states also adjust successfully to outside pressures, thereby alleviating economic disruption and reducing the prospects for induced internal change."[4] Klinghoffer concluded that "oil sanctions ... [were] a mild form of punishment rather than a lever effecting deinstitutionalization of apartheid" and that the embargo "failed to alter apartheid in any significant way."[5]

Were oil sanctions ineffective? I argue that, despite its leakiness, the oil embargo did have important direct effects on South Africa, driving up the cost of oil purchased by South Africa. This expense was largely borne by white South Africans, though the health effects of increased coal consumption may be felt by all South Africans for many decades. Oil embargoes may provoke resistance: conservation and/or rationing, stockpiling, resort to black markets, and import substitution. The consequences of these resistance strategies may simply be in the form of higher expense and decreased growth which may itself decrease the capability of the target to carry on the policies that led to the imposition of sanctions. Indeed, the most profound effects of oil sanctions were largely the result of South African resistance: the state went to great lengths to decrease its overall dependence on imported oil and this drive for self-sufficiency was enormously expensive as South Africa searched for domestic oil reserves and invested in the capital equipment to produce synthetic fuel. Further, developments in the energy sector that were probably in large part shaped by the oil embargo may have important consequences for post-apartheid South Africa as the new state deals with the inherited import substitution industries and reaps the benefits of an immense strategic fuel reserve.

HISTORY OF OIL SANCTIONS

The Conference of Independent African States made the first international call for oil sanctions against South Africa in 1960. A UN General Assembly resolution on Namibia in November 1963 urged an oil embargo on South Africa, and in July 1964 the Organization of African Unity (OAU) called for a general oil embargo of South Africa. The Organization of Arab Petroleum Exporting Countries called for a complete Arab oil embargo of South Africa, Rhodesia, and Portugal at the November 1973 Algiers Arab Summit, in exchange for African states' support of the Arab war against Israel. Iraq, Saudi Arabia, and Qatar immediately halted oil shipments to South Africa, which amounted to nearly 50 percent of South Africa's crude oil supplies.[6] Even after the embargo against other states ended in 1974, the sanctions against South Africa remained in force. But Iran, which already had a close relationship with South Africa, immediately stepped up its oil exports to South Africa in 1973, and though all other Organization of Petroleum Exporting Countries (OPEC) members proclaimed an embargo in 1977, Iranian oil continued to flow.[7] Iran then became South Africa's

105

Map 2 Energy-related assets

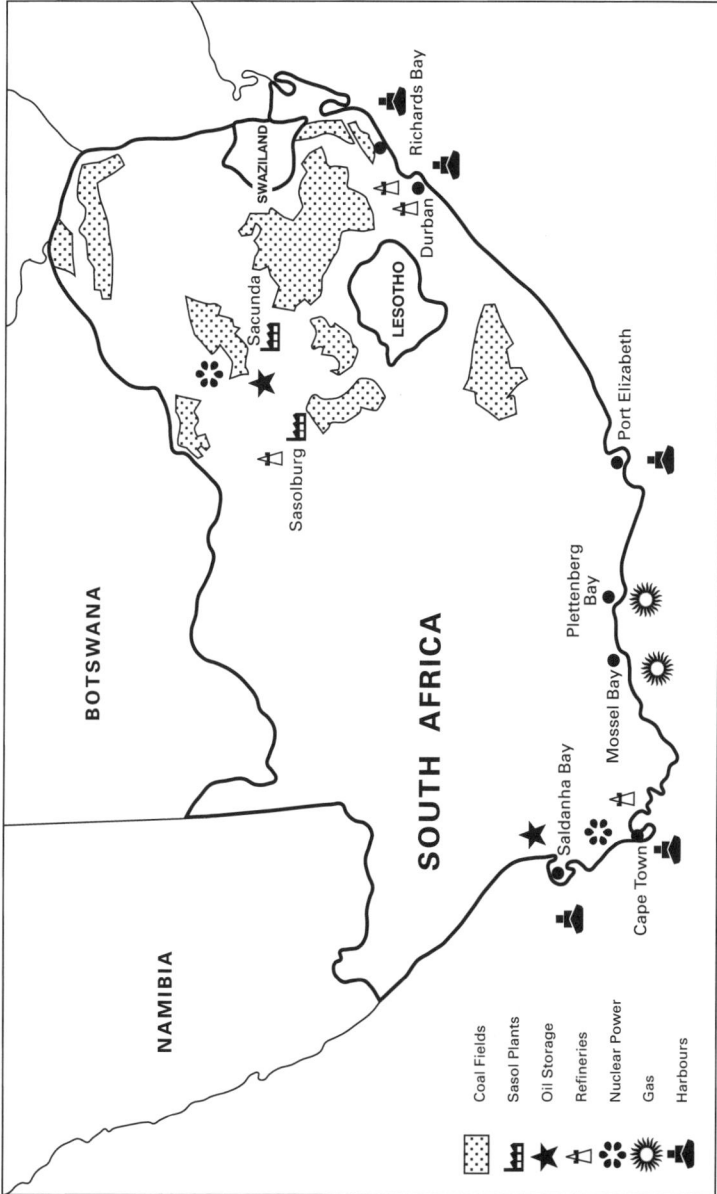

BOTSWANA

NAMIBIA

SOUTH AFRICA

SWAZILAND

LESOTHO

Richards Bay

Durban

Sacunda

Sasolburg

Port Elizabeth

Plettenberg Bay

Mossel Bay

Saldanha Bay

Cape Town

Coal Fields
Sasol Plants
Oil Storage
Refineries
Nuclear Power
Gas
Harbours

chief supplier of crude oil, directly and indirectly supplying on average over 90 percent of South Africa's oil from 1973–78, and by 1978 South Africa depended on Iran for 96 percent of its crude oil imports. Only after the revolution in Iran in 1979 did Iranian oil exports to South Africa cease and it became much more difficult for South Africa to import oil at market prices. South African oil imports dropped 40 percent in the first quarter of 1979 compared to the previous year.

Oil imports were extremely difficult to acquire for only a short time: after 1979 South Africa turned to the black market and bought oil more or less clandestinely, primarily from the Persian Gulf countries of Saudi Arabia, Oman, and the United Arab Emirates. South Africa was thus able to bounce back by diversifying its suppliers. The oil was shipped on tankers owned by private companies sailing under various flags, for example Transworld Oil of The Netherlands and Bermuda, Marc Rich and Co. based in Switzerland, and Marimpex based in the then Federal Republic of Germany.

Support for the embargo grew beyond OPEC. The UN General Assembly voted in support of an oil embargo several times from the late 1970s through the early 1990s. The UN Security Council never voted for a mandatory embargo since the US, France, and Britain did not favor a mandatory oil embargo against South Africa. Thus oil sanctions were never universal, and throughout the voluntary embargo, many private and government oil producers provided oil to South Africa. The European Economic Community banned oil sales to South Africa in September 1985 and the United States prohibited oil shipments to South Africa in its 1986 Comprehensive Anti-Apartheid Act.

South Africa had international assistance in evading oil sanctions. Even during the height of the embargo, dozens of ships bearing oil docked at ports in Durban and Cape Town each year; the Shipping Research Bureau documented 865 deliveries of oil between 1979 and 1993.[9] South Africa was able to refine the crude oil it obtained on the international market in refineries located in South Africa owned by British Petroleum, Caltex (Socal and Texaco) Royal Dutch/Shell, Total Oil, and at its own Natref refinery. The chairman of British Petroleum, visiting South Africa in 1974, said that international oil companies "intentionally set out to thwart Arab attempts at enforcing embargoes on countries like South Africa."[10] It appears that only Nigeria made a serious effort to halt private oil flows to South Africa when it seized a South African-owned tanker ship, the *Kulu,* then on charter to British Petroleum, and announced in May 1979 that it would not deal with any tankers in contact with South Africa.[11]

Table 5.1   South Africa's oil consumption by sector in 1974

Sector	Oil consumed in barrels/day (b/d)	Percent of energy in each sector provided by oil	Percent of total energy consumed by each sector
Transport	138 700 b/d	79%	13%
Household and agricultural	31 100 b/d	28%	14%
Industrial and commercial	35 900 b/d	8%	62%
Mining	3 900 b/d	3%	11%
Total	209 600 b/d		

Source: *Outlook for Energy in South Africa: A Report of the Subsidiary Committee of the Prime Minister's Planning Advisory Council* (Pretoria: Department of Planning and the Environment, 1977), p. xxxiv.

Embargoing states gradually lifted their sanctions after the release of political prisoners. For example, the US was the first to do so, resuming oil exports to South Africa in 1991, and Kuwait resumed exports in 1993. All oil sanctions ended in December 1993 after the Transitional Executive Council was installed in South Africa.

HOW VULNERABLE? ENERGY USE AND SUPPLY

In the 1970s, South Africa stopped publishing data on oil imports as well as much of the data that could be used to tell whether the embargo was having any effect and laws made it a criminal offense for anyone in South Africa to publish this information. Thus, though it is not easy to know exactly where and how South Africa acquired and used its energy during the embargo era, it is possible to sketch a general picture from available statistics. In 1974 road vehicles accounted for 87 percent of the oil consumed in transportation.[12] Households and agriculture were less dependent on oil, but since most household energy was supplied by electricity, agriculture was "highly dependent on oil for capital intensive commercial agriculture, mostly in the form of diesel for tractors."[13] It is clear that South Africa was quite dependent, when the embargo first took effect, on imported oil for transport. Other sectors were much less dependent on oil and most of South Africa's electrical power generation was supplied by coal. Table 5.1 shows the patterns of energy use and supply at the beginning of the embargo.[14]

Table 5.2   Number of licensed vehicles in South Africa, 1970–92

Year	Total	Motor Cars	Commercial
1970	2 067 619	1 544 501	393 841
1975	3 045 343	2 101 961	747 452
1980	3 395 365	2 313 866	803 378
1985	4 452 754	2 947 501	1 042 291
1990	5 092 462	3 375 277	1 207 088
1992	5 273 493	3 488 570	1 267 766

Source: RSA Central Statistical Service, *South African Statistics 1994* (Pretoria: Government Printing Office, 1994), "Transport Vehicles – South Africa: Historical Summary," p. 17.9.

Coal was extremely important, but because transport and agricultural sectors depended on oil, coal could not supply all of South Africa's energy needs. Nearly all of South Africa's liquid fuel was supplied by refined oil import products until 1954 when its first crude oil refinery opened in Durban. By opening local refineries South Africa was able to decrease imports of refined oil products and begin to import crude oil for local refinement. By 1989 several refineries were in operation (with a total capacity for refining about 430 000 barrels of crude oil per day), including two partially government-owned refineries. The multinational oil companies Caltex, Mobil, and Shell/BP ran refineries in Cape Town and Durban.[15] "Mobil panicked out of SA in 1989. Mobil's loss was [South African mining company] Gencor's gain. It acquired ownership of the refining and marketing operations of Mobil SA at a fire sale price."[16]

South Africa's transport sector probably became more, not less, dependent on oil during the 1970s and 1980s because the number of cars in South Africa grew. The number of vehicles rose even during the 1980s when prices, especially for imports, increased significantly, and despite US and Japanese companies' sanctions on automobile parts. Table 5.2 shows the enormous growth in the total number of vehicles, both commercial and private, that were licensed in South Africa from 1970 to 1992.[17]

South Africa's military and police shared the transportation sector's dependence on oil. Security forces used close to 30 000 barrels of oil per day according to Klinghoffer, though he does not specify whether this estimate includes operations in the theater of war or only in South Africa.[18] Bailey argued that "without oil, the armed

Table 5.3 Coal consumption and total electrical output
of Eskom by energy source, 1960–90

Year	Total GWh transmitted	Coal consumed in 1 000s of tons	Percent supplied by coal	Percent supplied by hydroelectric	Percent supplied by pumped storage	Percent supplied by diesel-gas turbine	Percent supplied by nuclear
1960	17 308	12 513	99.9	<1			
1965	24 583	16 727	100				
1970	37 321	21 631	100				
1975	61 498	34 232	98.2	1.8			
1980	83 362	46 755	98.7	1.1		<1	
1985	121 987	59 489	93.4	<1	1.7	0	4.4
1990	146 046	70 861	92.3	<1	1.3	<1	5.7

Sources: RSA Central Statistical Service, *South African Statistics 1992*, "Summary Statistics, Eskom," p. 14.7, and Eskom, *Eskom Statistical Yearbook 1990* (Johannesburg: Eskom, 1991). Percentages of Eskom output by source were calculated from data in table 4, "Summary of Operations," pp. 8–9.

forces and the police would lose their mobility," and he notes the advice a South African law firm gave Mobil Oil in 1976: "As oil is absolutely vital to enable the army to move, the navy to sail, and the air force to fly, it is likely that a South African court would hold that it falls within . . . the definition of munitions of war."[19]

Oil consumption and South Africa's vulnerability to an oil embargo must be seen in the context of overall patterns of energy production and consumption. Electrical energy use in South Africa increased from 1960 to 1990. Almost all electricity used by the public in South Africa was generated by the public utility Eskom (Electricity Supply Commission), though some was generated in municipalities or bought by Eskom from hydroelectric facilities in neighboring countries.[20] Table 5.3 shows trends over this period.[21]

Electricity consumption per capita more than quadrupled between 1958 and 1989, and domestic household consumption grew nearly ten times over the same period, about doubling between 1975 and 1989.[22] Like the ownership in private automobiles, this increased consumption occurred despite the fact that throughout these years, electrification of private households was almost exclusively a white privilege.

As the embargo continued, coal was increasingly important:

Prior to the price rise, the low price of oil had encouraged some domestic consumers to begin using oil. For example, in 1972 the

Cape Town power station converted from coal- to oil-burning boilers, resulting in a decline in demand from Tranvaal collieries. With the rapid rise in the oil price and the uncertainty of supplies, many consumers converted back to coal or recommissioned and redesigned their plants to use coal.[23]

Eskom's coal consumption also grew well over 500 percent during this period. Electricity also provided an increasing amount of transport energy, as Transnet Ltd., which operated South Africa's public trains and ports, more than tripled its electricity consumption between 1960 and 1989, and trains moved away from being directly powered by coal-generated steam.[24]

In sum, South Africa's electricity use increased during the embargo, but most commercially supplied electricity was produced by coal-fired plants. Still, it is likely that despite conservation and conversion to coal, demand for crude oil grew in the 1970s and 1980s and as increasing numbers of automobiles were manufactured and imported. How did South Africa meet the demand for oil in the context of the embargo?

RESISTANCE

The South African government pursued a multipronged energy policy from the 1960s to the early 1990s (including purchasing oil at whatever the price), conservation, starting a strategic oil reserve, exploration, increased coal extraction, synthetic fuel production, and diversifying into hydroelectric and nuclear power. But the same time that South Africa was under the oil embargo, the entire world experienced waves of OPEC oil price increases. Thus, it is hard to gauge just exactly how much of South Africa's efforts in the energy sector were due to the embargo or were reactions to oil price shocks. What is clear is that the South African state, and through liquid fuel taxes, the white public, bore almost the entire financial burden of these efforts.

Oil Purchases and the "Equalization" Fund

Perhaps the most immediately expensive aspect of resistance was South Africa's state-controlled and managed oil international purchases. South Africa bought oil directly from several sources, including those states such as Brunei and Iran (which resumed shipments in the 1980s), that had policies of selling oil to the apartheid regime. The entire effort involved clandestine deals and undercover oil shipments and South Africa even, in some cases, bartered its indigenously produced weapons for oil.[25] The Equalization Fund, a levy on liquid fuel consumption, was established in 1980 to help cover the extra costs of crude oil imports. White South Africans – who owned the majority of private and commercial automobiles – probably paid the most to the Equalization Fund.

The government noted that "During 1979 the Republic of South Africa found itself in a situation where it could no longer obtain crude oil without paying a price differential for delivery of crude oil to South Africa."[26] The Shipping Research Bureau estimated that in 1979 South Africa had to pay a premium up to 50 percent above world oil prices to obtain oil.[27] In the early 1980s, South Africa paid a premium of about $8 per barrel.[28] The South African government also used middlemen to broker oil deals on the black market. The Shipping Research Bureau reported that "companies and middlemen are making profits in the tens of millions of dollars in the illegal oil trade to South Africa."[29] One of these middlemen, Marino Chiavelli earned $7.5 million per month in 1980 for brokering the "Lucina Contract" which ensured that 120 000 barrels of oil per day were shipped to South Africa.[30]

Strategic Oil Reserve

The government began a strategic oil reserve program in 1964, primarily storing oil in unused coal mines in the Transvaal, and in 1979 South Africa opened a storage facility with a capacity of 45 million barrels at Saldanha Bay.[31] In addition, factories were required to stockpile enough fuel for 13 weeks and lubricants for a year. Managed by the Central Energy Fund's Strategic Fuel Fund, the amount in the government's strategic stockpile was secret information under apartheid.

Government secrecy worked. Most outside estimates of the government stockpile were wrong, usually underestimating the amount of crude oil South Africa had in storage.[32] Only the Afrikaner-dominated Sanlam overestimated South African crude oil stockpiles: in 1979, Sanlam said they "assume that it ought to be enough for about 3 years at present rate of consumption. If the fuel-saving measures are tightened up (it is estimated that consumption can be reduced by 30% without any serious effect on economic activity) the oil reserves ought to be enough for 4 to 5 years."[33]

Only with the democratic transition in 1994 did the Strategic Fuel Fund announce that total storage capacity for its strategic reserve was 180 million barrels, though the reserve was never more than 80 percent full (144 million barrels).[34] Assuming, conservatively, that South Africa's liquid fuel consumption was about 300 000 barrels per day (probably an underestimate of consumption) and that the stockpile was about 144 million barrels, South Africa had in storage enough fuel to last 480 days – nearly a year and a half. If consumption were cut to below 1974 levels, say to 250 000 barrels per day, the reserve could last 576 days, or an additional few months.

The stockpile varied in size. South Africa used the strategic reserve as a cushion against sharp oil price increases and sometimes sold oil for revenue. "Facing a sharp fall of the Rand against the US Dollar during 1984 and 1985, the South African government tried to keep the petrol pump price at its 1984 level by heavily drawing on the strategic stockpile. However this could be merely a temporary measure. In January 1985, the government was forced to raise the petrol price by more than 40 percent."[35] South Africa replenished the stockpile the next year when prices for crude oil fell. During 1990–91, after Iraq invaded Kuwait and Western countries went to war to push Iraq out, South Africa sold some of its strategic oil reserves.[36] In July 1993 the South African Cabinet decided that strategic reserves "be reduced to an imported crude oil consumption level equivalent to 6 months stockpiling."[37] In 1993 the government again sold oil reserves, generating an enormous amount of cash as of 31 March 1994, totaling R1 856 421 000.[38]

Conservation and Subsidy

Like much of the world, South Africa began oil conservation in earnest in the 1970s following the first oil price shocks. South Africa increased the pump price of gasoline, restricted the hours of filling stations, and lowered speed limits.[39] In addition, during the 1980s, ethyl alcohol (a by-product of the Sasol coal-to-oil processes discussed below), was added to premium-grade gasoline sold in the Transvaal, parts of the Orange Free State and Cape Province.[40] From 1974 to 1978, conservation kept petrol consumption down to a 0.8 percent annual increase, though diesel (used more for commercial and public transport, the military, and agriculture) consumption grew much more, 5 percent annually during that period.[41] Sasol reported that petrol consumption in South Africa decreased 3 percent during 1985–86 as prices increased, but that consumption increased in the late 1980s, growing, for example, 6.6 percent in 1988–89 and 3.4 percent in 1989–90.[42]

The South African government also subsidized liquid fuel prices. From 1979 to November 1993, to smooth out fluctuations in the retail price of oil, the government operated the Central Energy Fund's Equalization Fund, financed by taxes on liquid fuel consumption. Pump prices reflected consumption taxes while government subsidies also kept pump prices down: the retail price of liquid fuels in South Africa was government controlled, and on average, the price of petrol at the pump increased 13 percent each year from 1977 to 1989.[43]

Coal

The linchpin of South Africa's ability to survive the embargo was its large (mostly bituminous) coal reserves, located primarily in the western half of the country.[44] Between 1950 and 1970, South African coal mining corporations opened only two new coal mines (collieries) in South Africa and this period was associated with "frequent shortages of coal for the domestic market."[45] But the higher oil prices after the OPEC embargoes, and the threat of an oil supply cut-off, led South African coal producers to both increase the intensity of mining, and to invest in major improvements in efficiency by changing mining techniques and increasing mechanization. Between 1970 and 1990 South Africa's saleable coal output increased an average of 6 percent per year.[46] South Africa's Department of Mineral and Energy Affairs policy was to minimize reliance on oil: "Already most of the obvious areas where oil can be substituted for other fuels (primarily coal) have already been exploited, and there is therefore relatively little scope for further reductions."[47] As table 5.3 above shows, Eskom's coal consumption doubled between 1975 and 1990.

Though the US, Denmark, and France prohibited importation of South African coal in 1985, South Africa's total coal exports grew. By 1986 coal accounted for 13 percent of South Africa's revenue from mineral exports (second only to gold), and South Africa became the major supplier of coal to the European Community.[48] Coal exports continued to grow under the partial coal embargo, and by 1990 South Africa had become the world's fifth largest producer of salable black coal, and the third largest exporter.[49] Coal export revenues, which grew on average 21.2 percent per annum between 1974 and 1990 could then be plowed into oil purchases, while coal mined by Sasol was turned into oil at Sasol plants.[50]

The drive to boost coal exports (which tied South Africa as a coal supplier to multinational oil companies), combined with South African demand for coal-produced electricity and synthetic fuel, caused an employment and wage boom for coal mine workers. These gains occurred even as employment declined in the rest of South Africa's mining industry in the 1970s due to mechanization, a policy of reducing reliance on unskilled labor, and falling commodity prices. Between 1980 and 1990, 50 000 jobs were lost overall in the entire mining sector.[51] But in coal mining, despite increased mechanization, "employment rose from 77 244 in 1965 to 103 352 in 1983" and in 1990, coal mines employed 84 303 workers.[52] And though South Africa's coal mining wages remained perhaps the lowest in the world among major producers, wages for coal mining in South Africa increased. South African coal mining wages, in 1987, were also 18.8 percent higher on average than average mining wages.[53] In general, white coalmine workers got the more skilled jobs, but black workers' wages and working conditions also improved relative to white workers', and the number of black workers in unions also grew in the 1970s and 1980s.[54]

Oil from Coal

South Africa also used its coal deposits to make a substantial investment in getting oil from coal, primarily converted at Sasol refineries. Sasol used a conversion method adapted from the German Fischer-Tropsch process, and the technology was provided by the Fluor Corporation based in the United States.[55] Founded in 1950, the first Sasol plant began production in 1955 in Sasolburg, south of Johannesburg. After solving some technical problems, Sasol produced 5 000 barrels of oil per day. In 1974 the government decided to build a second plant, and in 1975 levied a tax of 2 cents per litre on fuel consumption, which increased to 4 cents per litre in 1977 to finance the plant.[56] In February 1979, after the Iranians cut off oil to South Africa, the government decided to build Sasol III. The additional Sasol plants, located in Secunda in the Transvaal west of Johannesburg, were completed in 1980 and 1982 respectively. Sasol II and III each produce 45 000 to 50 000 barrels of oil per day from coal, while Sasol I was gradually turned to producing other petroleum products.[57] A fourth plant was considered but never built.

Even if South Africa made several more Sasol plants, the Department of Mineral and Energy Affairs acknowledged that oil from coal would not solve all of South Africa's commercial diesel, public, and military transport needs: "Coal is, however, less suitable than oil for the production of diesel fuel under present technology. A possible alternative may be methanol, blended with appropriate additives."[58] Sasol also did not provide South Africa's commercial or military jet fuel. Although two test runs of producing jet fuel were conducted at Sasol plants in the 1980s, jet fuel production was too expensive compared to what South Africa could pay for imported fuel.[59]

Government subsidies were crucial for Sasol. In addition to the initial huge capital investments required to build and operate the Sasol plants, production, operations, and fuel sales were subsidized, even after Sasol was semi-privatized in 1979. The subsidies kicked in if imported oil prices fell below $23 per barrel. The subsidy was reduced in the early 1990s but in 1994, the year before subsidies were again cut, Sasol still received R1.1 billion (c. $31 million).[60] These subsidies were important because coal to oil conversion is expensive: though the cost of oil produced from coal was never released by Sasol, estimates range from $45 to $75 per barrel.[61] Moreover, local refineries, though run by outside multinational corporations, received payments from the South African government to compensate for Sasol's share of gasoline sales. One estimate put subsidies to non-Sasol refineries at $960 million in total from 1985–94.[62]

Despite the direct and indirect expense of the coal-to-oil program, Sasol was eventually able to provide fuel for a large portion of South Africa's transportation needs. During the 1980s Sasol provided roughly half of South Africa's gasoline, and in 1995, despite the end of the embargo, and before government subsidies to the industry entirely ended, Sasol accounted for 46 percent of South Africa's total gasoline sales.[63] Sasol also became one of South Africa's largest single employers, by 1989 employing 28 500 people, including several hundred in research and development.[64]

Trevor Bell argues that the construction of Sasol I during the 1950s "had nothing whatsoever to do with sanctions against apartheid."[65] Bell is probably partly right: though international criticism of apartheid and the occupation of Namibia dated to the 1940s, there was no widespread discussion of an oil embargo until the early 1960s. Sasol I was probably primarily a response to the strategic concerns raised during World War II of a cut-off of South Africa to international oil. Further, Bell argues that "Sasol Two was constructed for economic reasons, independent of the oil embargo."[66] But, Bell is likely wrong on this count: Sasol II and III were likely a response to the international oil embargo and to the general sense, felt by leaders in other oil-importing nations during the 1970s, that Middle Eastern oil supplies could be vulnerable to price shocks. South Africa was particularly vulnerable because of its relationship to Israel and sanctions became a strategic concern. In 1991 the Department of Mineral and Energy Affairs said, "In the past, the decision by the Government to proceed with a particular synfuel project was based on strategic rather than economic considerations. Future synthetic fuel projects will, however, have to be economically viable on their own."[67] So, at least Sasol II and III were built primarily as a way to decrease dependence on embargoed crude oil.

Exploration and Mossgass

Exploration of South Africa for oil and natural gas began in the nineteenth century but systematic surveys did not begin until 1965 when Soekor Limited began exploration. Under the 1967 Mining Rights Act, the right to prospecting was vested in the South African government which leased prospecting to Soekor which then subleased to other companies. After finding little oil or natural gas on land, Soekor ended onshore exploration efforts in 1978.

Offshore exploration, which began in 1969, was a little more successful. The first well found gas near Plettenberg Bay that was "too small to warrant exploitation."[68] Chevron made a major gas discovery in South West Africa/Namibian waters in the mouth of the Orange River, in 1974, but "the evaluation of the Orange River occurrence was hampered by political developments in SWA/Namibia."[69] Overall, the official figure spent on oil and natural gas exploration both onshore and offshore between 1965 and 1989 was R1591.58 million ($606.8 million), mainly by Soekor and its subsidiary companies (R1509.58 million).[70]

Soekor made its first and only major discoveries of natural gas south of Mossel Bay in 1980 and 1982, and the government began to make plans to exploit the gas fields.[71] Mossgas was designed to convert the gas to liquid fuel using similar technology to the Sasol II and III refineries. In 1989 the project was projected to cost R7.8 billion ($2.97 billion) and scheduled for final commissioning in July 1990.[72] The offshore plant finally began production in April 1992 and ran above capacity, and the onshore plant was commissioned in January 1993.[73] Mossgas produced about 30 000 barrels of oil per day but total reserves were limited.[74] In late 1995 the new government, with less than a year before already-tapped gas reserves ran out, decided to put an additional R443 million into Mossgas so that it could tap into nearby gas fields and extend its life by an additional 22 months. At the same time, the government decided to sell Mossgas. By 1995, the South African government had spent a total of R11.3 billion ($3.23 billion) on the plant for Mossgas, of which R2 billion was borrowed from outside South Africa.[75]

Other Synthetic Fuels

Sasol also produced methanol for mixture with diesel and automobile fuel because its coal-based diesel was not up to standard. In addition, during the 1980s some research was done on the idea of creating ethanol from sugar. The proposed scheme would have generated 200 million litres of ethanol per year at a plant in Richard's Bay. "The project could account for a saving of R50 million in oil imports and help sustain up to 25 000 jobs for rural workers."[76] In 1990 the government decided not to proceed with the plant because the world oil price had fallen.[77] The amount spent on research on alternative fuels was not revealed at the time.

Hydroelectric and Nuclear Power

South Africa diversified electricity sources by developing nuclear and hydroelectric power. Nuclear power plants in South Africa were probably primarily intended to be a source of highly enriched uranium and a cover for South Africa's nuclear weapons program. Nevertheless, commercial electrical power was generated at the Koeberg power stations which went into the Eskom grid in 1984. Hydroelectric power generation was never a reliable source of energy for South Africa during the embargo era. Eskom notes that hydroelectric use was "restricted to peaking and emergencies and availability of water in Hendrick Verwoerd and P. K. le Roux dams."[78] South African attempts to get hydroelectricity from Mozambique and Angola were also largely unsuccessful because of the wars in those countries.[79]

INDIRECT HEALTH CONSEQUENCES OF SANCTIONS

It is possible that South Africa's resistance to the embargo in the form of increased coal mining and consumption, along with the development of a large synthetic fuel production capacity, led to significant health and environmental effects. Greater attention to the health and environmental consequences of pollution, and significant advances in techniques for pollution reduction coincided with South Africa's scientific and technical isolation under sanctions. Thus sanctions combined with South Africa's apartheid energy policies may have indirectly caused a long-lasting environmental and health crisis. How did this happen?

The extensive coal mining that allowed South Africa to evade the most dire effects of the embargo caused water and air pollution. Nearly 40 percent of South African coal was produced by the open pit (strip mining) method in 1990 which can cause groundwater contamination.[80] During the 1980s South Africa began to experience the acid rain problems associated with massive industrialization in the region that housed most of South Africa's coal-fired power plants and industry: "Highly acidic rainwater frequently falls in the industrial heartland of the eastern Transvaal Highveld. This pollution comes from the power stations and industries" of the area.[81] In January 1989 a study of sulfur dioxide commissioned for South Africa's Council for Scientific and Industrial Research found that "emission densities are between five and just under ten times greater than those found in West Germany and the United States, and approximate the worst conditions found anywhere."[82] Moreover, South African coal is primarily bituminous (over 95 percent), burning less cleanly and efficiently than anthracite coal, and South African power stations put about half a million tons of smoke particles in the air each year.[83] The coal-to-liquid fuel process was also far from clean: though Sasol II and III were built to be cleaner, Sasol I, located south of Johannesburg discharged toxic waste into the Vaal River: "Tests have identified twenty seven chemicals listed as priority pollutants in the United States in Sasol's effluent."[84]

There were a few studies of the health effects of poor air quality in South Africa. Respiratory disease was the second major killer of children under five in the Johannesburg-Soweto area. A study of 2000 children by Professor Saul Zwi of the University of the Witwatersrand in 1988 showed that children in polluted towns were shorter in height than those in cleaner areas.[85] But poor air quality can also be attributed to apartheid policies. Those whom the state classified as "non-whites" were systematically denied access to electricity. In 1990 the head of Eskom said that 70 percent of black South Africans did not have access to electricity in their households.[86] The lion's share of coal consumption went to generate power for white-owned homes, manufacturing centers, and business. Most of the power used by township dwellers, until quite recently, was produced when they burned wood or coal in large cans for cooking while coal power stations tended to be located on the outskirts of cities, roughly the same areas occupied by townships. So, while benefiting little from coal-powered electricity generation, the majority population suffered the same or probably worse air quality than whites since they were burning coal and wood directly for heat and light. While the evidence that poor air quality hurt township poor more directly than those with access to electricity is far from definitive – and the availablity of medical care varied among population groups – overall morbidity rates are suggestive: whites were, not unexpectedly, healthier and tended to die of diseases like cancer and heart disease whereas black people died in greater proportion of respiratory disease than white South Africans.[87]

CONCLUSIONS

In a speech at Vereeniging in April 1986, South African State President P. W. Botha said:

> Between 1973 and 1984 the Republic of South Africa had to pay R22 billion more than it would have normally spent. There were times when it was reported to me that we had enough oil for only a week. Just think what we could have done if we had that R22 billion [\$9.6 billion in 1986] today . . . what could have been done in other areas? But we had to spend it because we couldn't bring our motor cars and our diesel locomotives to a standstill as our economic life would have collapsed. We paid a price, which we are still suffering today.[88]

Thus the direct consequences of the oil embargo on South Africa were the increased expenses, particularly after 1979, of acquiring oil from multiple sources for immediate sale and stockpiling. Peter Van Bergeijk argues that the direct costs of the embargo which "consists of premiums paid to middlemen, transporters and traders ... import substitution facilities for strategic oil reserves and obsolescence of specific parts of the capital stock. ... more than doubled South Africa's import bill." He argues that the "direct costs of the oil embargo in the 1980s equalled South Africa's gross foreign debt, which by the end of the decade was estimated at between \$15 to 20 billion."[89] Some effort at energy self-sufficiency would have been made by any government concerned with oil supplies in the wake of OPEC price increases. Still, it is clear that because of sanctions South Africa paid more dearly for decreasing dependence.

There were also indirect costs. The government's primary source of foreign exchange earnings throughout the oil embargo came from gold exports. It is likely that the government had to increase exports of both gold and coal to pay for oil on the spot market and the capital equipment to build Sasol II and III, and later, Mossgas. Finally, there were what might be considered positive consequences of the embargo. South Africa increased its oil conservation efforts for a time; there was probably increased black employment in the power industry and mining industries, especially coal mines; and after the transition to democracy in 1994 oil reserves were sold by the new government to generate foreign exchange.

Still, the oil embargo against South Africa never lived up to the fears of the Afrikaner elite or the hopes of the African National Congress – grinding the South African government and economy to a halt. Nelson Mandela recently argued "oil sanctions helped tremendously in the efforts to end apartheid."[90] How could it have been more effective? A complete oil embargo of South Africa would have required either a firmer international consensus among large multinational corporations and governments that South Africa must change its apartheid policies and/or a willingness by states to monitor South African ports in order to enforce a blockade or seize ships that delivered crude oil to Cape Town, Durban, Port Elizabeth or Walvis Bay. Few ports were able to take in large oil tankers (with Durban accounting for 85 percent of supplies docking in South Africa) and one port, in Richards Bay, was the main coal depot. A more effective embargo would also have targeted the multinational corporations and governments that supplied technology for Sasol South African coal exports much earlier which, along with gold and arms exports, supplied much of the foreign exchange used for South Africa's oil purchases. A tighter embargo of this sort would have required more sanctions on the sanctions busters, though there were governments and private organizations that were such busters.[91]

A complete embargo would have been immediately successful in 1979 and reduced the South African military and police to immobility within a few months. A complete embargo after Sasol II and III came on line in 1980 and 1982 would have meant a difficult choice for the South African government between fuel for the economy and fuel for the military abroad and police at home, with Sasol oil from coal fuel admittedly supplying poorer quality diesel for military and police vehicles than fuel from oil.

But, by the early 1980s, after Sasol II and III came on line and the strategic fuel reserve was well in place, it is clear that South Africa would not have fallen in a day or even a year after a complete oil embargo took effect. Even with Sasol, South Africa never completely got around its dependence on imported oil – and as table 5.3 suggests, due to the surge in motor vehicles used in South Africa, that dependence probably substantially grew even after the embargo went into effect. Thus, a tighter embargo would likely have been extremely disruptive.

Over the long run, South Africa could not have survived oil sanctions without large coal reserves. As it was, fear of a total embargo, and the consequences of the actual rather leaky embargo, were probably significant factors in apartheid government planning and policy. Though there were few public statements to that effect, and officials minimized the impact of all sanctions, the influence of oil sanctions on state policy can be inferred from the tremendous practical lengths the government went in order to diversify oil sources and to acquire an import substitution capacity. For example, the strategic oil reserve system was developed in the 1960s after the first international discussions of an embargo and grew in capacity after the opening of Saldanha Bay facilities in 1979. Plans to build Sasol II and III were decided upon in 1974 and 1979, as South Africa felt the first and second, more effective, embargoes. Official secrecy and efforts to minimize dependency through conservation, coal-powered electrification, and government-sponsored oil and natural gas exploration grew as the embargo intensified.

So, South African resistance allowed the state to adjust partially to outside pressure. It is unlikely that the oil embargo directly changed any minds in the South African government. It is also unlikely that the embargo caused considerable shortages for long enough periods to affect military and police operations; there was no evidence that fuel shortages caused military incapacity. Still, the direct impact of the leaky embargo, and indirect consequences of the resistance to it, were not without cost or consequences. Even leaky oil sanctions made the maintenance of apartheid more expensive – and that expense probably helped to slow South Africa's economic growth in the 1970s and 1980s, which in turn decreased the ability of the state to maintain apartheid.

In sum, contrary to conventional wisdom, it is not necessary to have a complete oil embargo in place to affect the target; the threat of an embargo – and even leaky sanctions – may have important consequences. Embargoes that at least partially decrease oil flows could cause costs to increase and/or create shortages that affect the target's ability to maintain the policies that sparked the embargo. Finally, though the evidence is far from complete, oil embargoes can have indirect counterproductive environmental consequences which may be aggravated by inequalities of income distribution.[92] This raises issues about the ethical responsibility of sanctioners for the environmental and health consequences of oil embargoes.

Notes

1. Amy Nash provided research assistance. Jacklyn Cock, Audie Klotz, and Kim Richard Nossal made useful suggestions on an early draft.
2. Under the 1977 Petroleum Products Act, and the 1979 and 1985 amendments to it, disclosing information regarding the source, manufacture, transport, destination, storage, consumption and quantity of petroleum used in South Africa was subject to fines of up to R7000 and/or up to seven years imprisonment.
3. "Sanctions and the South African Economy," *Sanlam's Economic Review* (February 1979), 1–12: 1, emphasis in the original.
4. A. J. Klinghoffer, *Oiling the Wheels of Apartheid* (London: Lynne Rienner, 1989), p. 87.
5. Ibid., pp. 87 and 91.
6. M. Bailey, "Oil Sanctions: South Africa's Weak Link," *Economic Sanctions Against South Africa* 5 (Amsterdam: 1980), p. 23.
7. Iran was part-owner of South Africa's Natref refinery in Sasolburg, and in 1975 the two countries reached an agreement for South Africa to supply Iran with uranium.
8. Klinghoffer, *Oiling the Wheels of Apartheid*, pp. 35–8.

9. R. Hengeveld and J. Rodenburg, eds., *Embargo: Apartheid's Oil Secrets Revealed* (Amsterdam: Amsterdam University Press, 1995), pp. 206–21. Shipping Research Bureau (SRB), *Secret Oil Deliveries to South Africa, 1981–1982* (Amsterdam: SRB, 1984). On shippers, also see Klinghoffer, *Oiling the Wheels of Apartheid*, pp. 50–3; also see J. Waldendorp, "The Oil Embargo Against South Africa: Effects and Loopholes," in R. Edgar, ed., *Sanctioning Apartheid* (Trenton, NJ: Africa World Press, 1990), p. 175. This is part of a larger pattern of multinational corporations evading the sanctions against South Africa.

10. Originally quoted in the *Rand Daily Mail*, 5 March 1974, and quoted in Bailey, "Oil Sanctions," p. 23.

11. Bailey, "Oil Sanctions," p. 24.

12. Ibid., p. 10.

13. Ibid.

14. Excludes "oil consumed as refinery fuel, oil used in energy conversion, and exports and bunkers," as given in Bailey, "Oil Sanctions," pp. 9–10.

15. "World-Wide Refining Report," *Oil and Gas Journal* 90, no. 51 (21 December 1992), pp. 41–95: 81.

16. R. Friedland, "Engen: An Oil Giant Stirs," *Financial Mail* 127, no. 8 (22 May 1992), 24–27: 24.

17. The total does not include tractors, trailers, caravans, and vehicles that were exempt from being licensed.

18. Klinghoffer, *Oiling the Wheels of Apartheid*, p. 2.

19. Bailey, "Oil Sanctions," p. 10.

20. Municipalities also sold electricity to industry. Economist, *Economist Intelligence Unit Country Profile, South Africa, 1990–1991* (London: Economist, 1991), p. 36.

21. Pumped-storage facililities are "net users of electricity and are used for peaking. Water is pumped during off-peak periods to generate electricity during peak periods." The contribution of nuclear power to the electricy of South Africa is complicated. See D. Fig, "Sanctions and the Nuclear Industry," previous chapter in this volume.

22. RSA Central Statistical Services (CSS), *South African Statistics 1992*, "Production and Consumption of Electricity, All Undertakings," p. 14.3. Though the numbers for the black majority population are unreliable, since so few blacks received electrical power during most of this period, one can safely say that the minority white population's electrical usage accounts for most growth.

23. J. Leger, "Coal Mining: Past Profits, Current Crisis?" in S. Gelb, ed., *South Africa's Economic Crisis* (Cape Town: David Philip, 1991), pp. 129–55: 134.

24. RSA CSS, *South African Statistics 1992*, "Production and Consumption of Electricity, All Undertakings" (RSA: Pretoria, 1992), p. 14.3. "Steam locomotives as a form of traction are being phased out, partly for reasons of efficiency and environmental protection and partly because of the shortage of suitable and convenient water supplies." RSA Department of Mineral and Energy Affairs (DME&A), *South Africa's Mineral Industry 1990* (RSA: Johannesburg, 1991), p. 44.

25. See Hengeveld and Rodenburg, eds., *Embargo*, for a discussion of clandestine shipping.
26. RSA, *Report of the Auditor General on the Financial Statements for 1993–1994 of the Central Energy Fund* (RSA: Pretoria, 1995), p. 28.
27. SRB, *Secret Oil Deliveries to South Africa 1981–1982*, p. 29.
28. P. A. G. Van Bergeijk, "The Oil Embargo and the Intellectual: The Academic Debate on Economic Sanctions Against South Africa," in Hengeveld and Rodenburg, eds., *Embargo*, pp. 338–45: 343.
29. SRB, *Secret Oil Deliveries to South Africa 1981–1982*, p. 29.
30. E. Koch, "How Chiavelli Earned His Tax-Free Millions," *Weekly Mail and Guardian*, 13 October 1995, citing SRB data in Hengeveld and Rodenburg, eds., *Embargo*.
31. Klinghoffer, *Oiling the Wheels of Apartheid*, p. 26; J. Yeld, "Full Steam Ahead – To Disaster?" *African Wildlife* 49, no. 5 (1995), p. 5.
32. Estimates of strategic oil reserve varied from eighteen months to five years. In 1988, the SRB estimated the stockpile to be seven to eight million tons (about 1 million barrels) – enough for six or seven months of supplies. Cited in *Africa Research Bulletin*, 30 September 1988, p. 9265B. Jaap Waldendorp estimated that 16–17 million tons, or enough for 15 months of consumption, was stockpiled. Waldendorp, "The Oil Embargo Against South Africa," p. 169. This is equivalent to about 2.1 to 2.3 million barrels.
33. Sanlam, "Sanctions and the South African Economy," p. 7.
34. K. Davie, "Apartheid and the Cost of Energy Self-Sufficiency," in Hengeveld and Rodenburg, eds., *Embargo*, p. 250.
35. Waldendorp, "The Oil Embargo Against South Africa," p. 169.
36. T. Bell, "The Impact of Sanctions on South Africa," *Journal of Contemporary African Studies* 12 (1993), pp. 1–28: 24–5.
37. RSA, *Report of the Auditor General on the Financial Statements for 1993–1994 of the Central Energy Fund*, p. 39.
38. Ibid., p. 5.
39. See Klinghoffer, *Oiling the Wheels of Apartheid*, pp. 26–8.
40. DME&A, *South Africa's Mineral Industry 1989*, p. 56.
41. Bailey, "Oil Sanctions," p. 13.
42. Sasol, *Annual Report 1989* and *Annual Report 1990*.
43. DME&A, *South Africa's Mineral Industry, 1989* (RSA: Johannesburg, 1990), p. 57.
44. Only 2 percent of coal in South Africa is anthracite and 1.6 percent metallurgical (DME&A, *South Africa's Mineral Industry 1990*, pp. 39–41).
45. Leger, "Coal Mining," p. 131.
46. DME&A, *South Africa's Mineral Industry, 1990*, p. 39.
47. Bailey, "Oil Sanctions," p. 14.
48. J. Leger, "Coal Mining," p. 128; DME&A, *South Africa's Mineral Industry 1986*, p. 4.
49. DME&A, *South Africa's Mineral Industry 1990*, p. 41.
50. Ibid., p. 39.
51. C. M. Rogerson, "The Unemployment Challenge in a Democratic South Africa," in A. Lemon, ed., *The Geography of Change in South Africa* (New York: John Wiley and Sons, 1995), pp. 169–94: 174.

52. Leger, "Coal Mining," p. 134; DME&A, *South Africa's Mineral Industry, 1992–1993*, p. 32.
53. Calculated from figures in DME&A, *South Africa's Mineral Industry, 1992–1993*, p. 5, and Leger, "Coal Mining," p. 149.
54. Leger, "Coal Mining," pp. 134, 138, 144.
55. Gas from coal is produced at Sasol plants and in gasworks located in Johannesburg, Cape Town and Port Elizabeth, for use in those metropolitan areas. Other oil from coal schemes besides Sasol were much less productive. South Africa tried to get oil from torbanite shale, but reserves were small and expensive to turn into oil and work on this process was discontinued. DME&A, *South Africa's Mineral Industry 1989*, pp. 56 and 58.
56. The levy was discontinued in 1988. RSA *Report of the Auditor General on the Financial Statements for 1993–1994 of the Central Energy Fund*, p. 11.
57. In the 1980s, the ANC also targeted Sasol facilities for sabotage. See Hengeveld and Rodenburg, eds., *Embargo*, pp. 25–55.
58. DME&A, *South Africa's Mineral Industry, 1990*, p. 43.
59. SA Air Force Colonel P. B. Willcock, interview with the author, Pretoria, South Africa, 5 March 1996.
60. R. Hartley, "Cabinet Set to Slash Sasol's R1.1bn Subsidy," *Sunday Times* (Johannesburg), 3 December 1995.
61. K. Davie, "Apartheid and the Cost of Energy Self-Sufficiency," pp. 242–53: 243; Klinghoffer, *Oiling the Wheels of Apartheid*, p. 24. The expense of coal to oil and gasoline production is illustrated by the behavior of Sasol after the embargo ended: Sasol accelerated diversification into petrochemical production to the point where petrochemicals provided more than 50 percent of its revenue, and international consultants were brought in to facilitate reengineering of their synfuels program. M. Collins, "Sasol: Phasing Out its Subsidy," *Financial Mail* (15 December 1995), pp. 23–4: 24.
62. D. Knott, "South Africa's Synfuel Issue," *Oil and Gas Journal* 93, no. 23 (5 June 1995), p. 26.
63. Ibid., 24.
64. *Financial Mail*, special supplement, 116 (22 June 1990).
65. Bell, "The Impact of Sanctions on South Africa," p. 9.
66. Ibid.
67. DME&A, *South Africa's Mineral Industry, 1990*, p. 55.
68. DME&A, *South Africa's Mineral Industry, 1989*, p. 53.
69. Ibid.
70. Ibid., p. 54.
71. Soekor and Gencor also explored the feasibility of a mobile floating production system in the late 1980s in the Bredasdorp Basin. "Extended testing of one reservoir yielded encouraging results and some 120 000 barrels of oil was recovered into a tanker at an average flow rate of approximately 5 000 barrels per day." DME&A, *South Africa's Mineral Industry, 1989*, p. 58. In 1988 the government's Central Energy Fund and Industrial Development Corporation were joined in developing Mossgas by the private company Gencor which took over project management.

72. DME&A, *South Africa's Mineral Industry, 1989*, p. 58.
73. C. Ryan, "R443m to Wash Government's Hands of Mossgas," *Sunday Times* Johannesburg, 3 December 1995.
74. Davie, "Apartheid and the Cost of Energy Self-Sufficiency," p. 243.
75. Ryan, "R443m to Wash Government's Hands of Mossgas."
76. DME&A, *South Africa's Mineral Industry, 1989*, p. 59.
77. DME&A, *South Africa's Mineral Industry, 1990*, p. 55.
78. Eskom, *Eskom Statistical Yearbook 1990*, table 4, "Summary of Operations," pp. 8–9.
79. In 1969, South Africa agreed with Portugal to construct a hydroelectric power station on the Zambezi River in Mozambique. Cahora Bassa station was completed in 1977 and operated until Renamo rebels, backed by South Africa, sabotaged the dam. Only in 1988 did South Africa, Mozambique, and Portugal come to an agreement to repair the dam at an estimated cost of $75 million. Another hydroelectric facility, the Calueque dam, was constructed in southern Angola and became one of the reasons South Africa gave for its 1975 invasion of Angola. *Africa Research Bulletin*, 31 July 1988, p. 9172.
80. DME&A, *South Africa's Mineral Industry 1990*, p. 41.
81. H. Coetzee and D. Cooper, "Wasting Water," in J. Cock and E. Koch, eds., *Going Green: People, Politics and the Environment in South Africa* (Cape Town: Oxford University Press, 1991), pp. 129–38: 132.
82. Report quoted in J. Clark, "The Insane Experiment: Tampering with the Atmosphere," in Cock and Koch, eds., *Going Green*, pp. 139–57: 144.
83. M. Gandar, "The Imbalance of Power," in Cock and Koch, eds., *Going Green*, pp. 94–109: 98.
84. Coetzee and Cooper, "Wasting Water," p. 135.
85. Clark, "The Insane Experiment," pp. 140–1.
86. Ian McRea quoted in Clark, "The Insane Experiment," p. 149.
87. RSA CSS, *South African Statistics 1994* data on principal causes of death.
88. In the *Windhoek Advertiser*, 25 April 1986, quoted by Waldendorp, "The Oil Embargo in South Africa," p. 172.
89. Van Bergeijk, "The Oil Embargo and the Intellectual," p. 343.
90. N. Mandela, "Preface" in Hengeveld and Rodenburg, eds., *Embargo*, p. ix.
91. See Hengeveld and Rodenburg, eds., *Embargo*, pp. 95ff.
92. In Haiti, sanctions on fuel exacerbated deforestation. S. Zaidi, "Humanitarian Effects of the Coup and Sanctions in Haiti," in T. G. Weiss, D. Cortright, G. A. Lopez and L. Minear, eds., *Political Pain and Civilian Gain: Humanitarian Impacts of Economic Sanctions* (Oxford: Rowman and Littlefield, 1997), pp. 189–212: 200.

Part III

Economic Sanctions

6 The US Divestment Movement

Meg Voorhes

US universities, pension funds, local governments, and other institutions faced ethical pressures to sell off their investments in companies doing business in South Africa. These demands originated with the campus divestment movement, which concentrated – almost by definition – on 150 or so highly endowed colleges and universities. This anti-apartheid activism began in the mid-1960s, accelerated after the Soweto rebellion and its aftermath, and peaked in response to the South African state of emergency imposed in 1985. A growing number of state and local governments in the US also added their weight to the divestment campaign from the late 1970s onward. By 1993, 40 of the top 50 colleges and universities (ranked by size of endowment) had some sort of divestment policy, as did the governments and pension funds of more than 100 states, counties, cities, and US territories.

Activists claimed that divestment would – to paraphrase the introduction to this book – send a clear signal to companies operating in South Africa, to policymakers, to the broader public, and to the people of South Africa. But like most popular movements, the divestment campaign comprised a broad range of actors with varying viewpoints, sophistication and strategies. Students and their faculty allies called for total divestment from companies doing business (generally defined as having assets or employees) in South Africa. At least initially, administrations generally resisted these demands. Many institutions eventually developed corporate codes of conduct as well as guidelines for communicating their anti-apartheid concerns through correspondence with companies and by voting on shareholder resolutions. Thus the movement embraced more than students and city councillors pressing for total divestment. Endowment and pension fund administrators also shaped the campaign to encourage companies to improve their labor practices, to step up their actions in opposition to apartheid, and to limit their sales or operations in South Africa.

US and South African businesses took note of these pressures and policies. The divestment campaign, including student protests, shareholder resolutions, or meetings between corporate executives and representatives of institutional shareholders, moderated the policies of US banks and corporations. However, divestment had no direct economic impact on companies. Those corporations that did pull out by 1985 responded, by their own admission, to the increasing number of selective contracting policies adopted by local governments.

More fundamentally, divestment and shareholder activism increased US public awareness of apartheid, creating a political environment conducive to Congressional sanctions against South Africa. Furthermore, the movement received extensive international media coverage, heartening many South African anti-apartheid activists. Thus this chapter's assessment of the overall impact of the US divestment campaign underscores the importance of viewing social movement mobilization as a component of both the causes and consequences of sanctions.

DIVESTMENT PRESSURES AND POLICIES

Initiated by students, the divestment movement grew in three progressively larger waves, during the late 1960s, the late 1970s, and the mid-1980s. These stages reflected events in South Africa and prompted corresponding phases in university, pension-fund and government policies. Investors gradually accepted increasingly stringent criteria for divestment.

Phase 1: Ethical Investment

The first wave of US anti-apartheid activism began in 1965, when members of Students for a Democratic Society demonstrated at Chase Manhattan's headquarters on Wall Street to protest its loans to the South African government; 17 were arrested. Throughout the late 1960s and early 1970s, student protesters urged administrations at Cornell, Princeton, Wesleyan, the University of Wisconsin at Madison, and Union Theological Seminary to sell their South African holdings.[1] Some responded by selling off securities in particularly controversial companies, but most resisted. Rather, the divestment debate prompted many administrations and faculty to consider their responsibilities as ethical investors and to develop appropriate guidelines.

This examination resulted in publications, primarily by academics at Harvard, Princeton, and Yale, which concluded that universities should follow certain principles as socially responsible investors. *The Ethical Investor*, published in 1972, proved particularly influential.[2] Although recognizing that a shareholder does not cause "social injury in the same sense [as] the manager who fashions corporate policy," the book argued that a shareholder still "bears responsibility for harm resulting from corporate business practices," because of proximity to, and capability to influence, the corporation. Moreover, if a shareholder fails "to seek to bring about corrective action by the shareholders as a group, that individual shareholder contributes – however fractionally – to the continuation of the corporate wrong." Not voicing objections "amounts to participation in the injurious practice." That said, the authors cautioned against the sale of securities for ethical rather than economic reasons, except "where the company is committing grave social injury and where all methods of correcting these policies have failed or appear doomed to failure."[3]

In response, many universities established committees to advise trustees on investment and shareholder issues. One of the first, formed at Harvard in 1972, had equal representation from faculty, students and alumni, a pattern similar to the composition of committees formed at other universities (although some included administration, staff or even community representatives). By 1979 more than 30 of the 89 universities polled by the Investor Responsibility Research Center (IRRC) had established advisory committees on investments involving South Africa.[4] Thus, by the 1970s, a significant number of administrations had accepted a responsibility to exercise influence as shareholders when corporate activities caused "social injury." The basis for divestment had been established.

Phase 2: Partial Divestment

The Soweto uprisings and Steve Biko's death in detention provoked another wave of anti-apartheid activism on US campuses. In early 1977, more than 700 students were arrested in various protests; at Stanford University, one protest alone led to nearly 300 arrests. The student-led South African Catalyst Project, headquartered at Stanford, coordinated actions throughout the country.[5] In response, several colleges and universities adopted total divestment policies, including Antioch, Hampshire, Howard, Michigan State, the University of Massachusetts, Ohio University, and the University of Wisconsin.[6]

By and large, however, most administrations, following the reasoning of *The Ethical Investor*, argued that divestment would be a premature step. Although sensitive to student demands, they defined ethics and responsibilities differently. Many administrations remained unconvinced that a corporation's presence in South Africa constituted social injury, or they thought that the social injury could be corrected if the company modified its behavior. Rather than divest, these universities sought to persuade companies, through correspondence and by voting on shareholder resolutions, to implement exemplary labor practices and philanthropic activities, to lobby against apartheid laws, and to ban sales to the South African security forces. They claimed that divestment either would not send a signal (because someone else would buy the stocks) or would deprive them of a means of conveying signals (because they would no longer vote at corporate annual meetings).

These arguments received powerful support from the development of the Sullivan Principles. Developed by Rev. Leon Sullivan, a civil rights activist and a director of General Motors, in concert with representatives of other leading US corporations, the code called on companies to promote equal pay and opportunities within the workplace, and to improve the quality of life for their black workers outside the workplace through social investment projects. Announced in 1976, this voluntary code of conduct gave legitimacy to the position that corporations could act as a force for progress within South Africa. Many university advisory committees developed guidelines for voting on shareholder resolutions dealing with South Africa. In some cases, universities and colleges sponsored or cosponsored shareholder resolutions. As a general rule, these colleges and universities supplemented their votes on shareholder resolutions with direct communication with the company to elicit information and to explain their policies. By the early 1980s most schools with South Africa-related investment policies voted in favor of resolutions that requested companies to sign the Sullivan principles.

A smaller number also favored resolutions restricting sales of goods to the South African government, especially its security and apartheid-enforcing agencies. Several schools, including Brandeis, Carleton, and Macalester, forbade investment in companies that were involved in strategic sectors of the South African economy (such as computers or oil) or that sold to the South African military or police.

Many administrations accepted that they should divest from companies that failed to respond to queries or refused to counter the social injury caused by their presence in South Africa. The Sullivan Principles also made it more justifiable to sell shares in companies that failed to comply.[7] By early 1983, at least 34 colleges and universities had developed policies that required them to sell off securities, or to forego purchasing additional shares, in companies that did not measure up. More than a dozen schools, including Cornell, the University of Pennsylvania, Wesleyan, and Yale, announced that they would not hold stock in companies that failed to adopt the code of conduct.

Some universities also adopted policies calling for divestment of stock in companies that refused to disclose information on their operations or labor practices. From 1978 to early 1983, schools sold more than $80 million in investments.[8] But most continued to oppose resolutions calling for corporate withdrawal from South Africa. These administrations generally viewed such resolutions, as they did divestment, as a step to be taken only if all other remedies failed.

Meanwhile, several state, county and city governments adopted similarly mixed policies. First, Connecticut passed a partial divestment law in 1982. In January 1983, Massachusetts banned all investments by its pension funds in companies doing business in South Africa. The city council of Madison, Wisconsin, agreed in 1976 to avoid contracts with companies that have "economic interests in South Africa." In 1978, Cotati, California, became the first US jurisdiction to prohibit the investment of its funds in corporations with business ties to South Africa. Berkeley and the Oakland Unified School District, in May 1979, restricted their relationships with banks that retained ties to South Africa.[9] These increasingly tough restrictions set the stage for the next wave of pressure for more comprehensive divestment.

Phase 3: Total Divestment

The third and most intensive wave of US divestment activism started in the 1984/85 academic year, sparked by the increased turmoil in South Africa that was covered extensively by US and international media. As part of escalating global anti-apartheid mobilization calling for comprehensive economic sanctions, demands for US companies to withdraw from South Africa increased. Divestment proponents also hoped that campus activism would educate the broader public about apartheid and galvanize a larger sanctions movement. Jerry Herman, working with the American Friends Service Committee, advocated divestment as "an extremely effective tool to get people moving on South Africa. People need and want something to do on South Africa, and divestment provides them with such an opportunity."[10]

Student blockades of administration buildings at Columbia, Rutgers, and Berkeley in April 1985 galvanized similar actions across the country. Protests reached unprecedented numbers and caught many college administrations by surprise. More than 1000 Cornell students clashed with police, while those at Columbia blockaded Hamilton Hall for three weeks. At the University of California at Berkeley, 650 students were arrested in a series of demonstrations, and 3 000 boycotted classes to join rallies.[11] The following October, about 130 Wesleyan University students were arrested while blocking entrances to administration buildings, 1200 Berkeley students once again convened, and at least two protesting Cornell students were arrested every weekday. Overall, more than 20 campuses across the country experienced rallies, sit-ins and marches.[12]

To these proponents of total divestment, corporations – whatever their intentions or actions – could not be a net force for good in South Africa. As Stanford University's public affairs office summarized this argument, "By their very existence in South Africa, US companies contribute to the continuation of the apartheid system. They pay taxes, enhance economic stability and lend credibility to the racist government in South Africa, and thus they strengthen the system of apartheid."[13] There could be no distinctions between companies, since efforts to ameliorate apartheid were doomed to failure. Activists equated holding securities as encouraging companies to remain in South Africa and, therefore, as signaling support for apartheid. In the words of Professor Peter Walshe, a member of the University of Notre Dame's Ad Hoc Committee of the Board of Trustees on South African Investments, "to encourage corporations to remain in South Africa in these circumstances, is to abdicate moral responsibility."[14]

Some activists theorized that if enough institutions adopted total divestment policies, the stock prices of the targeted corporations would be deflated, making it more difficult to finance new stock issues and to resist hostile takeovers. But most conceded that divestment would have little, if any, direct economic impact on the targeted companies; the economic pressure argument, therefore, did not feature prominently in debates. Some activists also said their universities should divest as a signal to its immediate community of students, faculty and alumni that it rejected apartheid. However, few divestment proponents argued that their universities should follow through in the interests of moral purity by refusing to purchase supplies or to accept gifts from companies operating in South Africa. One respondent to a survey by the University of Pennsylvania's Committee on University Responsibility to the Trustees captured the views of many divestment advocates by suggesting that "Investors, as owners, are accountable for the behavior and location of companies in a way that consumers and gift/grant beneficiaries are not."[15]

By the mid-1980s, institutional investors proved far more willing to adopt total divestment policies.[16] Nearly half of the 49 institutions which implemented new South Africa-related policies opted for total divestment. By early 1986, 40 of the 100 top schools (by size of endowment) chose partial divestment policies and seven had total divestment policies. Anti-apartheid investment restrictions tightened further throughout the rest of the decade. From April 1986 through the end of 1989, another 19 US colleges and universities, most of which were among the 100 most highly endowed schools, adopted total divestment. These included the University of Pennsylvania, Bowdoin College, Colgate University, Duke University, New York University, the University of Pittsburgh, the University of Rochester, and Tufts University. By 1992, 15 of the top 50 US colleges and universities (by size of endowment) had total divestment policies and 25 had partial divestment policies.[17]

Similarly, at the local government level, pension funds increasingly adopted partial or total divestment policies. In 1984 and 1985 alone, 13 state and city governments or agencies adopted partial divestment provisions, and 38 adopted total divestment policies; others joined the trend throughout the late 1980s. Even more significantly, major municipalities restricted their purchases of goods and services from companies doing business in South Africa. In 1985 and 1986, Chicago, Houston, Los Angeles, New York, Oakland, Pittsburgh, San Francisco, and Washington adopted such provisions. More than 70 localities had adopted selective contracting laws

restricting their procurement of goods and services from companies with South African business ties by 1993.

Even institutions and pension funds that still resisted total divestment now voted in favor of resolutions that called on companies to withdraw from South Africa. For example, TIAA–CREF
(the Teachers Insurance and Annuity Association–College Retirement Equities Fund), one of the largest US institutional investors,
remained unpersuaded about the virtues of divestment but did spon-
sor stockholder resolutions asking companies to withdraw. In 1987,
with the New York State Common Retirement Fund, it sponsored
shareholder resolutions asking companies to cut economic ties with
South Africa; they pursued the campaign through late 1991.[18] This
shift, by two of the country's largest single institutional investors,
ensured that virtually every US company with operations in South
Africa received a shareholder resolution asking it to end those
operations, which required the directors or top executives to for-
mulate responses. Similar resolutions received record levels of more
than 12 percent overall support, on average, at each company to
which they were submitted in 1987 and 1988 – nearly double the
6.6 percent such proposals received, on average, in 1986.[19]

Another by-product of student anti-apartheid activism was the
formation of a consortium of colleges and universities under the initial sponsorship of Wesleyan University in early 1984. Over the
next ten years the consortium commissioned research papers and
briefings to help members refine their investment and shareholder
voting guidelines, and to develop scholarship and faculty development programs aimed at black South Africans. On two occasions,
the consortium engaged collectively in political lobbying. In January 1985, members urged the American Chamber of Commerce in
South Africa to more actively oppose apartheid.[20] Several months
later, 20 university presidents signed a letter to Senate Majority
Leader Robert Dole urging the passage of sanctions strong enough
"to demonstrate the depth and sincerity of this country's disapproval of apartheid."[21]

One reason for the growing acceptance of total divestment (and
sanctions) was the situation on the ground in South Africa. In the
context of violent unrest and the South African government's harsh
response, investors had difficulty defending the role of corporations in promoting peaceful change. Even Leon Sullivan admitted,
in May 1987, that his code of conduct had not eliminated apartheid and called for economic sanctions. Within five months of

Sullivan's dramatic shift, five colleges and universities adopted total divestment policies, and the governor of Connecticut signed a law imposing a total divestment policy on its pension funds that superseded its 1982 partial divestment policy.

Another factor making total divestment more acceptable to institutional investors was the dramatic exodus of corporations from South Africa. Previously, institutions had argued that fiduciary and fundraising responsibilities should temper divestment. Similarly, many schools had soft-pedaled any divestment motivated by non-financial reasons, in an effort to avoid retaliation by the target companies in the form of decreased donations and research grants. But in contrast to the early 1980s, when nearly 300 US companies had investments or employees in South Africa, by 1991 the number had fallen to 104. Total divestment no longer seriously restricted portfolio managers.

Finally, ethical investment policies that stopped short of total divestment proved cumbersome. They tied up the time of investment policy committees, treasurers, and trustees in case-by-case reviews of individual companies' activities, in letter-writing campaigns, and in deliberations over shareholder resolutions. Many university administrations recognized that all this activity still failed to satisfy total divestment proponents or to restore calm to their campuses.

Student activism slowed after the 1985/86 academic year, in large part because of the anti-apartheid movement's success. Not only had corporations begun to divest; from 1985 on, the divestment movement was supplemented – and even superseded – by the adoption of selective contracting laws by US municipalities and the imposition of economic sanctions by the US federal government. The question remains, then, how the divestment campaign affected South Africa.

OUTCOMES OF THE DIVESTMENT MOVEMENT

The significant consequences of the US divestment movement became most evident starting in 1985. Two dimensions are worthy of attention. First, the campaign contributed to popular mobilization in the US for anti-apartheid sanctions, thus contributing indirectly to any results of international pressure on South Africa. Activism focusing on corporate investments and practices also bolstered the psychological effects of sanctions on business and political elites in South Africa. Overall, the divestment campaign is most noteworthy for its ability to signal international rejection of apartheid and to warn of the likelihood of more stringent economic measures on the horizon.

Impact in the US

Divestment and shareholder activism by US institutional investors attracted the notice of US companies but not because it depressed stock prices; targeted companies could count on the self-interest of institutions to lead them to divest incrementally, precisely in order to avoid depressing the sale price.[22] Rather, US companies were aware of ethically motivated sales of their stock because these actions so often responded to highly visible student protests, accompanied by press releases or correspondence from universities and pension funds to corporate management.

By 1982, when IRRC interviewed several corporate representatives on their impressions of shareholder activism on South Africa, many conceded that concern over (potentially escalating) domestic pressures motivated their involvement in the Sullivan Principles program. Colgate-Palmolive, Goodyear and Mobil, for example, wanted their companies to be perceived as socially responsible, so they were beginning to contemplate taking a higher profile within South Africa to speak out against oppressive laws. Several other corporate officials reported receiving a spate of mail from shareholders during the late 1970s. An official from Gillette presciently predicted that student and shareholder demands would increase if South Africa did not proceed with social and political reforms.[23]

Domestic anti-apartheid pressure may even have played a part in persuading General Electric to order its then-subsidiary, Utah International, not to go ahead with a major mining investment in the KwaZulu homeland. Church shareholders opposing the project wrote to the parent company, which also sat on the Connecticut advisory panel that had recommended the state's partial divestment policy. Although General Electric said only that the project "didn't meet the criteria upon which allocation of resources are made," an official at the State Department told IRRC that the company "didn't want to become the largest investor in South Africa."[24]

Similarly, from the late 1970s, several banks prohibited new loans to the South African public sector, at least in part in response to concerns of shareholders, particularly church groups. Banks sensed the potential damage to their public image. Moreover, by raising the issue, activists prompted bank officials to become more knowledgeable about South Africa. One official at J. P. Morgan told IRRC that, without the debate over lending raised by church groups and other shareholders, "American banks would be making more loans to the South African public sector than they are now."[25]

The third wave of anti-apartheid activism had an even more profound impact on US companies. For example, corporate concern for public image led the American Chamber of Commerce in South Africa (Amcham) to be the first business organization in South Africa to call publicly for the white government to enter into negotiations with representative black organizations, including the African National Congress. In a March 1985 news release, Amcham said that its memorandum to the government "deals with virtually all of those issues which currently form the basis of the disinvestment lobby's arguments."[26]

Although corporate executives responded to heightened divestment and shareholder activity, they worried most about the adoption by US cities and local governments of severe restrictions on purchases from companies doing business in South Africa. For the companies who counted these cities as major customers, the calculus was straightforward: potential loss of sales in major US cities versus sales in South Africa. The passage of the Comprehensive Anti-Apartheid Act (CAAA) in October 1986, while having little direct impact on most companies operating in South Africa, sent a warning shot that these domestic pressures would only escalate, especially as the political situation in South Africa looked bleak. The inclusion of the Rangel Amendment to the 1987 Omnibus Budget Reconciliation Act, ending credit to US companies for income tax paid to the South African government, added further incentives. From 1985 through 1987, 149 US companies sold or closed their operations in South Africa – an average of 50 a year.

By helping to publicize concerns about apartheid, the divestment movement appears to have played an indirect role in influencing some city council members to pass these selective contracting measures. Certainly, the chronology of sanctions activity by municipalities and of divestment activity by major universities within their boundaries or in neighboring areas is suggestive. For example, Madison, Wisconsin, restricted purchases from companies operating in South Africa in 1976, eight years after University of Wisconsin students first rallied against Chase Manhattan. Similarly, in April

1979, the University of California sold a block of investments in the Bank of America and Stanford University sold off investments in Wells Fargo Bank. Just one month later, Berkeley and Oakland schools limited their relationships to banks with ties to South Africa. As two components of anti-apartheid mobilization, the municipal selective contracting movement and the campus divestment movement developed in parallel.

With divestment, shareholder activism, and municipal selective contracting in full swing in 1985 and early 1986, Congress, emphasizing popular will, could more easily justify the CAAA, passed despite a presidential veto. This moderate package of partial economic sanctions remained compatible with the political philosophy of the partial divestors at US colleges, states, and city government. The CAAA did not order US companies to withdraw from South Africa, but it restricted their ability to invest new funds. Moreover, it required US companies with more than 25 employees to sign and meet the minimum standards of the Sullivan Principles.

Thus the divestment campaign directly influenced corporate policy, reinforced grassroots anti-apartheid mobilization, and contributed to the dramatic public shift in favor of sanctions against South Africa. The movement at least indirectly contributed to whatever effects these sanctions policies, as a critical component of US policy, had on South African reform. In addition, the campaign had some direct effects on South Africans, as the following section suggests.

Impact in South Africa

The divestment movement hoped that publicity would reach the attention of South Africans, both black and white. It did. Campus anti-apartheid activism in the US quickly got picked up by South Africa newspapers. For example, during the second wave of campus activism, fairly broad circulation English-language South African newspapers, such as *The Star, Sunday Tribune, Rand Daily Mail*, and *The Citizen* reported on divestment activity from 1977 to 1979, as did the annual survey of the South African Institute of Race Relations.[27] One American, who traveled throughout South Africa on a fellowship in the 1984/85 academic year, recalls that "every grunt, whisper and sneeze of the US anti-apartheid movement was covered breathlessly – and derisively – by the South African media."[28]

The college divestment movement captured the attention, too, of South Africa's growing and increasingly influential black trade union movement. An article in the *South Africa Labour Bulletin*, examining trade union options with regard to sanctions, heralded divestment as "part of the broader campaign for disinvestment, which involves also putting pressure on companies by means of, for example, consumer boycotts, withdrawal of public sector contracts, and ultimately legislation."[29] Thus developments on US college campuses heartened sanctions supporters in South Africa, who recognized that US public opinion was changing and hoped that US policymakers would react. Even anti-apartheid campaigners who opposed sanctions welcomed the campus movement as a message to Pretoria that the American people condemned apartheid.[30]

South African businesses also absorbed and reacted to these signals. In the mid-1980s, leading corporations and their associations began to speak out about the need for major political reforms, openly acknowledging the role of overseas pressure. Michael Rosholt, executive chairman of Barlow Rand, identified two reasons for businesses to voice opposition to influx control and forced removals: these policies created tensions within the black community, and they were "probably the one single issue most likely to ensure the success of the US disinvestment lobby."[31]

However, before 1985, the US divestment movement had little direct impact on the South African government. Certainly, government officials were aware of the campaign because of the South African media coverage, the related decisions by leading US banks to stop lending to the South African public sector, and US companies signing the Sullivan Principles. While the divestment movement may have embarrassed and annoyed government officials, it did not disable government functions.

But after 1985, the exodus of US companies increased the psychological pressures on South African officials and increased the perceived costs of repressive measures. For example, Geoff Budlender, for many years an attorney with the Legal Resources Center (an organization that defended clients against apartheid and worked to get many of these policies repealed), believes that the Sullivan Principles combined with the growing threat of disinvestment "had a very significant impact at a particular moment" in the mid-1980s. Signatories' support of the Legal Resources Center, he said, along with the government's "genuine concern about the possibility of further withdrawals" by US companies, to some extent discouraged the government from pursuing forced removals of black communities and from enacting repressive legislation.[32]

Overall, then, the divestment campaign was one component of increasing economic pressures. Its psychological impact, as a signal of harsher measures to come, weighed more heavily than its actual financial costs on South African business or political leaders. These signals also galvanized the resistance movement.

CONCLUSIONS

Grassroots divestment activism, and media attention to it, helped to persuade major US corporations to reduce their involvement in the South African economy. Business leaders also joined in publicly condemning the economic and social practices of apartheid. The success of divestment and shareholder activism can be traced to its public nature – campus demonstrations and annual meetings of major US corporations – which sparked concerns among executives about their public images. Ironically, the divestment movement would have had much less impact had administrators immediately and quietly divested their portfolios, obviating the need for divestment proponents to hold rallies and other public protests.

The visibility of the global condemnation of apartheid, furthermore, enabled the divestment movement to play a more significant role in South Africans' minds than its (small) economic impact would imply. An ever-increasing threat of corporate withdrawals and Congressional sanctions played a role in both persuading South African businesses to lobby against apartheid legislation and South African government officials to refrain from certain repressive actions. Similar patterns of activism in Britain and other European countries (detailed discussion of which is beyond the scope of this chapter), supplemented the power of anti-apartheid mobilization in the United States. As the anti-apartheid movement understood early on, the global public wanted to do something about South Africa; divestment offered a highly visible and low-cost method.

The role of divestment as a political signal underscores the interrelationship between various components of anti-apartheid sanctions. Without the threat of escalating pressures, divestment alone may not have substantial effects on the economic or political leaders in the target state. Grassroots mobilization appears essential – but not sufficient – for the effective use of sanctions, at least when countries initially have friendly strategic and economic ties.

Notes

1. D. Hauck, M. Voorhes, and G. Goldberg, *Two Decades of Debate: The Controversy over US Companies in South Africa* (Washington, DC: Investor Responsibility Research Center [IRRC], 1983), pp. 8–9. See also J. G. Simon, C. W. Powers, and J. P. Gunnemann, *The Ethical Investor: Universities and Corporate Responsibility* (New Haven: Yale University Press, 1972), p. 1.
2. Simon, Powers and Gunnemann, *The Ethical Investor*; its authors were a Yale law professor, a Yale ethicist, and a Pennsylvania State religious studies professor.
3. Ibid., pp. 48–63, 91.
4. Hauck, Voorhes and Goldberg, *Two Decades of Debate*, p. 68.
5. C. A. Coons, *The Response of Colleges and Universities to Calls for Divestment* (Washington, DC: IRRC, 1986), p. 4.
6. Ibid.
7. See M. P. Mangaliso, "Disinvestment by Multinational Corporations," in this volume.
8. Hauck, Voorhes and Goldberg, *Two Decades of Debate*, p. 69.
9. W. F. Moses, *A Guide to American State and Local Laws on South Africa* (Washington, DC: IRRC, 1993), p. 1.
10. Quoted in Hauck, Voorhes, and Goldberg, *Two Decades of Debate*, p. 19.
11. Coons, *Response of Colleges and Universities*, p. 6.
12. Ibid., pp. 7–8.
13. *Stanford and South Africa* (Palo Alto: Stanford University Office of Public Affairs, 1985), p. 13.
14. P. Walshe, "Divest Now," *Notre Dame Scholastic Special Edition: Notre Dame and South Africa* (28 October 1995), p. 4.
15. Report of the Committee on University Responsibility to the Trustees, University of Pennsylvania, 19 June 1986, Appendix C, p. 10.
16. Coons, *Response of Colleges and Universities*, p. ii.
17. J. D. Kibbe, *Divestment on Campus: Update on the Top 50 Schools* (Washington, DC: IRRC, 1992), p. 2. Given the vagaries of the stock market, portfolio composition and other factors, endowment ranking varied from year to year.
18. "New York State Fund Switches Gears; Files 'No Expansion' Resolutions for 1992," *News for Investors*, October 1991, p. 1; see also "CREF Suspends Sponsorship of South Africa Resolutions," *News for Investors*, December 1991, p. 3.
19. H. J. Welsh, *How Institutions Voted on Social Responsibility Shareholder Resolutions in the 1987 Proxy Season* (Washington, DC: IRRC, 1987), p. 14, and R. A. Williams, *How Institutions Voted on Social Responsibility Shareholder Resolutions in the 1988 Proxy Season* (Washington, DC: IRRC, 1988), p. 14.
20. Press release issued by Wesleyan University Office of Public Information, 7 January 1985.
21. Coons, *Response of Colleges and Universities*, p. 42.
22. None of the corporations that IRRC has interviewed in many years

of examining the US anti-apartheid movement has cited falling stock price as a cause of concern. ⸱

23. Hauck, Voorhes, and Goldberg, *Two Decades of Debate*, pp. 119–20, 121–2, 126.
24. Ibid., p. 12.
25. Ibid., pp. 138–41.
26. D. Hauck, *Can Pretoria Be Moved? The Emergence of Business Activism in South Africa* (Washington, DC: IRRC, 1986), pp. 8, 36–7.
27. *Survey of Race Relations in South Africa 1977* (Johannesburg: South African Institute of Race Relations, 1978), p. 192; *Survey of Race Relations in South Africa 1978*, pp. 144, 154; and *Survey of Race Relations in South Africa 1979*, pp. 180, 187.
28. William F. Moses, telephone interview, March 1996.
29. S. Gelb, "Employment and Disinvestment," *South African Labour Bulletin* (1985), pp. 58–9. Also see Mangaliso, "Disinvestment," and T. Maloka, "'Sanctions Hurt but Apartheid Kills!': The Sanctions Campaign and Black Workers," in this volume.
30. Interviews with Renfrew Christie, Cas Coovadia, and Helen Zille, February 1996.
31. Hauck, *Can Pretoria Be Moved?*, p. 8.
32. W. F. Moses and M. Voorhes, *Corporate Responsibility in a Changing South Africa* (Washington, DC: IRRC, 1991), p. 27.

7 Disinvestment by Multinational Corporations
Mzamo P. Mangaliso

What role did foreign multinational corporations (MNCs) play in South Africa's transition to democratic rule? At best, corporate codes of conduct, adopted by foreign MNCs as an alternative to sanctions, provided comfort for only a few South Africans, mostly company employees. Only disinvestment from critical industries enabled MNCs to be an effective catalyst for socio-political transformation.

The experience of MNCs in South Africa refutes the liberal claim that links economic growth to prosperity for the entire population through a "trickle down" effect. Instead, evidence supports the underdevelopment thesis that growth in the central economy simultaneously disadvantages peripheral areas. In South Africa's racially stratified society, huge gaps in income and standards of living widened between the white-dominated central economy and peripheral black areas – the homelands and townships. Under these circumstances, any further injection of foreign capital exacerbates those disparities. Only coercive measures, like trade embargoes, financial sanctions, and disinvestment, could induce government reforms.

In making the claim that corporate withdrawal contributed to the end of apartheid, this chapter first briefly surveys the debates between liberal and underdevelopment theories. I argue that evidence in the South African case demonstrates that multinational investment increased economic disparities. In this context, I then examine the controversy over corporate codes of conduct and conclude that such ameliorative measures failed. Only corporate withdrawal could prompt the dismantlement of apartheid. I focus on corporations based in the United States (US) because of their sheer number and visibility, the amount of scrutiny they received as a result of the Sullivan Principles, and the intensity of the divestment campaign.[1] Many of the experiences of US companies are generalizable to other MNCs.

DIRECT FOREIGN INVESTMENT

One of the most contentious issues in the sanctions debate has been the role of foreign investment and its economic, social, and political impacts. Any developing country depends on inflows of foreign capital in order to finance its domestic investment and current account deficits. Although foreign direct investment (FDI) can be linked to economic development, analysts remain divided over the specific consequences of multinational corporations in South Africa.

Liberals argued that economic growth, in the context of a finite pool of white skilled labor, would increasingly incorporate blacks in the central economy. Job creation would "trickle down" to benefit the entire population. As black upward mobility increased, FDI advocates stressed, so would social and political gains.[2] Foreign capital could thus serve as a progressive force for change. In sum, liberals claimed that increased investment in South Africa would make apartheid less and less feasible, eventually leading to the dismantlement of systematic racial segregation.[3]

On the other hand, those articulating an alternative underdevelopment thesis argued that the spread of capitalism in South Africa depended on the marginalization of African communities in the region.[4] Land dispossession, large reservoirs of cheap labor created in homelands, hut taxes, and stringent controls to prevent black labor mobility characterized economic "development." For example, the migrant labor system conscripted African men to work in the mines for very low wages, while it prevented them from bringing their families with them. The result was two economies within the same country: an advanced one controlled by whites and an underdeveloped one of cheap homeland labor to support apartheid.[5] In sum, critics contended, FDI fuelled such policies, entrenching and perpetuating racial domination.

Even though foreign capital in South Africa dates back to the last century, consistent or complete data on its distribution by home country remains unavailable, making a systematic analysis of its impact more difficult. One source estimated that approximately 1000 MNCs operated in South Africa in the mid-1980s, mostly from Britain, the US, West Germany, France, and Switzerland.[6] In terms of market capitalization through direct and portfolio investment, it estimated that the largest inflows came from Britain (38 percent) and the US (32 percent), with Germany, France, and Switzerland lagging further behind.[7] Initially, MNC subsidiaries proved most important, contributing over 50 percent of total foreign investment. The escalation of sanctions and other global economic changes in the 1970s and 1980s led to a shift from direct to indirect investments (portfolio investments and bank loans).[8]

US involvement remained limited ($2.6 billion in the early 1980s), accounting for about one percent of total US capital exports and only a small fraction of foreign investment in the South African economy.[9] US corporations employed approximately 180 000 workers, and the shift to indirect investment further reduced the number of employees.[10] Withdrawal would, therefore, seemingly be inconsequential.

The importance of MNCs in South Africa rested less on the amount of capital invested and more on the strategic nature of the industries in which US investment was concentrated.[11] These industries required sophisticated technology from either the US or Japan. Advocates of sanctions argued that withholding access to crucial inputs in these key sectors – starving South Africa of access to foreign capital goods – would undermine the economy. Corporate withdrawal and other economic sanctions could, thereby, force economic and political leaders to reconsider apartheid. Thus to compare the competing liberal and underdevelopment perspectives on sanctions, I examine the implications of FDI in three critical sectors: electronics, petrochemicals, and automobiles.[12]

Electronics

South Africa has been most dependent on Western investments in the computer industry. Until the departure of MNCs due to sanctions, every major sector of the economy used US computers extensively. International Business Machines, Hewlett-Packard, National Cash Register, Sperry Rand, and Control Data Corporation maintained extensive sales and service networks. Before the Japanese began to chip away at their lead, US computer corporations controlled 75 percent of sales and 77 percent of rentals.[13] In addition, computers serviced other key South African industries, including motor vehicles, tire and rubber industry, mining, and banking. As one South African executive noted, "We're entirely dependent on the United States. The economy would grind to a halt without access to the computer technology of the West".[14]

In addition, US equipment enabled South Africa to administer its infamous pass laws, to maintain a high degree of control over its black population, and to keep extensive police files. US Commerce Department restrictions on supplying computers to law enforcement agencies eliminated only a fraction of sales. The head of a computer division at the Anglo American Corporation said that there was no way the US authorities would be able to prevent the defense and the police departments from gaining access to this technology.[15] Computer sales also generated $33 million per year in local taxes for the South African government.[16]

Thus, data-processing companies underpinned South Africa's industrializing economy by supplying crucial technology. Computers also enabled the minority government to automate apartheid. Yet these corporations provided few jobs, especially for blacks.

Petrochemicals

Any economy needs a dependable supply of energy, and South Africa is no exception. Lacking in the most crucial source of energy – petroleum – the country has relied heavily on coal. For many years, it successfully kept secret the figures on oil imports, consumption and reserves. At the time of the adoption of the Sullivan Principles, multinational corporations including Mobil, Caltex (an alliance of Chevron and Texaco), and Exxon, controlled an estimated 45 percent of South Africa's oil supplies.[17]

In an attempt to gain self-sufficiency, South Africa also experimented with the coal-to-oil conversion.[18] To obtain the necessary technology, including engineering designs, procurement, construction, and management, the government turned to Fluor Corporation, a California-based MNC and one of the world's largest engineering and construction firms. Fluor contributed an estimated 4500 jobs to the black community, most among the lowest paid in the country.

US oil companies thus contributed a vital commodity to the South African economy. And without oil, its military and police could not function effectively.

Automobiles

Until recently, US companies dominated the South African automobile industry; the Japanese have made inroads since the mid-1980s. But the market is small, saturated, and depressed, offering variable employment across racial categories.[19] Here, again, the contribution made by US companies to the apartheid regime far outweighed any efforts to promote reform. For example, in spite of a 1978 US prohibition, Ford and General Motors (GM) provided vehicles to the South African military and police. These companies circumvented restrictions by claiming they provided these agencies with South African vehicles made without any US components.

These companies also pledged to be obedient to any host country's laws. South Africa's passage of the National Key Points Act of 1980 created a critical issue.[20] Companies operating in certain prescribed industries at specific sites were required to cooperate with the South African Defence Force by forming and training commando units to prevent industrial sabotage and civil unrest. Under this act, these industries could be paid to manufacture weaponry and machinery for the apartheid government.

MNCs in the motor industry, therefore, contributed vehicles to the South African police and military, despite anti-apartheid restrictions in their home country. And as the government's "total strategy" increased the militarization of the South African economy, these corporations became directly tied to the defence forces.

Overall, the computer, petrochemical and motor industries demonstrate the critical role of foreign investment in underpinning a South African economy that did little to benefit the majority of the South African population. In addition, MNCs became increasingly tied directly to the apartheid police and military. Such activities seriously undermine the liberal contention that foreign economic involvement would bolster the welfare of blacks and gradually bring about the elimination of racial segregation. Not surprisingly, in the face of this evidence, anti-apartheid activists increased demands for corporate withdrawal. The following section explores the evolution of MNC reactions to these critics.

CORPORATE CODES OF CONDUCT

In response to complaints that their involvement in South Africa bolstered apartheid, several corporations signed codes of conduct. The Sullivan Principles, formulated in 1977 by a member of GM's board of directors, became the model. After initially campaigning for the company's withdrawal from South Africa, Rev. Leon Sullivan became persuaded that reform from within the country was the best strategy. MNCs, in his view, needed guidelines to regulate their conduct. Failure to meet the guidelines, however, ultimately fuelled demands for corporate withdrawal; in that sense, codes of conduct were a necessary precondition for the success of the disinvestment campaign.[21]

The Europeans (1978), Canadians (1978), Swiss (1978), Australians (1985), Japanese (1985), and others, developed similar codes.[22] Common elements included calls for desegregated workplace facilities; equal and fair employment practices; equal pay for equal or comparable work; training programs to prepare blacks for supervisory and technical jobs; more blacks in managerial jobs; and improved quality of life for black employees. As anti-apartheid pressures mounted, some codes supported unrestricted rights of black business to locate in the urban areas, called on other companies in South Africa to follow similar principles, and rejected all apartheid laws.[23] For example, the Sullivan Code escalated its challenge to the South African government by calling for signatory companies to practice corporate civil disobedience against all apartheid laws and to use their financial and legal resources to assist blacks in the equal use of all public and private amenities.

Innocuous as most of these principles appeared to be, skeptics, such as the Motor Assemblers and Component Workers Union (operating at the Ford Motor Company, a Sullivan Principles signatory), criticized their failure to challenge the basic apartheid structures.[24] Each component of the codes came under criticism.[25]

Workplace Desegregation

By 1985, positive – but misleading – progress reports indicated that all facilities had been desegregated.[26] In many cases, discrimination simply took a new form, because categories of workers correlated highly with race. For the 75 percent of African workers employed in job categories with hardly a white worker, apparent desegregation meant little.[27] Also, some companies consciously perpetuated racial discrimination by more subtle means. GM, for example, supposedly desegregated comfort facilities in its Port Elizabeth plant in preparation for an overseas visitor from the corporate headquarters. Color-keyed signs replaced racially discriminatory signs on toilet doors: blue for whites and Chinese (considered honorary whites for toilet purposes) and orange for blacks and coloreds. Similarly, the practice of assigning lunch rooms and locker areas formerly used by blacks to hourly workers, and those previously used by whites to salaried staff, only perpetuated racial segregation.[28] But more importantly, according to a South African Institute of Race Relations study, blacks tended to see the desegregated facilities as cosmetic, not as a barometer of fundamental change; they perceived desegregating facilities as little more than a distraction from the more fundamental problem of social and economic injustice in these firms and the country.[29]

Fair Employment

In general, the codes rarely required signatories to accept the right of black workers to bargain collectively. Many hesitated to recognize unions that were not legal, claiming that South African law tied their hands. However, after legal reforms following recommendations by the Wiehahn Commission, the same businesses claimed that the companies constituted a "progressive" force. Several Sullivan signatory companies, including Fluor and Colgate-Palmolive, reportedly engaged in serious anti-union activities. Some companies also provided different health policies for black and white employees.[30] Nor were academic qualifications treated equally. For example, Ford reportedly evaluated black workers by more stringent standards; whites, who could hardly write or speak fluent English and had a sparse formal education, filled supervisory and even senior positions.[31] Ford was not unique.

Equal Pay

According to the third Sullivan progress report, blacks occupied 70 percent of the lowest job categories, and only 2 percent were white. White workers represented 99 percent of the top category, and only 1 percent were black. At Ford, for example, 84 percent of the workers employed in the lowest job categories were black, and 98.5 percent of the workers employed in the top category were white.[32] Furthermore, although the disparity between black and white incomes appeared to be narrowing, in absolute terms it actually widened.[33] One reason was the Industrial Council agreement which required, among other things, that whites be paid more than blacks. In addition, under the provisions of the Job Reservation Act – especially enforced in the mining industry where white unions had the strongest influence – whites had to fill certain jobs. Along with the practice of "last hired, first fired," these rules implied that blacks would never reach parity in seniority (and, therefore, wages) with whites. At Ford, the union claimed that the company actually practiced just the opposite of equal pay for equal work. Of course, certain individual firms operated in a more positive way. But the practice of using local labor meant that whites filled the ranks of middle management; their psychological conditioning by apartheid created a further barrier for the advancement of blacks in management.[34]

Training Programs

Corporations reluctantly accelerated training programs for blacks. Despite the historical inequities in education and the intentions of the Principles, signatory companies spent more money on white participants in training programs than on blacks. In 1982, for example, the union at Ford alleged that 99 percent of black workers were misinformed about the education and training center.[35] Some companies reported legal barriers to training blacks. In the mines, for instance, blacks could not earn Certificates of Competence. Also, closed-shop agreements between white unions, which controlled the apprenticeship programs, and employers placed a ban on blacks doing skilled work. Finally, the misleading nature of the reporting process has been well documented.[36] Signatory companies tended to report the number of black trainees in the programs instead of the dollar amount spent on programs for training the different groups.

Management Jobs

Some reports lauded the progress made by signatory companies between 1981 and 1990, noting that the percentage of managerial positions filled by Africans, coloreds and Indians had increased from 3 to 13 percent.[37] However, many critics regarded this principle simply as tokenism. A thorough scrutiny of reported figures reveals little improvement. For example, between 1982 and 1984, the number of black managers in Sullivan signatory companies decreased from 76 of 3829 managers to 68 of 4136, a low and declining percentage. In addition, these scarce black managers typically occupied junior positions, often in charge of lowly clerical staff whose main duties were keeping records of black employees. The rare exception was a black manager in charge of any critical functions, such as finance or operations. Extraordinary was a black supervising whites; only 0.007 percent of all black employees in Sullivan companies held positions overseeing whites.[38] Asians, and to some extent coloreds, fared better. Yet this strategy of selectively offering opportunities to the more privileged among the oppressed drove a wedge between these groups and reduced the momentum for dismantling apartheid.[39] Companies thus abided by the spirit of apartheid; even black managers had no real authority or decision making power.

Quality of Life

Notable achievements in this area included the creation of the Teacher Opportunity Programs to improve black schools and the establishment of the East Rand Legal Aid Clinic in Springs (a town east of Johannesburg), to provide legal aid in housing, residence rights, influx control, and other human rights cases.[40] But improvements had limited reach since signatories employed such a limited number of blacks. For example, given the proportions of the national housing crisis, any piecemeal effort amounted to a drop in the ocean. And aid in effect helped government-run, legally segregated schools, whose curricula were designed by law to give blacks an inferior education. Overall, the education, health, and housing efforts of US companies worked within the framework of the apartheid system. In short, many critics claimed that US corporate social responsibility practices in South Africa ameliorated the impact of apartheid on some blacks but could not root out apartheid itself.

In sum, these principles of desegregation, equal employment, training, promotion, and community aid all failed to help dismantle apartheid in South Africa. Either they were not implemented fully by the signatories or, even if they were, they were not structured to change social, economic, and political discrimination. Codes of conduct coexisted with the disenfranchisement of blacks, population controls, forced removals, bannings, and detention without trial. Predictably, they met with severe criticism from the black population. In the words of Nobel Laureate Desmond Tutu, "Our objection to the code is on the basis that it does not aim at changing structures. The Sullivan Principles are designed to be ameliorative. We do not want apartheid to be made more comfortable. We want it to be dismantled."[41]

By 1985, Sullivan, skeptical about the sluggish progress made by the signatory companies, warned that he would call for withdraw if apartheid had not been dismantled within two years. Indeed, in 1987, he followed through, noting that although conditions had improved for a few blacks, the core of apartheid remained.[42] As the South African crisis intensified, corporate resistance to disinvestment also decreased. For example, the British Industry Committee on South Africa, which included the largest British corporations in South Africa, urged Prime Minister Margaret Thatcher to accept the pending European ban on new investments and imports of certain South African products.[43]

From the mid-1980s, many foreign MNCs began to withdraw from South Africa by closing down their operations, selling to local management, or reducing the size of their holdings. Many cited deteriorating economic conditions in South Africa, while others acknowledged pressure from activist groups. In announcing GM's withdrawal, Chairman Roger Smith expressed frustration with the slow speed of change and noted that the South African government lagged behind world opinion.[44] Soon after, several other MNCs followed suit. The US Corporate Council on South Africa, a group of 100 US corporations which sought to oppose apartheid from within South Africa, even placed a full-page advertisement in South African newspapers calling on the South African government to negotiate with black leaders. In an unprecedented move, a group of South African business leaders, including Gavin Relly, chairman of Anglo American Corporation, met with Oliver Tambo and other African National Congress members in Lusaka.

Thus disinvestment sent a much stronger signal to Pretoria than the inherently flawed corporate codes of conduct ever could. Its success lay in ratcheting up the pressure on South Africa which, in turn, helped to persuade key elements within the white community and the government to take a strong stand against apartheid and to turn to the bargaining table to negotiate with legitimate representatives of the black population.[45]

CONCLUSION

Growth through investment and the adoption of codes of conduct, as a strategy to abolish apartheid, proved to be a failure in South Africa. While foreign investors challenged some aspects of petty apartheid, they proved incapable of transforming more fundamental socio-economic conditions. Conciliatory corporate positions only succeeded in letting the National Party consolidate its grip on power. As Kevin Danaher noted, the apartheid government gained "breathing space to pummel its neighbors with a wide variety of economic and military aggression, and modernize the system of control within the country."[46]

Advocates of the gradualist approach believed that the minority government would change its philosophical position on human rights and race relations. The government's failure to deliver meaningful reforms led to disillusionment both inside the country and internationally. Subsequent MNC disinvestment starved South Africa of access to important resource inputs – capital and technology – that were necessary to keep a modern economy buoyant. The consequences were felt through double digit inflation, currency devaluation, and a climate of heightened uncertainty due to isolation. These pressures, along with additional sanctions discussed in the other chapters of this volume, contributed to the end of grand apartheid.

But under what circumstances could corporations have engaged South Africa constructively? It is conceivable that a greater impact could have been felt if investors had agreed on a code based on a set of principles that spelled out more clearly the conditions under which companies would cease to do business in South Africa. For example, Thomas Donaldson suggests a "condition of business" principle to guide corporate reactions to the violation of human rights.[47] These corporate policies would be accompanied by a specific deadline after which punitive measures would be adopted.

Of course, this strategy is not without risk, cost, or other limitations. Oftentimes, MNCs can only move some of their assets from a host country and not always quickly. Or, as companies discovered when pulling out of South Africa in the late 1980s, a quick departure compelled them to sell their assets to local management at fire-sale prices. Host countries may also retaliate by preventing the outflow of resources. Access to rare but essential commodities (like gold or platinum), on the other hand, may prevent MNCs from challenging the host country at all; in most cases, however, substitutes are available, albeit at an increased price.

Multinational corporations inevitably influence the social and economic conditions of the countries in which they operate. In this capacity, however, they can create background conditions which are conducive to more explicitly political struggles, such as the anti-apartheid movement. Moreover, it is precisely their ability to take their business elsewhere that makes the MNC a powerful political agent. The ability to inject investments in, or remove them from, key industries gives corporations a powerful weapon to change host government policy.

Notes

1. See M. Voorhes, "The US Divestment Movement," in this volume.
2. See J. Chettle, "Economic Growth and Political Change in South Africa," *Study Commission on US Policy toward Southern Africa* (New York: Study Commission, October 1979), p. 6; R. Horwitz, *The Political Economy of South Africa* (London: Praeger, 1967); M. O'Dowd, "The Stages of Economic Growth and the Future of South Africa," in L. Schlemmer and E. Webster, eds., *Change, Reform and Economic Growth in South Africa* (Johannesburg: Ravan, 1978).
3. H. Oppenheimer, "Why the World Should Continue to Invest in South Africa," International Monetary Conference, Mexico City, 22 May 1978.
4. S. Greenberg, "Economic Growth and Political Change," *Journal of Modern African Studies* 19 (1981), pp. 667–704. See also C. Bundy, "The Emergence and Decline of a South African Peasantry," *African Affairs* 71 (1972), 369–88, and H. Wolpe, "Capitalism and Cheap Labor-Power in South Africa: From Segregation to Apartheid," *Economy and Society* 1 (1972), pp. 433–9.
5. Many scholars have challenged the "trickle down" theory in South Africa. For example, Elizabeth Schmidt notes that the South African gross domestic product increased by more than 2000 percent between 1945 and 1975, but very little of that increase benefited the black majority; see E. Schmidt, *Decoding Corporate Camouflage* (Washington, DC: Institute for Policy Studies, 1985), p. 6. Joseph Hanlon and Roger Omond also point out that 81 percent of blacks in the rural areas in 1980 lived below the poverty line; see J. Hanlon and R. Omond, *The Apartheid Handbook* (Harmondsworth, UK: Penguin, 1987), p. 89.
6. R. Leonard, "The Crisis in South Africa: Rising Pressures on Multinationals," *Multinational Business Quarterly* 3 (1986), pp. 17–28.
7. Ibid.
8. This chapter focuses only on direct investment. For analysis of indirect investments and loans, see X. Carim, A. Klotz, and O. Lebleu, "The Political Economy of Financial Sanctions," next chapter in this volume.
9. J. D. Holladay, "The Limits of American Influence," *Business and Society Review* 57 (1986), pp. 17–21.
10. The number of people employed varies depending how a US company is defined. One widely accepted view cites majority US equity (51 percent or more), but other sources use different percentages of ownership. See R. Knight and R. Walke, *Unified List of United States Companies Doing Business in South Africa and Namibia* (New York: American Committee on Africa, 1988).

11. J. Nielsen, "Time to Quit South Africa?" *Fortune*, 30 September 1985, pp. 18–26; Schmidt, *Decoding Corporate Camouflage*; T. Conrad, "Computers Programmed for Racism," *Business and Society Review* 42 (1982), pp. 61–4.
12. Heavy foreign involvement in finance will not be considered here; see Carim, Klotz and Lebleu, "Political Economy of Financial Sanctions."
13. See Conrad, "Computers Programmed for Racism," p. 61.
14. Schmidt, *Decoding Corporate Camouflage*, pp. 68–9.
15. Ibid., p. 69.
16. Conrad, "Computers Programmed for Racism," p. 62.
17. Schmidt, *Decoding Corporate Camouflage*, p. 70.
18. See N. C. Crawford, "The Costs of Oil Sanctions," in this volume.
19. For an extended discussion of the motor industry, see T. Maloka, "'Sanctions Hurt but Apartheid Kills!': The Sanctions Campaign and Black Workers," in this volume.
20. *Newsweek*, 29 September 1980; D. Hauck, *US Companies and Support for the South African Government: The Legal Requirements* (Washington, DC: Investor Responsibility Research Center [IRRC], 1986), p. 5; W. J. Pomeroy, *Apartheid, Imperialism and African Freedom* (New York: International, 1986), p. 139.
21. See Voorhes, "US Divestment."
22. The Japanese code was of particular interest because its corporations had no direct investments; it would be unusual to impose a set of standards for employee relations on licensees and distributors. See Leonard, "The Crisis in South Africa," and South African Council of Churches, *Towards a Code of Investment* (Edenvale: South African Council of Churches, 1992).
23. D. Hauck, *Can Pretoria Be Moved? The Emergence of Business Activism in South Africa* (Washington, DC: IRRC, 1986).
24. P. E. Andrews, "Corporate Codes of Conduct under Apartheid: An Assessment," *TransAfrica Forum* 3 (1986), pp. 21–8.
25. I can testify to the similarity between observations made in Sullivan signatory companies and my experiences in the 1970s and early 1980s as a black manager at Unilever, an MNC whose conduct was monitored by the European code.
26. Arthur D. Little, Inc., *Reports on the Sullivan Signatory Companies to the Sullivan Principles* no. 8 (Philadelphia: International Council for Equality, 1985).
27. Schmidt, *Decoding Corporate Camouflage*, p. 22.
28. Ibid. and H. Nickel, "The Case for Doing Business in South Africa," *Fortune*, 19 June 1978, pp. 60–74.
29. K. Rothmeyer and T. Lowenthal, "The Sullivan Principles: A Critical Look at US Corporate Role in South Africa," revised by G. Morlan and R. Knight, *Southern Africa Perspectives* 1 (1981), p. 4.
30. C. Brown and M. Watts, *UC Faculty for Full Divestment: Alternative Treasurer's Report* (Berkeley: University of California Press, 1985).
31. Andrews, "Corporate Codes under Apartheid," pp. 21–8.
32. Ibid.
33. Schmidt, *Decoding Corporate Camouflage*. Also see M. P. Mangaliso,

"Predicting the Closing of the Black–White Wage Gap in South Africa," Working Paper, University of Massachusetts, Amherst, 1986, p. 40.
34. See M. P. Mangaliso, "The Corporate Social Challenge for the Multinational Corporation," *Journal of Business Ethics* 11 (1992), pp. 491–500.
35. Andrews, "Corporate Codes under Apartheid," p. 24.
36. See K. Paul, "The Inadequacy of Sullivan Reporting," *Business and Society Review* 57 (1986), pp. 61–5.
37. South African Council of Churches, *Towards a Code of Investment*, p. 65.
38. *New York Times*, 6 December 1983; Schmidt, *Decoding Corporate Camouflage*, p. 399.
39. Paul, "The Inadequacy of Sullivan Reporting," pp. 61–5.
40. South African Council of Churches, *Towards a Code of Investment*, p. 68; Mangaliso, "The Corporate Social Challenge," p. 494.
41. Quoted in E. Schmidt, "The Sullivan Principles: A Critique," in D. Mermelstein, ed., *The Anti-Apartheid Reader: South Africa and the Struggle against White Racist Rule* (New York: Grove, 1987), p. 399.
42. *New York Times*, 3 June 1987.
43. Leonard, "The Crisis in South Africa," p. 23.
44. R. Smith, "Why GM Decided to Quit South Africa," *New York Times*, 30 October 1986, p. 27.
45. See S. Davis, "Economic Pressure on South Africa: Does It Work?" in G. W. Shepherd, *Effective Sanctions on South Africa: The Cutting Edge of Economic Intervention* (New York: Greenwood, 1991), pp. 65–80.
46. K. Danaher, "The US Struggle over Sanctions against South Africa," in M. Orkin, ed., *Sanctions against Apartheid* (Cape Town: David Philip, 1989), p. 135.
47. T. Donaldson, *The Ethics of International Business* (New York: Oxford University Press, 1989).

8 The Political Economy of Financial Sanctions

Xavier Carim, Audie Klotz, and Olivier Lebleu

By the mid-1980s, a seemingly unstoppable tide of strikes, boycotts and other protests threatened to make South Africa ungovernable, while the international community simultaneously increased the campaign for sanctions. Already weakened by anti-apartheid pressures from shareholders, consumers, and governments in the 1970s and 1980s, and a US Congressional amendment blocking International Monetary Fund (IMF) loans since 1983, domestic and foreign investors' confidence in the economy plunged in the wake of the state of emergency declared in July 1985. Chase Manhattan Bank decided neither to extend ("roll-over") credit nor to provide new loans to South Africa. Other bankers and investors immediately moved to switch their funds out of the country, leading the Johannesburg Stock Exchange (JSE) to decline rapidly and the rand to plummet on foreign exchange markets. In an attempt to stem capital flight, the South African government quickly imposed a moratorium on debt repayments to public and private creditors, suspended foreign exchange dealings, and temporarily closed the JSE. As this crisis unfolded, the international anti-apartheid movement called for intensified financial sanctions.

The short-term nature of South Africa's foreign debt between 1985 and 1990 created exceptional opportunities for sanctioners, international bankers, and domestic business leaders to pressure the government to eliminate apartheid. The complex relationship between politically motivated restrictions on lending and market-induced investment decisions by international bankers becomes crucial for understanding why South Africa became unusually susceptible to demands for political reforms. A host of external economic influences, including the price of gold, fluctuating exchange rates, and country-risk assessments by investors affected financial decisions and the South African economy. To unravel the specific role of "bankers' sanctions" in the process of political change, we first place South Africa's financial vulnerability in historical context. Attempts to manage the debt crisis between 1985 and 1990 reveal the economic and perceptual importance of sanctions, as international bankers and the domestic business community increased direct demands for political reforms. After a series of ineffectual attempts to placate its opponents with minor changes, the government conceded major reforms by the end of the decade.

ORIGINS OF FINANCIAL VULNERABILITY

South Africa's economic vulnerabilities had roots in the nature of its incorporation into the world economy. Historically an exporter of primary products, the country has always maintained international links. For over a century, since the discovery of diamonds and gold, foreign capital has played a critical role, first in mining and later in manufacturing. Like many developing countries in the 1950s and 1960s, South Africa pursued import-substitution policies, which fostered local manufacturing by raising tariff barriers. The resulting high costs of production undermined significant export growth. In addition, the country's highly skewed, racially based income distribution exacerbated the limitations of a small domestic market, foreclosing more autonomous economic development.

Since industry remained critically dependent on imported technology, machinery, and transport equipment, an expansion in local production of intermediate and consumer goods spurred the need for foreign capital. By the 1980s, capital goods comprised over 40 percent of imports.[1] Any growth in the domestic economy, therefore, increased the demand for foreign exchange, which the country could acquire either from exports or inflows of foreign investment.[2] Thus for South Africa, like many newly industrializing countries, sustained economic growth hinged on a healthy balance of payments.

Lacking a competitive manufacturing base, South Africa paid for many imports with proceeds from mineral, agricultural, and other raw material exports. Primary products comprised over 80 percent of total exports in the 1980s, with gold earning over 40 percent of South Africa's export trade and over 50 percent of its gross domestic product (GDP) derived from trade in the 1980s.[3] Through the 1960s, foreign direct (productive) and indirect (portfolio) investment inflows supplemented the country's capacity to import capital goods. Most South African foreign loan liabilities entailed medium- to long-term debt, borne mainly by the government and parastatals underwriting the expansion of infrastructure. The IMF supported such lending, and large foreign banks, such as Citicorp, National Westminster, Barclays, Deutschebank, and Credit Suisse, viewed South Africa as highly profitable and politically stable.

The first exception to this picture followed the 1960 Sharpeville killings, when, in an attempt to forestall capital flight, the government established a two-tier exchange rate. This "financial rand" system devalued capital exports and rewarded capital inflows.[4] Combined with repression that quieted domestic unrest, the government's policies calmed investors' concerns over the political situation, and capital inflows soon resumed.

In the 1970s, capital inflows fluctuated significantly as a result both of market forces and of reactions to apartheid. First, the US went off the gold standard in 1971 (creating sharp and unpredictable price swings), followed by two global oil shocks. But gold cushioned the South African economy. For example, following the first petroleum price increase in 1973, investor enthusiasm for South Africa spurred lending to the private sector.[5] Then, in the wake of the 1979 oil shock, gold soared as investors feared defaults by other countries. South Africa once again profited, with global capital flowing to public and private borrowers.[6]

Downturns, however, tempered these peak investment periods, most notably in the wake of the Soweto riots in 1976 and South Africa's military strikes into Angola in 1977, when medium- to long-term loans to South Africa dried up almost entirely. South Africa switched from being a capital importer to an exporter. For example, in 1976 the country recorded a net inflow of R501 million, but the next year this figure reversed to negative R552 million and continued to slide to negative R2.472 billion in 1979. In 1985, South Africa exported R10.4 billion.[7]

Anti-apartheid sentiments as well as risk assessments contributed to this capital flow reversal. Various governments, including the Nordic states and Switzerland, either limited or completely banned loans, while the US placed restrictions on import–export credits. Japan had already banned direct investment by 1964 and loans in 1975. Some private banks, such as the Bank of Boston and Citicorp, also halted loans to the South African government in 1978, and many extended these restrictions to private sector loans by early 1985.[8] Multinationals began shifting from equity to loans, first converting direct investment to portfolio holdings.[9] In addition, the end of the petrodollar boom created a global capital shortage, manifest in market volatility and an emerging global debt crisis (notably the threat of Mexican default in 1982).[10]

Volatility in international commodity markets affected gold in particular, with prices falling from a peak over $800 in the late 1970s to a low near $300 by 1984. Rising import prices and declining currency earnings put severe pressure on South Africa's balance of payments. After the government abolished the financial rand and lifted some exchange controls in February 1983, non-residents quickly reacted to declining returns on investment and increased risk by selling stocks and shares, and transferring proceeds abroad.[11] Rising domestic double-digit inflation, expanding money supply, low personal savings, and high interest rates spurred the search for lower rates abroad, particularly through short-term loans. The Reserve Bank, furthermore, encouraged foreign borrowing.[12]

In the past, South Africa had turned to the IMF for bridging loans during such periods of temporary recession and balance-of-payments difficulties. A founding member, South Africa first borrowed from the Fund in 1957, followed by a series of additional payouts in the mid-1970s (91.2 million Standard Drawing Rights [SDRs] in 1975, SDR 390 million in 1976, and SDR 162 million in 1977), which made it the third largest borrower. In November 1982 the IMF granted a controversial $1.1 billion (SDR 902.2 million, R1.24 billion) loan.[13] Unexpected increases in the price of gold early in 1983 further bolstered the economy. The Minister of Finance calculated that a $100 increase in the price of gold produced a R2 billion change in the balance of payments and a R1 billion increase in government revenue. Price increases also enabled marginal mines to stay in operation, propping up employment, and contributing to government revenues.[14] Yet international investors still preferred the dollar to gold, thus limiting the extent to which South Africa's gold boom could translate into imports of dollar-based goods or ease current account pressures.

Then in an unprecedented move, the IMF refused to grant additional funds to South Africa in 1983, as a result of a US anti-apartheid initiative led by the Congressional Black Caucus. Adding an amendment to a House of Representatives bill authorizing contributions to the Fund, this group of African-American legislators (at that time, all Democrats) proposed banning loans to countries practicing apartheid. Irate Republicans objected because their previous similar attempts to block IMF loans to communist countries had been rejected.[15] In the midst of this domestic controversy, the Fund released a report that confirmed its view that apartheid was an economic impediment and not solely a political problem, thus undermining conservative objections to anti-apartheid restrictions.[16] A series of political compromises between the House, the Senate, and the Reagan Administration resulted in a law tightly restricting loans to South Africa. The US was charged to use its preeminent power in the IMF to "actively oppose" loans to South Africa unless the Secretary of the Treasury certified that the money would economically benefit the majority population and reduce constraints on labor and capital markets.[17] Although technically not forbidden from borrowing, the South African government ceased to apply for loans in order to avoid additional discussion of apartheid in Congress and embarrassment for its friends.[18]

Although these first anti-apartheid financial sanctions did not prevent South Africa from securing private international loans, the absence of IMF approval made foreign finance more expensive (generally at a 1 percent premium) and precluded access to bridging loans from the Bank of International Settlements.[19] In addition, in the wake of the Mexican crisis, international access to debt finance generally became more difficult, with short-term loans becoming the preferred tool to service emerging market demand for finance. Thus, the absolute levels of South Africa's foreign liabilities grew substantially, with short-term debt amounting to $14 billion by 1985, while longer-term outstanding loans came to $10.3 billion.[20] The proportion of South Africa's short- to long-term debt (66 percent) grew even higher than other developing countries (44 percent), involving even greater risks that any drop in the value of the rand would increase the debt burden in dollar terms.[21]

Pressures by sanctioners exacerbated South Africa's growing financial difficulties. While incomplete, trade boycotts imposed additional costs on the economy, including "sanctions busting" strategies.[22] At the same time, intensified pressures from the disinvestment campaign combined with declining profitability encouraged many firms to leave.[23] Between 1984 and 1990, over one-third of all foreign companies, especially those based in the US, departed.[24] Disinvestment provided a few South African conglomerates, notably Anglo American, Barlow Rand, Sanlam, and Gencor, with windfall gains as they bought out departing firms at discount prices. Although foreign multinationals frequently maintained licensing, franchising, and trademark agreements, trade sanctions and disinvestment further undermined already precarious business confidence. Repatriating earnings from these sales (before the reimposition of the financial rand) placed additional pressure on South Africa's balance of payments.

Decisions by the South African Reserve Bank and other financial institutions aggravated the situation. In an attempt to counter high inflation, the Reserve Bank raised prime lending rates to 25 percent, thereby increasing the search for short-term international loans offering lower rates. Nedbank in particular borrowed heavily in New York and London. Lacking adequate reporting and information systems, the Reserve Bank failed to keep track of the dramatic rise in accumulating debt as well as its maturity structure.[25] This spate of uncontrolled borrowing became so serious that by mid-1985 South Africa's external finances were being described as chaotic.[26]

Simultaneously, the price of gold and the value of the rand both dropped, causing the dollar value of the loans to soar. In 1980, $16.9 billion of debt converted to R12.6 billion (20 percent of GDP); by 1984, it climbed to $24.3 billion, valued at R48.2 billion (46 percent of GDP). Further depreciation boosted the debt to 50 percent of GDP by 1985, far above the 30 percent which analysts generally consider to be dangerous. The Reserve Bank responded by using gold swaps and partially paying the mines in rands rather than dollars. The Bank of England and Citibank, among others, expressed concern about the country's level of short-term debt.[27]

This bleak financial picture, compounded by the wave of political unrest by civic, student, youth, and worker organizations, made foreign lending to or investing in South Africa difficult to justify.[28] The self-reinforcing nature of the deteriorating economic and political situation became so acute that the government recognized the need for political change to control the economic malaise. Seeking to repeat previously successful repressive moves to restore law and order, which had improved investor confidence and reversed capital outflows following Sharpeville and Soweto, it declared a (partial) state of emergency on 20 July 1985. This time, however, the situation appeared intractable. Within one week of the imposition of emergency measures, the market value of shares on the JSE fell by R11 billion and the flow of money out of the country pushed the rand exchange rate down almost 18 percent. The gold mines share index fell to a three-year low, despite recent net increases in foreign buying. The French government added a ban on investments.[29]

While once again gold partially counterbalanced other economic pressures, it could not completely protect South Africa from the fears of foreign commercial lenders.[30] On 31 July, Chase Manhattan announced that it would call in its short-term loans and freeze new credit. As other banks quickly followed suit, South Africa faced a liquidity crisis.[31] With R43.3 billion debt due within a year, net reserves of R784 million and a current account surplus for the first half of the year at R5 billion, South Africa was in no position to meet its obligations.[32]

As a large portion of South Africa's foreign liabilities came due at the end of August, hopes rose that President P. W. Botha would announce major reforms to ease investors' concerns. In his speech on 15 August, however, he failed to "cross the Rubicon." The following morning, the rand fell by an additional 20 percent, and it became clear that the debt due at the end of the month would not be rolled over. The situation deteriorated dramatically as the rand reached a record low and capital flight accelerated. In addition, the Governor of the Reserve Bank, Gerhard de Kock, failed in his attempt to negotiate debt relief in international banking capitals, in part because of hostile public opinion.[33]

Criticism of the government increased, including calls in the financial press for Botha's resignation. South Africa's main business organizations, the Association of Chambers of Commerce, the Federated Chamber of Industries, the National African Federated Chamber of Commerce and Industry, and the Urban Foundation, as well as Gavin Relly, the chairman of Anglo American, called on the government to eliminate apartheid and negotiate with black leaders. Similarly, the US Corporate Council on South Africa, a group presenting over 80 US companies, took out newspaper ads in both the US and locally. In September 1985, furthermore, Anglo American sent a delegation to meet with the exiled African National Congress, and numerous other business leaders followed in the "trek to Lusaka" in subsequent months (and years). Even de Kock, a strong National Party supporter, claimed that the drop in the value of the rand was caused by the government's social policies, not economic factors. Despite disagreements over the extent of constitutional changes, both business and government recognized that solving the debt crisis would require significant political reforms.[34]

The combined effects of dependence on foreign capital and technology imports, persistent actual and potential capital flight, volatile gold earnings, anti-apartheid sanctions on investments and loans,

rising debt, a depreciating rand, and a marked rise in the proportion of debt due within one year, created an unsustainable balance
of payments situation. On 27 August 1985, the South African government announced a moratorium on repayment of $13.63 billion of
its total debt (57 percent of $23.72 billion) due at the end of the
month. Simultaneously, it suspended all trading on the JSE and
foreign exchange markets until 2 September. In an attempt to sta-
bilize the exchange rate, reduce capital flight, and create a dollar
pool for leverage against lenders, on 1 September it reintroduced
the financial rand with exchange controls. Foreign bankers decided
to reduce their exposure. In the end, private international bank
loans which appeared to free the government from political conditions turned into a fundamental source of vulnerability: the short-
term nature of expanding debt set the stage for increased political
leverage.

RESPONSES TO THE DEBT CRISIS

South Africa hoped both to negotiate a rescheduling plan to repay
its debts in a way that would preserve the most favorable credit
rating possible and to forestall further political pressures. Unlike
most other debtor countries in crises, South Africa's gold and other
mining sector earnings enabled it to continue to meet interest and
principal payments and, while it prohibited the repayment of commercial bank debt including interbank credit lines, the debt standstill did not apply to payments for ordinary current transactions
nor credits that facilitated trade. In addition, the moratorium excluded privately placed public sector notes and Eurobonds, obligations to the IMF, debts guaranteed by foreign governments or export
credit agencies, Reserve Bank debt, and new loans extended after
2 September that did not replace existing loans. In part trying to
placate creditors, Botha announced reforms at the opening session
of parliament in January 1986.[35]

Lenders, especially in West Germany, inclined to cooperate with
the apartheid government in working out a repayment scheme, but
US banks adopted a tougher stance. After months of arbitration,
the First Interim Arrangement in March 1986 covered the period
until June 1987. The deal stipulated a 5 percent ($500m) repay-
ment on maturing affected debt (that is, debt in the "standstill net"),
offered an additional 12 months to negotiate repayment of the

balance, and provided an "exit option" that allowed creditor banks to convert affected debt into three-year loans outside the net. Renewed loans would earn interest 1 to 1.25 percent higher than premoratorium rates (in some cases, that meant 2 percent above Libor, The London Inter-Bank Offered Rate). Mediator Fritz Leutwiler, former President of the Bank of International Settlements, persuaded South Africa to commit to more meaningful political change.[36]

Opponents of apartheid, unconvinced by Botha's pledges, escalated pressures for international financial sanctions as additional debt negotiations approached in September 1986. Undeterred by South Africa's threats of default, the Commonwealth adopted further sanctions in August, followed by the US Comprehensive Anti-Apartheid Act in October, which included restrictions on loans to South Africa.[37] Anti-apartheid pressures also contributed to international bankers' demands for South African political reforms. For example, protests and account-closings against Barclays Bank, organized by the End Loans to South Africa movement, deprived it of a substantial portion of its market in Britain by 1985. In response, Barclays declared a halt to loans in March 1986 and sold its direct stake in the South African banking industry in November 1986, apparently at a heavy loss (in part due to the financial rand system). Powerful pension portfolios operating in the US adopted similar restrictions, and several banks, such as Citibank in June 1987, cut ties to South Africa. Many of those that remained refused to lend to the apartheid government.[38] De Kock, the Reserve Bank governor, criticized "misinformed" foreign investors for denying "normal access" to credit for political reasons and acknowledged that such measures hurt the South African economy.[39]

In this increasingly hostile environment, the South African government sought to placate its critics without abolishing apartheid. Increased repression combined with severe restrictions on media coverage of domestic violence temporarily quieted unrest as well as business concerns. Hoping to bolster his international image before the next debt talks in early 1986, Botha declared the repeal of the notorious pass laws, but in ways that merely recognized *de facto* practice. Proposals to incorporate blacks into the political system granted only minimal, non-elected, positions at local levels, creating the appearance of reform without undermining white minority rule. In a similar tactical move, Botha lifted the partial state of emergency just before a critical meeting with the country's creditors in March, only to reinstate more severe restrictions in June.[40]

The second round of debt negotiations, without the aid of a mediator, concluded in February 1987. The Interim Arrangement stipulated a $1.5 billion repayment over a three-year period, July 1987 to June 1990. Terms were more favorable to South Africa than before: minimal political conditions and an exit option significantly less favorable to the banks. Debt within the standstill net could be converted into medium-term (ten-year) loans. In April 1988, both Citibank ($670 million) and Manufacturers Hanover ($230 million) publicly took the exit option (as did others, less visibly), thus helping South Africa. In addition, Asian banks and corporations (especially in South Korea, Taiwan and Hong Kong) showed increasing interest in South Africa.[41] This relatively favorable agreement eased the balance of payments crisis.

As the Reserve Bank and government officials struggled to refinance debt, the local business community turned inward in order to stave off bankruptcies. The JSE offered a short-term solution. In 1986 and early 1987, equity issues totaled over R17 billion – R6 billion more than the total issued between 1981 and 1985. These huge cash calls were successful as local insurance companies and other institutional investors, eager to diversify out of underperforming government bonds but prohibited from investing abroad, took up new stock issues while simultaneously absorbing the massive (R850 million) foreign sell-off in 1986.[42] The global crash in equity markets in October 1987, however, wiped out the impressive gains by the JSE and dampened local enthusiasm for further equity issues. Compounded by the government's stated intention to privatize several parastatals to finance growing fiscal deficit, the domestic equity market's ability to provide financing flexibility withered in early 1988 as institutions hoarded remaining cash resources.

A mini-boom in late 1987 and early 1988, reflecting a rise in the price of gold (following the crash in global equity markets), expanded consumer imports, weakened the current account, and added pressure on foreign exchange.[43] Once again, South Africa faced the prospect of being unable to repay its international debts, with the threat of additional sanctions looming on the horizon as the US Congress considered more anti-apartheid legislation. Business, fearful of declining economic conditions and the escalating sanctions environment, renewed calls to scrap apartheid in order to relieve the country from sanctions pressures.[44] The Botha government declared more (double-edged) reforms to lift certain segregation measures.

Thus far, South Africa had succeeded in rescheduling $2.5 billion into medium-term loans and repaying its IMF obligations completely, but its total foreign debt still stood at $21.2 billion in 1989, with $9.1 billion inside the net.[45] The Reserve Bank, furthermore, remained concerned about $7.5 billion public debt outside the net.[45] Noting South Africa's continued vulnerability and the upcoming expiration of the second repayment schedule in June 1990, sanctions advocates targeted finance.

Before its October 1989 meeting, the Commonwealth widely circulated a study of South Africa's financial predicament. The report encouraged further restrictions on new lending and investment, and highlighted the crucial area of trade credits that were not yet subject to sanctions. Church leaders petitioned creditors to place strict political conditions on South Africa, the anti-apartheid movement threatened to boycott banks, and discussion of possible gold sanctions became more widespread.[46] Once again, the Botha government hinted at the possibility of default, hoping to quiet international pressures and enhance its bargaining leverage with its creditors.[47] Just before the debt negotiations, furthermore, the government released high-profile political prisoners, in a move that most saw as presaging the imminent release of Nelson Mandela.

South Africa succeeded in preempting Commonwealth measures by announcing a favorable Third Interim Arrangement on 18 October 1989, to cover a three-and-a-half year period until December 1993. Since the country had continued to meet its repayment obligations and decreased the level of debt within the standstill, both by debt repayment and conversion through the exit option, the new agreement set significantly lower repayment installments, averaging only $352 million per year (a total of $1.5 billion) with interest remaining at a one percent premium. Payments inside and outside the net were coordinated for the first time to prevent coinciding obligations which would put additional liquidity pressure on the balance of payments.[48] South Africa had effectively eased economic and political pressures by rescheduling to medium-term debt.

Nevertheless, South Africa remained starved of finance. Maintaining current account surpluses led to deflationary measures – high interest rates and low levels of investment. As South Africa's deputy governor of the Reserve Bank and key debt-negotiator, Jan Lombard, observed, "We had to depress the domestic economy deliberately to be able to produce a surplus on the balance of payments so that we could service our debt. That depression brought about the feeling that we couldn't get out of this."[49] No rescheduling or restructuring could put the debt on a new footing. One study estimated that lack of foreign investment lowered the growth of capital stock from three percent per year to one percent.[50] Economic and political isolation, furthermore, led to investment decisions which, in retrospect, "look pretty silly."[51] Although South Africa avoided political and economic collapse in 1985, the financial situation weakened long-term prospects for sustainable economic growth, and with it, the foundations of apartheid. As a result of this economic and political conundrum, NP leaders increasingly acknowledged the need for some type of "power sharing" and negotiations. Botha's removal as party leader opened the door for more substantial change.[52]

This series of interim debt renegotiations revealed that the South African government responded to anti-apartheid pressures linked to debt rescheduling by proffering reforms while simultaneously escalating repression to hide domestic upheaval. Since foreign banks preferred to recover their money (especially at premium rates), South African threats of default tempered their demands for the elimination of apartheid.[53] Indeed, the anti-apartheid movement complained that international banks had missed the opportunity to force deep political concessions.[54] However, the possibility of further political pressures loomed in the background as sanctions advocates shifted focus to the possibility of applying restrictions to trade credits and of locally mandated sanctions.[55] Financial sanctions thus contributed significantly to the economic and political climate which fostered F. W. de Klerk's path-breaking reforms.

CONCLUSION

The South African state increasingly confronted challenges to its legitimacy and hegemony. Anti-apartheid pressures on banks and the IMF's refusal of bridging loans from 1983 contributed substantially to the country's economic and political crisis in the 1980s. Government strategies to meet its debt obligations, such as curbing imports and restricting capital exports, combined with burgeoning unrest, undermined already precarious levels of business confidence, itself a cause of capital flight and economic stagnation. Politically, financial sanctions sharpened divisions within the white oligarchy and strained the alliance between business and the NP, further exacerbating the government's weakness in the face of all types of international pressures. Sanctions, in this context, denied South Africa policy space within which to address the roots of its economic and political malaise.

The usefulness of "bankers sanctions" beyond South Africa, however, will depend on the particular nature of the economic and political vulnerability of the target. South Africa, for example, remained less vulnerable to financial strains than most developing countries during the 1970s and 1980s because of its gold production and the sophistication of its domestic capital markets. Many other countries would not have the mitigating strength of a resource base that increases in value during times of global economic turbulence or the institutional capacity to oversee a two-tiered exchange rate. Thus, we should expect most other countries to be *more susceptible* to financial pressures, if their economic and institutional weaknesses are accurately identified.

Some of the specific measures that enhanced leverage over the apartheid government may be exceptional, particularly because of coincident proliferation of short-term loans with countrywide political upheaval in the mid-1980s. Yet many other countries face similar financial vulnerabilities at times of attempted transitions to democracy. Globalizing financial markets, furthermore, will only increase susceptibility to international political constraints.[56] With such a wide range of financial tools available, including restrictions on trade credits (in the short term) and direct or portfolio investments (over the long term), sanctioners should be able to adapt to a particular country's weaknesses. The South African experience also indicates that bans on immediate financing are more likely to offer direct bargaining leverage, as panic easily sets in when bankers fear default because once one bank refuses loans, others quickly follow for fear that they will be the only ones not getting repaid. Capital and technology shortages, meanwhile, will undermine growth, contributing to indirect political pressures in the medium to long run.[57]

But the dynamic is different for trade, where suppliers have an incentive to stay in sanctioned markets. One implication, therefore, is that "bankers' sanctions" can be enforced by market mechanisms, whereas trade sanctions are more difficult to implement because they require government restrictions on the economic incentives to profit from being the only supplier. Debt repayment offers immediate possibilities for reclaiming good standing, thus increasing incentives to bargain.[58] Combined, financial sanctions offer more opportunities than trade sanctions to work with, rather than against, market forces.

Another question related to bargaining leverage is whether or when political conditions will be linked to a financial crisis. As the anti-apartheid experience demonstrates, social movements can influence economic actors. Some governments, notably the US, were more responsive than others to anti-apartheid protests. Congressional restrictions on loans to South Africa legally bound banks and other investors, while US corporations allow for a substantial degree of shareholder activism, unlike those in Europe. Thus the adoption and consequences of financial sanctions depend considerably both on the strength of domestic concern and the relationship between governments and banks. For example, in Germany and Japan, sanctions can be tools of central governments, rather than pension funds, city councils, and other grassroots activists. The resulting bargaining dynamics between sanctioners (either governments or bankers) and the target will depend in part on these variations of government control. We should also expect the degree of political conditionality to vary. In the South African case, for example, political pressures intensified because anti-apartheid measures proliferated in the one country, the US, whose bankers held the greatest proportion of short-term loans. Swiss or Hong Kong banks, in contrast, remained less concerned about political conditions.

Clearly, financial tools of pressure influenced the South African government and domestic economic elites. Yet these measures also did not live up to their full potential. Similar pressures are likely to be effective against more vulnerable targets or in pursuit of less ambitious goals than total social, economic, and political transformation. The successful application of these types of sanctions requires a sophisticated understanding of the political economy of the target, as well as the global market conditions which will create incentives (or disincentives) for adoption of international political demands.

Notes

We thank Neta Crawford, David Fig and especially Herman Schwartz for detailed comments on earlier drafts. Views expressed in this paper are the opinions of the authors and in no way attributable to the Government of South Africa.

1. R. Moorsom, "Foreign Trade and Sanctions," in M. Orkin, ed., *Sanctions Against Apartheid* (Cape Town: David Philip, 1989), p. 256.

2. See D. Kaplan, "The South African Capital Goods Sector and the Economic Crisis," in S. Gelb, ed., *South Africa's Economic Crisis* (Cape Town: David Philip, 1991), p. 173; A. Hirsch, "The Origins and Implications of South Africa's Continuing Financial Crisis," *Transformation* 9 (1989), p. 32.
3. Moorsom, "Foreign Trade and Sanctions," pp. 255–6.
4. There are numerous technicalities in the two-tier system. In this chapter, we refer only to rules for non-residents.
5. B. Kahn, "The Crisis and South Africa's Balance of Payments," in Gelb, ed., *South Africa's Economic Crisis*, p. 78; V. Padayachee, "Private International Banks, the Debt Crisis and the Apartheid State, 1982–1985," *African Affairs* 87 (1988), p. 362.
6. Padayachee, "Private International Banks," p. 363.
7. M. Lipton, *Sanctions and South Africa* (London: Economist Intelligence Unit, 1988), p. 37, based on the South African Reserve Bank, *Quarterly Bulletin*.
8. D. Geldenhuys, *Isolated States: A Comparative Perspective* (Cambridge: Cambridge University Press, 1990), pp. 394, 404–5; International Labor Organization, *Financial Sanctions against South Africa* (Geneva: ILO, 1991), pp. 25–8.
9. Moorsom, "Foreign Trade," p. 258.
10. On the global debt crisis, see M. Kahler, ed., *The Politics of International Debt* (Ithaca, NY: Cornell University Press, 1986).
11. F. Cassim, "Growth, Crisis and Change in the South African Economy," in J. Suckling and L. White, eds., *After Apartheid: Renewal of the South African Economy* (London: James Currey, 1988), p. 8. Lifting exchange controls signified a general policy shift toward liberalizing the economy, upon the recommendation of the de Kock Commission on Monetary Policy (published in 1979).
12. Padayachee, "Private International Banks," pp. 364–6.
13. Only 51.9 percent of the board favored the loan. Implicitly it critiqued apartheid by requiring a review of the country's labor training and mobility. Economist Intelligence Unit, *Quarterly Economic Report: South Africa*, 1983, no. 1, p. 30.
14. J. D. F. Jones, "Pretoria Takes Cautious View of Cheerful Economic Atmosphere," *Financial Times*, 17 February 1983, p. 3.
15. *Congressional Quarterly*, 15 January through 26 November 1983.
16. The report cited apartheid-instigated shortages of skilled labor as a medium-term constraint on potential growth which required policy changes affecting labor mobility. It strongly urged the South African government to target education and training. See R. Bonner, "Economic Problems Tied to Apartheid," *New York Times*, 17 November 1983, D6.
17. As part of the compromise, similar restrictions applied to communist countries. The anti-apartheid provision succeeded because of the overwhelming desire of the Administration and most Republicans to bolster IMF funding at the peak of the international debt crisis. Reagan's commitment to money for public housing sealed the deal by ensuring Democratic approval. See C. H. Farnsworth, "Senate Votes IMF Increase," *New York Times*, 18 November 1983, D1.

18. Interview with Chris Stals in *Euromoney*, August 1991, as quoted in Investor Responsibility Research Center (IRRC), "US Banks and South Africa," *Social Issues Service: Proxy Issues Report*, 1993 Background Report B, Supplement #3, 12 March 1993, p. 5. At the time of the interview Stals was governor of the South African Reserve Bank.

19. According to Stals, "One should not exaggerate this, but just about every foreign banker that comes into my office asks me when we will have normal relations with the IMF again. . . . If you do not have access to IMF facilities, there's not much that you can pull out of the hat to support your economy if you have a balance of payments problem. So the bankers give you a high risk rating" (quoted in IRRC, "US Banks and South Africa," p. 5).

20. Reserve Bank estimate, cited in L. Harris, "South Africa's External Debt Crisis," in B. Onimode, ed., *The International Monetary Fund, the World Bank and African Debt* (London: Zed, 1989), pp. 182–3. Also see Cassim, "Growth, Crisis and Change," p. 7.

21. *Financial Mail*, 9 August 1985, p. 41; M. Lipton, "The Challenge of Sanctions," Center for the Study of the South African Economy and International Finance, London School of Economics, Discussion Paper Series, 1990, p. 9.

22. See, for example, N. C. Crawford, "Oil Sanctions Against Apartheid," in this volume.

23. See M. P. Mangaliso, "Disinvestment by Multinational Corporations," and M. Voorhes, "The US Divestment Movement," both in this volume. Investors in gold remained more confident, however.

24. Lipton, "Challenge," p. 7.

25. *The Economist*, 7 September 1985, pp. 13–14, 83–4; A. Hirsch, "Sanctions, Loans and the South African Economy," in Orkin, ed., *Sanctions Against Apartheid*, p. 273; Economist, *Quarterly Economic Report*, 1984, no. 4, p. 33.

26. Padayachee, "Private International Banks," pp. 365–6.

27. *Financial Mail*, 9 August 1985, p. 41; Hirsch, "Sanctions," p. 273. Nevertheless, net buying of gold shares increased in 1984 and the first half of 1985.

28. V. Padayachee, "The Politics of South Africa's International Financial Relations," in Gelb, ed., *South Africa's Economic Crisis*, pp. 98–101, based on South African and international financial papers. Nevertheless, it is important to distinguish between the perspectives of equity investors and commercial lenders; we focus here primarily on the latter.

29. European investors generally reacted more negatively than those in the US, while local South African buyers – prohibited from investing abroad – absorbed many of these shares. The weak rand also stemmed disinvestment. Thus South Africa avoided massive sell-offs. See J. Jones, "Nervous Foreigners Ditch Shares," *Financial Times*, 27 July 1985, p. 3; A. Bachar, "Foreign Capital Leaving South Africa But No Alarm Noted," *Reuters*, 7 August 1985; T. Hawkins, "Currency Specter Haunts Analysts," *Financial Times*, 7 September 1985, p. 3; Harris, "South Africa's External Debt Crisis," p. 174.

30. *The Mining Journal*, 15 October 1985, p. 1. Gold holdings, unlike the industrial sector, tend to reflect investors' long-term price considerations rather than short-term political conditions.
31. US banks held 85 percent short term loans, British banks about 57 percent and Germans approximately 31 percent; Hirsch, "Sanctions," p. 274.
32. J. Leape, "South Africa's Foreign Debt and the Standstill, 1985–1990," Research Paper Series No. 1, Center for the Study of the South African Economy and International Finance, London School of Economics, undated (c. 1990), p. 4.
33. M. Holman and P. Montagnon, "Business Leaders Urge Pretoria to Open Political Talks," *Financial Times*, 30 August 1985, p. 1; Harris, "South Africa's External Debt Crisis," p. 175; Hirsch, "Sanctions," p. 274.
34. R. Davies, "The Fight of the Little Tiger: The State's Response to Sanctions," in Orkin, ed., *Sanctions Against Apartheid*, p. 224; N. Sheppard, Jr., "South Africa Reform Gets Unlikely Ally," *Chicago Tribune*, 1 September 1985, p. 1; Holman and Montagnon, "Business Leaders"; Lipton, *Sanctions*, p. 64; D. Hauck, *Can Pretoria Be Moved? The Emergence of Business Activism in South Africa* (Washington, DC: IRRC, 1986), p. 17. Relly especially came under criticism for not using his power as head of the country's largest conglomerate to make politicians meet his demands; *Economist*, 2 February 1986, p. 58. The organizations' statements are reprinted in Hauck, *Can Pretoria Be Moved?*, Appendices A-D.
35. Leape, "South Africa's Foreign Debt," p. 5; Economist, *Country Report*, 1986, no. 2, pp. 37–8; *Reuters*, 6 September 1985; Lipton, *Sanctions*, p. 59.
36. South Africa initially proposed much more lenient terms. See Economist, *Country Report*, 1986, no. 2, p. 38; Commonwealth Committee of Foreign Ministers on Southern Africa, *Banking on Apartheid: The Financial Links Report* (London: Commonwealth Secretariat, 1989).
37. Hirsch, "Sanctions," p. 275; Economist, *Country Report*, 1986, no. 3, p. 38.
38. Hirsch, "Sanctions," pp. 276–7; ILO, *Financial Sanctions*, pp. 36–40; Voorhes, "US Divestment."
39. However, he also rejected a "siege economy" because it restricted the free market, with long-term adverse effects on economic growth and stability. A. Robinson, "Investor Doubts Hit S. Africa, De Kock Says," *Financial Times*, 27 August 1986, p. 1.
40. Hirsch, "Sanctions," p. 276.
41. J. D. Battersby, "South Africa Looks East and Extends Its Markets," *New York Times*, 22 November 1987; Padayachee, "Politics," p. 104; Economist, *Quarterly Economic Report*, 1986, no. 1, p. 36.
42. J. Jones, "South Africa 5; Record Year for New Issues," *Financial Times*, 10 July 1987, p. 5; R. Tucci, "Foreign Shareholders Join Business Exodus from South Africa," *Reuters*, 8 Jan. 1987. Some conglomerates also circumvented restrictions on capital exports, as evident in the Minorco scandal; *Weekly Mail*, 23 December 1988 to 12 January 1989, and 31 March to 6 April 1989.

43. Unlike in the past, the JSE did not recover along with gold. J. Jones, "South Africa 4; Decline Expected for Rest of Year," *Financial Times*, 9 June 1988, p. 4.

44. Hirsch, "Sanctions," p. 288; *Weekly Mail*, 26 August to 1 September 1988, p. 13. In part, the liberal business community sought to distance itself from the rightward shift in the May 1987 elections; *Reuters*, 20 July 1988. Public opinion surveys confirm that sanctions motivated business demands for reform, especially after 1986. See K. van Wyk, "State Elites and South Africa's International Isolation: A Longitudinal Comparison of Perception," *Politikon* 15 (1988), pp. 73–5; J. Hofmeyr, *The Impact of Sanctions on South Africa: Whites' Political Attitudes* (Washington, DC: IRRC, 1990); South African Institute of International Affairs, *What Do We Think? A Survey of White Opinion on Foreign Policy Issues* (biannual), especially 1986, pp. 12–13; 1988, pp. 24–7; 1990, pp. 19–22; 1992, pp. 32–3. (Surveys in 1982 and 1984 did not contain a sanctions question; the survey ceased following the 1992 study.)

45. Lipton, "Challenge," pp. 11–12.

46. Commonwealth, *Banking on Apartheid*; K. Ovenden and T. Cole, *Apartheid and International Finance: A Program for Change* (New York: Penguin, 1989); H. Joffe, "Churchmen Set Terms for Easing of SA Debt Pressure," *Weekly Mail*, 2–9 June 1989, p. 2; H. Joffe, "Economy, Not Faith, Tells Churchmen Where to Squeeze," *Weekly Mail*, 23–29 June 1989, 15; M. Levy, "ANC Campaigns to Stop Debt Rescheduling," *Weekly Mail*, 21–28 July 1989; *New Nation*, 21–27 July 1989, 8; D. Pallister, "US Team in London to Look at Gold Sanctions," *Weekly Mail*, 10–17 March 1989, p. 1.

47. Hirsch, "Sanctions," p. 281.

48. Leape, "South Africa's Foreign Debt," p. 16; ILO, *Financial Sanctions*, p. 12.

49. Quoted in J. Goodwin and B. Schiff, *Heart of Whiteness: Afrikaners Face Black Rule in the New South Africa* (New York: Scribner, 1995), p. 140.

50. D. Woods, *Engagement in South Africa: The International Monetary Fund Involvement 1990–92* (Johannesburg: South African Institute of International Affairs Occasional Paper, October 1992), p. 5.

51. D. Keys, "The SA Government View on Foreign Trade and Investment," *South Africa International* 22 (1992), p. 171. Keys later became Minister of Finance.

52. Among these were Justice Minister Kobie Coetsee, who was a key player in the transition (quoted in *Southscan*, 6 September 1991, p. 274).

53. South Africa continued to get funds, either clandestinely (at a two percent sanctions-busting premium) or through bonds and export trade credits. See M. Duggan, "Out from the Cold: South Africa and International Capital Markets," *South Africa International* 22 (1991), pp. 4–6.

54. Padayachee, "Politics," p. 107. In retrospect, Reserve Bank Governor Chris Stals concurred by acknowledging in his testimony to the Truth and Reconciliation Commission that "Maybe we should not have re-

scheduled SA's foreign debt so well"; quoted in *Business Day*, 13 November 1997, p. 1.

55. IRRC, "US Banks and South Africa." In the US, municipalities increasingly implemented restrictions, regardless of trends in national level policymaking. See J. Gray, "New York City to Rate Banks on S. Africa Ties," *New York Times*, 11 July 1991, A11, and Voorhes, "US Divestment."

56. See L. E. Armijo, "Mixed Blessings: Foreign Capital Flows and Democracy in Emerging Markets," in L. E. Armijo, ed., *Financial Globalization and Democracy in Emerging Markets* (Basingstoke, UK: Macmillan, 1999).

57. See Lipton, *Sanctions*, p. 72.

58. Lipton, "Challenge," p. 32.

9 "Sanctions Hurt but Apartheid Kills!":[1] The Sanctions Campaign and Black Workers

Tshidiso Maloka

> As the sanctions campaign gains momentum internationally, it is important never to lose sight of the fact that the initial call for the isolation of South Africa came from inside South Africa itself.
>
> South African Congress of Trade Unions, c. 1983[2]

> [W]e do not conceive of sanctions as a substitute for our struggle and our sacrifices; it is additional. So we will continue, we will certainly embark on massive strike actions, we will do all the things that we can and must do for our own freedom, but sanctions are additional and sanctions alone would not bring about any results.
>
> Oliver Tambo, President of the African National Congress, October 1985[3]

One of the strongest arguments against the use of economic sanctions is that often ordinary people in the target state – rather than the political elite – are most hurt. This unintended effect may be counterproductive, especially if sanctions begin to lose popular support within the target state as a result of job losses and deepening poverty. It is important to keep in mind, therefore, that in the South African case, the call for isolation was part of the overall political strategy of the internal black opposition.

At the genesis of the global sanctions campaign, the African National Congress (ANC) despatched some leading members of its Youth League to London in January 1959 to launch the "Boycott of South African Goods."[4] The Sharpeville massacre of March 1960 inspired a month-long British boycott of South African goods – a campaign called for by Chief Albert Luthuli, then president of the ANC. This campaign culminated in the formation of the British Anti-Apartheid Movement in 1960. The American Committee on Africa also began a sanctions campaign in August of that year. By the end of 1963, 25 countries had imposed an official boycott of South African goods (albeit affecting only 1.7 percent of its total exports).[5] By 1969, the ANC placed the isolation of racist South Africa at the center of its political strategy. But not until the mid-1980s did the exiled ANC and anti-apartheid lobbies successfully pressure major Western powers for stronger economic measures. A significant number of multinational corporations (MNCs) began to pull out of South Africa during 1985–88.[6]

The impact of these sanctions and related disinvestment on employment were hotly debated. Now that sanctions have been lifted, a more sober discussion is possible; in the past, both proponents and opponents of sanctions tended deliberately to overlook some realities and facts. Proponents, concerned with intensifying the campaign for sanctions, tended to downplay the negative effects that these measures did have. Opponents, meanwhile, resorted to "scare statistics" to inflate the strength of their case. Yet even in retrospect, economic statistics and public opinion polls remain inconclusive, as this chapter demonstrates. And these debates lost sight of the most critical role of popular support for the anti-apartheid sanctions campaign.

The South African case demonstrates that the effects of sanctions are mediated by preexisting socio-economic and political factors. Both the imposition of sanctions and the legitimacy of their costs are contested and negotiated by different social forces (including workers and corporations) within the target state. As much as some measures may unintentionally hit the poorest and most disadvantaged sections in the civil society hardest, whether sanctions are bad or good largely depends on the extent of popular support. In South Africa, where the sanctions campaign started with the internal struggle against apartheid, oppressed communities were prepared to sacrifice for a long-term objective.

SANCTIONS AND JOBS

An array of often contradictory statistical data derived from various econometric models fuelled debates over the effects of sanctions on employment.[7] Opponents of international pressures manipulated these numbers for the purpose of "proving" that sanctions primarily hurt black people, and workers in particular. In the mid-1980s, some economists and social scientists predicted that sanctions would cost South Africa 700 000 jobs over a five-year period; others claimed that two million jobs would be lost by the year 2000. The Trust Bank estimated in March 1990 that sanctions cost South Africa 500 000 jobs, $8 billion in GDP, $32 billion of total production, as well as $16 billion in foreign exchange, since 1985.[8]

But questions arise about the derivation of such figures. First of all, unemployment in South Africa is a structural problem. Recession plagued the economy from the mid-1970s. Average annual growth rates dropped from 5.5 percent (1962–72) to 3 percent (1972–81), then 1.1 percent (1981–86). With average annual population growth ranging from 2.5 to 2.82 percent during these decades, the total employment growth rate consistently declined from 2.82 percent (1960–70) to 2.38 percent (1970–75), then down to 1.15 percent (1975–85), and finally a mere 0.7 percent (1985–90). As a result, the percentage of new entrants absorbed into the economy dropped from 90 percent in the 1960s to 8.5 percent in the 1980s.[9]

The racial composition of the labor force ensured that these downward trends, including the impact of sanctions, were distributed differentially. Figures released by the National Manpower Commission show that in 1991 almost half of the employees in "professional, semi-professional and technical" jobs were white, with Africans concentrated mainly in education and health. Whites also occupied more than half of the 348 157 "managerial, executive and administrative" positions.[10] Similarly, surveys by a human resources consulting firm, sampling 71 companies in 1989 and 1992, concluded that whites held almost 100 percent of the senior managerial positions in the private sector. Whites also accounted for about 60 percent of sales, administration and information system staff in the corporate sector. Africans were concentrated (about 60 percent) in the lower-skilled category.[11] This racially skewed distribution of positions was perpetuated by the disproportionate number of whites in universities, technikons and technical colleges.[12]

Wages also reflected apartheid practices. In 1990, for example, per capita monthly income for Africans was estimated (by the South African Advertising Research Foundation) at R160, as opposed to R470 for whites. A South African Advertising Research Foundation survey found that the average monthly household income for Africans between 1987 and 1992 was R912 while that of their white counterparts was R5163. In 1992, no African household earned more than R11 000 per month, while 7.6 percent of white households did. The highest proportion of African households (30 percent) earned monthly R1399, compared to only one percent of white households. The proportion of African households in relation to a monthly income bracket decreases after the R2000 mark, while the proportion of white households increases from the R2500 mark; the highest white proportion (25 percent) was in the R6000 to R10 999 monthly income bracket.[13]

Given these disparities, economic sanctions could hurt black workers. Undoubtedly, disinvestment would cost jobs. The boycott of South African exports, especially mining and agricultural goods, and capital outflows threatened employment. International pressures could also exacerbate the general recessionary conditions of the 1980s.[14] But it remains unclear to what extent sanctions were to blame for these unfortunate circumstances.

The experiences of the motor industry epitomize the combined impact of structural economic factors and sanctions. This manufacturing sector depends on imported technology and raw materials; vehicles and parts remain the country's largest single import (some 20 percent). With weak exports, it relies on domestic sales. Yet the country's racially skewed income distribution meant that Africans accounted for less that one percent of purchases in the 1980s. Total car sales declined from 1964 to 1987. The industry faced a crisis.

Mergers, disinvestment, and rationalizations led to job losses. For example, Ford's merger with SAMCOR (the South African Motor Corporation) in January 1985 resulted in a plant relocation from Port Elizabeth to Pretoria and 1 300 lost jobs; a second relocation cut another 950 positions. In September, Alfa Romeo closed its Transvaal plant, cutting 611 jobs. An additional 500 workers lost their livelihoods when Renault withdrew. Volkswagen reduced its Port Elizabeth – Uitenhage workforce by 49 percent between 1983 and 1986. When General Motors (GM) withdrew in October 1986, a three-week strike cost employees 209 jobs (867 were fired, then 338 were reinstated, along with 320 new recruits). The new management, restructuring the company, retrenched 100 employees, including senior executives and clerical staff.[15] Overall, between December 1984 and December 1986, African employment in the industry declined from 19 458 jobs to 15 276; coloureds from 9 922 to 4 858; and whites from 12 662 to 9 044.[16]

Some retrenched workers in Pretoria and Bophuthatswana opted for the mining industry, notorious for harsh working and living conditions.[17] Others found it difficult to repay loans, and many moved to less comfortable shelter. At the same time, as trade unions noted, MNC withdrawal benefitted local white capital. For example, rationalization and disinvestment resulted in a higher proportion of vehicles sold by majority or locally owned companies; sales increased from 9.6 percent in 1960, to 26.7 percent in 1970, 48.3 percent in 1984, and 72 percent in 1987. African entrepreneurs lacked resources and political muscle to bid for a departing MNC.

Overall, unemployment and poverty rose in the 1980s, during the peak of sanctions. Even for whites, the cost of living accelerated. Reaching its highest level in 66 years, the consumer price index rose 18.4 percent from 1984 to 1985. The average wage increase between 1985 and 1986 was 11 percent for all racial groups, while consumer prices rose 17 percent during the same period. From 1980 to 1987, personal disposable income for all racial groups only increased 1 percent annually, with a low of negative 4 percent in 1986.[18]

However, sanctions alone cannot explain the deepening economic crisis and consequent acceleration of unemployment and poverty. Despite trade sanctions, the composition and volume of exports showed little change. While the US, Commonwealth, and European markets increasingly rejected South African products, the country found new partners in East Asia and parts of Latin America. Moreover, the loss of 80 000 jobs in mining (which accounted for over 60 percent of total exports) between 1985 and 1990, cannot simply be attributed to trade sanctions; some 50 000 lost positions were due to marginal mines closing in 1990.[19]

Furthermore, disinvestment did not necessarily close plants and eliminate jobs, just as investment does not automatically boost employment.[20] Of 114 US MNCs that disinvested between 1 January 1986 and 30 April 1988, 57 kept non-equity ties with their South African partners; the number of non-US MNCs with non-equity ties increased from 134 in November 1990 to 147 in May 1991.[21] As a result, South Africans were little affected by disinvestment in the mid-1980s: stores stocked US consumer goods, and industry still obtained equipment, chemical supplies and computers.[22] In addition, the imposition of oil and arms embargoes created some new jobs, through import substitution.

Mechanization of certain sectors of the economy and the priva-

tization of government parastatals also contributed to unemployment in the 1980s. For example, the introduction of a R40 million
robot at the GM plant in Port Elizabeth in 1985 led to 465 workers being temporarily laid off, in addition to 320 retrenchments.
The process of preparing the "big four" parastatals – the Iron and
Steel Industrial Corporation, the Transport Service, the Post Office, and the Electricity Supply Commission – for privatization also
cost jobs. Despite boycotts, new markets in East Asia increased
the steel corporation's annual profits by 40 percent (and production by 3.8 percent) between 1984 and 1988. Yet rationalization
cut 23 000 jobs between 1985 and August 1989. In the same vein,
employment in transportation declined by 6.5 percent between 1986
and 1987, while electricity (responsible for 94 percent of South
Africa's needs) shed 14 000 jobs between 1985 and August 1989.[24]

Corporate managers also fired workers to undermine the increasingly militant labor movement.[25] In the 1970s, unions pushed for
recognition; the government conceded to this demand in 1979 (following the recommendations of the Wiehahn Commission). Unions
then focused on strengthening their membership and fighting
for better working conditions, including higher wages. 1987 was a
watershed in terms of the number of strikes and work stoppages.
The National Automobile Allied Workers Union played a pioneer-
ing role. Not only was it the first group to organize the majority of
workers in one industry along non-racial lines, it was also the first
to win the R2 per hour minimum pay in 1980 and the R3 per hour
minimum pay in 1983. In 1982, it became the first to organize an
industry-wide strike, which affected Ford, GM, and Volkswagen.[26]
To avert union pressure and weaken the bargaining power of workers,
several companies resorted to mechanization and rationalization
of the production process. Some MNCs even relocated their plants
to towns bordering homelands, where workers were less organized.[27]
In response to the 1987 National Union of Mineworkers' strike,
for example, the mining industry targeted activists for retrenchment.

A 1990 survey of about 200 companies representing 26 000 retrenchments found that most (52.4 percent) of those companies
attributed their action to economic downturn; the second highest
category (11.6 percent) pointed to rationalization; mechanization
accounted for 9.5 percent. Only 2.7 percent cited relocation as a
cause, while closure was a factor in 4.8 percent of the companies.[28]

Thus, there is no direct relationship between the high unemployment rate in South Africa and sanctions measures in the mid-1980s.

How sanctions reinforced structural causes of recession is an area left to other chapters in this volume to explain. The point here is simply that there is insufficient evidence that job losses among black workers are a legitimate reason to forego sanctions, especially if the majority of the population supports international pressure. The following section explores this second question.

UNIONS AND POPULAR SUPPORT FOR SANCTIONS

Opponents of sanctions also used surveys of black opinion to "prove" that the majority of South Africans opposed sanctions, particularly disinvestment. In 1979 Lawrence Schlemmer, then the Director of the Centre for Applied Social Science at the University of Natal in Durban, conducted the first systematic poll. 75 percent of the respondents expressed opposition to disinvestment. He conducted an additional, widely publicized survey in May 1984, with 551 black industrial workers from all metropolitan areas; 75 percent opposed disinvestment. He concluded that survival, rather than politics, guided black workers. On the basis of a third survey later in 1984, with 1000 respondents in eight metropolitan centers, he argued that the black middle class was more prone to support sanctions.[29]

As the sanctions campaign escalated in the mid-1980s, Schlemmer's work sparked considerable debate and triggered interest in black attitudes.[30] Consequently, more than 12 surveys followed, from 1984 and 1989. Three that confirmed Schlemmer's findings (two conducted by the Human Sciences Research Council between June 1984 and May 1985, and one conducted in February 1985 by the Johannesburg-based newspaper, *The Star*) were most notable among opponents of sanctions. But proponents of sanctions, especially the United Democratic Front (UDF), the ANC, and the Congress of South African Trade Unions (COSATU), attacked Schlemmer's findings. In particular, they objected to the way Schlemmer phrased his questions. For example, dichotomous choices between divestment or no divestment left no middle ground; his questions also inaccurately equated investment with the building of factories and disinvestment with closing them down. Thus, critics rejected the surveys as misleading and politically biased.

In response, COSATU commissioned its own researchers to critique Schlemmer's findings, culminating in a survey conducted by the Community Agency for Social Enquiry in September 1985, with

800 respondents drawn from all major metropolitan areas.[31] 49 percent of the respondents opted for conditional divestment (where corporations actively supported the anti-apartheid movement), with 24 percent encouraging total sanctions and 26 percent advocating unrestricted investment. This survey also sought to gauge the extent to which blacks were prepared to sacrifice for the anti-apartheid struggle. 26 percent indicated their willingness to suffer; 25 percent indicated an intermediate position, and 48 percent were referred to as "cautious."[32] Clearly, the construction of the survey questions had an impact on the results.

Timing created another difficulty in comparing the rival sets of surveys – the political climate changed rapidly in the mid-1980s. Schlemmer conducted his surveys before the September 1984 township uprisings. By July 1985, turmoil engulfed the country, and the government imposed a state of emergency in the Witwatersrand, Eastern Cape and the Western Cape regions. In retaliation, the UDF and COSATU called for consumer boycotts; street and defense committees sprouted across the country as "organs of people's power" to replace the collapsed local apartheid authorities. A countrywide state of emergency followed in June 1986, and troops were despatched to most black residential areas. These measures, and not least the detention and assassination of political leaders, established relative stability by 1988. But the following year, the UDF and COSATU renewed defiance, which continued until the unbanning of exiled organizations in February 1990.[33] This period, in other words, critically influenced black attitudes – not only toward sanctions but the anti-apartheid struggle in general. Surveys conducted during this period suggest hardening views toward investment, as well as increasingly militant support for the struggle. Blacks were now more prepared to suffer personally as long as they contributed toward overthrowing the apartheid government.

At this stage, unions played a critical role in the sanctions campaign. In the 1960s, the South African Congress of Trade Unions (SACTU), convinced that black workers would be relatively unaffected, had backed the ANC sanctions campaign. Furthermore, as early as 1963, SACTU declared that, "we do not shrink from any hardship in the cause of freedom. . . . The working people of our country do not eat imported food or wear foreign clothes; nor do we benefit from the export of South African mealies, wool, wine, or gold. *To our friends abroad we say that trafficking in the fruits of apartheid can never be in the interest of the workers who suffer under*

apartheid" [emphasis in original].[34] Research conducted in the early
1980s underscored this union position: MNCs had a higher white
to black worker ratio as compared to South African companies,
and approximately 30 percent of all African workers found employment in the informal sector. Therefore, the argument went,
MNCs pulling out would most affect white, rather than black, workers.
Conversely, economic isolation would slow technology imports, especially benefitting miners and farm workers (sectors most affected
by mechanization).[35]

But independent unions, especially the Federation of South African Trade Unions (FOSATU), developed a different position in
the 1970s. Unlike those tied to the exiled movements, internal unions
preferred various codes of conduct (such as the US Sullivan Principles and the European Community Code) to control activities of
MNCs. Only in the early 1980s, after some companies started pulling out and the rate of retrenchments increased, did unions (particularly FOSATU) develop a more coherent position. These workers
insisted that, as products of South African labor, the assets of MNCs
should not leave the country. Nevertheless, they acknowledged that
significant disinvestment was taking place. But they insisted that
unemployment was a structural problem, not simply the consequence
of corporate withdrawal.[36] By mid-1985, FOSATU opposed disinvestment (withdrawal of MNC assets), as distinct from divestment (selling shares), which it favored. Certainly concern for jobs
motivated the federation's view, since unions depend on employed
(not unemployed) workers. Organized workers also hoped that divestment (and codes of conduct) would force affected companies
and institutions to improve conditions for their employees.[37] The
exiled movement understood FOSATU's position.

FOSATU merged with other unions to form COSATU in November 1985, initiating a new phase in the union movement. Politically, COSATU inclined more toward positions of the exiled
movements; the new federation also supported sanctions (but without
explicitly calling upon MNCs to disinvest). In particular, sanctions
affected four affiliated unions the most. Boycotts of South African
sugar and deciduous fruit exports hit members of the Food and
Allied Workers Union. Restrictions on South African coal and other
mineral exports concerned the National Union of Mineworkers. The
National Union of Metal Workers (NUMSA) and the Chemical
Workers Industrial Union (CWIU) also operated in sectors with a
significant MNC presence. The food union publicly refused to state

its position, but the mine workers actively campaigned for sanctions, including sending its leaders overseas to promote the cause.[38]

Then, GM announced in 1986 that it intended to disinvest, in response to the US Comprehensive Anti-Apartheid Act, the crisis facing the South African motor industry, and the overall global reorganization of its operations. Negotiations between GM and the National Automobile and Allied Workers Union (later to be part of NUMSA) in October 1986 failed; a two-week strike ensued. The workers demanded severance pay and the right to appoint their representatives to the new board of directors, as well as the payment of their pension contributions. The GM management responded by firing some 570 workers, hiring scab labor, and calling in the police. After the workers' defeat and GM's withdrawal, Delta Motors (with which GM had signed non-equity agreements) took over, reorganized the production process (retrenching some workers in the process), and re-established links with the South African police and military (links which GM had to cut because of pressure in the US).[39]

The union leadership learned two things: corporate withdrawal could be deceptive, and it could benefit white capital instead of the struggling masses.[40] Disinvestment, now characterized as "corporate camouflage," was widely condemned. COSATU adopted resolutions at its 1987 congress calling for comprehensive sanctions, attacking deceptive disinvestment, and demanding that MNCs negotiate terms of their withdrawal with the unions.[41]

Other parallel developments in the motor industry taught the union leadership another set of lessons. As indicated above, in 1985 Ford merged with SAMCOR, relocating to Pretoria at the expense of its Port Elizabeth plant. Then, in June 1987 Ford announced its intention to disinvest (without, of course, completely severing ties with SAMCOR). Part of its shares in SAMCOR would go to workers individually. Critical of this scenario, NUMSA convened a meeting where its shop stewards agreed that shares should be used for community development instead. But in April 1988 (when the agreement was to go into effect), some workers organized against the union's position, insisting that the money be distributed individually as Ford had proposed. A strike ensued, clearly indicating the degree of division between the workers and the union leadership. In the end, Ford implemented individual share ownership.[42]

Other unions also sought to prevent a reoccurrence of the GM experience. In the chemical industry, the union clashed with MNCs.

In fact, COSATU's resolutions on sanctions and disinvestment had been largely due to the work of CWIU. In July 1987, the union sent letters to 41 MNCs operating in the chemical sector, requesting a meeting to negotiate. Their set of demands included one year's notice of any intention to disinvest; full disclosure of their reasons for disinvestment; and details about the sale of assets. None of the MNCs agreed to meet. CWIU sent another letter, this time threatening strike action. Still none of the MNCs responded. The union then asked the government to set up a conciliation board. In response, three MNCs took legal action against the union. Although the corporations' court application got turned down and the government refused to set up the board, some MNCs attempted to evade a strike by approaching the union. They preferred plant-level rather than industry-wide negotiations. In January 1989, the union convened a national meeting where the idea of a joint forum was dropped in favor of plant-level negotiations.[43]

But some important chemical corporations, including Shell, British Petroleum, and Mobil, still refused to negotiate with CWIU, claiming that they had no intention of disinvesting. Once the unions, especially in the metal industry, realized that some MNCs were indeed committed to staying in South Africa, they shifted focus to pressing for improved wages and working conditions. For example, NUMSA used the support of German unions to pressure German companies to sign a 14 point program, which gave South African workers the same rights as their German counterparts. But by 1990, only six MNCs had signed this program.

At another level, MNCs intending to remain in South Africa also attempted to neutralize anti-apartheid pressure groups by adopting more humane industrial relations as well as socially responsible programs. For example, before its subsequent disinvestment in 1989, Mobil established a $20 million charity fund to be spent over a period of five years. Later it also established an internal fund for its employees to be used for community projects. Shell also established its own community and education programs; British Petroleum, for its part, set up a fund for the restoration of District Six in Cape Town.[44]

Overall, worker attitudes toward sanctions and disinvestment were mixed, but unions predominantly supported international pressures. Moreover, their strategies evolved over time, adapting to changing circumstances. By the late 1980s, organized labor sought corporate disinvestment under negotiated circumstances which would most benefit black workers.

CONCLUSION

The 1980s marked a difficult decade for black workers in South Africa. Recession, due to global economic changes, mechanization, rationalization, trade sanctions, disinvestment, and numerous other pressures, led to considerable job losses and escalating poverty. But the use of sanctions cannot be judged solely by their negative economic effects on the masses. Many blacks, especially those in the ranks of organized labor, accepted that eliminating apartheid entailed heavy costs. Yet life under apartheid also meant significant hardships. Which costs, on balance, were most tolerable remained a political question – not one that could be measured by econometric models or public opinion polls, no matter how accurate these data may (or may not) be.

The experiences of black workers in South Africa offers insights into the use of sanctions against other targets. First and foremost, the political salience of these measures depends fundamentally on the popular reaction. At the symbolic level, these measures reinforce the demands of domestic opposition groups (such as the ANC and its allies, UDF and COSATU). In the private realm, businesses acknowledge them as bargaining partners; in the public sphere, governments accept them as legitimate voices. Presumably, sanctions will be most effective in similar circumstances – where international pressures are designed to supplement and support domestic movements. Thus the "naive" theory of sanctions, which equates international pressures with mass deprivation and rebellion, contains elements of insight. Economic restrictions can increase domestic opposition to the target regime. But the domestic political and social context matters immensely.

Notes

1. Moses Mayekiso, General Secretary of the National Union of Metalworkers, quoted in *The Weekly Mail*, 20–26 October 1989, p. 7.
2. South African Congress of Trade Unions, "The Case for Sanctions against Apartheid," unpublished pamphlet, c. 1983.
3. Cited in J. Hanlon and R. Omond, *The Sanctions Handbook: For or Against?* (Harmondsworth, UK: Penguin, 1987), p. 92.
4. T. Lodge, "Sanctions and Black Political Organizations," in M. Orkin, ed., *Sanctions Against Apartheid* (Cape Town: David Philip, 1989).
5. Ibid., Africa Research Center, *The Sanctions Weapon* (Cape Town: Buchu Books, 1989), pp. 11–13.

6. See M. P. Mangaliso, "Disinvestment by Multinational Corporations," in this volume.
7. For a discussion of some of these figures and econometric models, see C. Mesh, "Sanctions and Unemployment," in Orkin, ed., *Sanctions Against Apartheid*, and S. Gelb, "Unemployment and the Disinvestment Debate," *South African Labour Bulletin* 10 (1985).
8. Institute of Race Relations, *Survey*, 1989/90, p. 272.
9. C. Jenkins, "The Effects of Sanctions on Formal Sector Employment in South Africa," Institute of Development Studies, Discussion Paper 320, University of Sussex, 1993, pp. 4–7.
10. National Manpower Commission, *Annual Report*, 1993, p. 74.
11. Institute of Race Relations, *Survey*, 1993/94, p. 467.
12. National Manpower Commission, *Annual Report*, 1993, p. 78.
13. Institute of Race Relations, *Survey*, 1993/94, p. 484.
14. On the causes and magnitude of disinvestment and divestment, see Mangaliso, "Disinvestment by Multinational Corporations," and M. Voorhes, "The US Divestment Movement," in this volume.
15. Institute of Race Relations, *Survey*, 1985, p. 162; 1986, p. 748. See also J. Chataway, "The South African Motor Industry," in J. Hanlon, ed., *South Africa: The Sanctions Report, Documents and Statistics* (London: James Currey, 1990). GM will be discussed in more detail below.
16. Institute of Race Relations, *Survey*, 1985, p. 162; 1986, p. 748.
17. W. G. James, *Our Precious Metal: African Labour in South Africa's Gold Industry, 1970–1990* (Cape Town: David Philip, 1992), p. 63.
18. Institute of Race Relations, *Survey*, 1987/88, p. 290.
19. Jenkins, "The Effects of Sanctions," pp. 12–15. See also C. Jenkins, "Sanctions, Economic Growth and Change," in N. Natrass and E. Ardington, eds., *The Political Economy of South Africa* (Cape Town: Oxford University Press, 1990).
20. See Mangaliso's critique of foreign investment in "Disinvestment by Multinational Corporations."
21. Institute of Race Relations, *Survey*, 1991/92, p. 416; 1993/94, p. 392.
22. R. Knight, "Sanctions, Disinvestment, and US Corporations in South Africa," in R. E. Edgar, ed., *Sanctioning Apartheid* (Trenton, NJ: Africa World Press, 1990), p. 74.
23. See N. C. Crawford, "Oil Sanctions Against Apartheid" and "How Arms Embargoes Work," both in this volume.
24. CRIC (Careers Research and Information Center), "Privatization in South Africa," *South African Labour Bulletin* 14 (1989); CRIC, "Privatization: Selling off the Public Sector," *South African Labour Bulletin* 14 (1989).
25. R. Lambert and E. Webster, "The Re-emergence of Political-Unionism in Contemporary South Africa," in W. Cobbett and R. Cohen, eds., *Popular Struggles in South Africa* (London: James Currey, 1988); A. Fine and E. Webster, "Transcending Traditions: Trade Unions and Political Unity," *South African Review* 5 (Johannesburg: Raven Press, 1989), pp. 256–74.
26. *FOSATU Worker News* 35/36 (1985).

27. *Sunday Star*, 24 October 1985.
28. Andrew Levy and Associates, *Annual Report on Labour Relations in South Africa, 1990–91*, pp. 54–8.
29. L. Schlemmer, "The Sanctions Survey: In Search of Ordinary Black Opinion," *Indicator SA* 4 (1986); L. Schlemmer, "Disinvestment and Black Worker Attitudes in South Africa," *Review of African Political Economy* 38 (1987).
30. Hanlon and Omond, *Sanctions Handbook*, pp. 48–9; M. Orkin, "Politics, Social Change, and Black Attitudes to Sanctions," in Orkin, ed., *Sanctions Against Apartheid*; M. Orkin, *Disinvestment, the Struggle, and the Future: What Black South Africans Really Think* (Johannesburg: Ravan, 1986); and R. Bloom, *Black South Africa and the Disinvestment Dilemma* (Johannesburg: Jonathan Ball, 1986), pp. 58–74. See also D. Hirschmann, "The Impact of Sanctions and Disinvestment on Black South African Attitudes Toward the United States," in Edgar, ed., *Sanctioning Apartheid*.
31. Orkin, *Disinvestment*.
32. Ibid., Also see Orkin, "Politics," where he discusses another confirming survey conducted in 1987.
33. J. Seekings, "Origin of Political Mobilization in the PWV Townships, 1980–84," and M. Swilling, "The United Democratic Front and Township Revolt," both in Cobbett and Cohen, eds., *Popular Struggles*; T. Lodge and B. Nasson, *All, Here, and Now: Black Politics in South Africa in the 1980s* (Cape Town: David Philip, 1991).
34. SACTU, "The Case for Sanctions," p. 2.
35. See especially B. Rogers and B. Bolton, *Sanctions against South Africa: Exploding the Myths* (Manchester: Manchester Free Press, 1981).
36. See A. Erwin, "Why COSATU Has Supported Sanctions," and H. Joffe, "The Policy of South Africa's Trade Unions towards Sanctions and Disinvestment," both in Orkin, ed., *Sanctions Against Apartheid*.
37. "Local Response to Disinvestment: No Simple Equation," *Work in Progress* 37 (June 1985). Also see D. Innes, "A Force for Change? The Great Sanctions Debate," *Work in Progress* 44 (1986).
38. Joffe, "The Policy of South Africa's Trade Unions," p. 59.
39. G. Adler, "Withdrawal Pains: General Motors and Ford Disinvest from South Africa," *South African Review* 5 (1989); G. Adler, "What's Good for General Motors? Black Workers' Response to Disinvestment, October–November 1986," *Journal of Southern African Studies* 15 (1989); G. Jaffe and K. Jochelson, "The Fight to Save Jobs: Union Initiatives on Retrenchment and Unemployment," *South African Review* 3 (1986).
40. D. Innes, "Multinational Companies and Disinvestment," in Orkin, ed., *Sanctions Against Apartheid*, pp. 232–9.
41. J. Baskin, *Striking Back: A History of COSATU* (London: Verso, 1991), pp. 155–7.
42. J. Matiko, "Samcor – Workers Strike against Share Ownership," *South African Labour Bulletin* 13 (1988).
43. R. Rafel, "Chemical Workers – the Struggle over Disinvestment," *South African Labour Bulletin* 14 (1989).

44. District Six is a neighborhood that symbolizes non-racialism and the struggle against forced removals. A. van Heerden, "Trade Union Gains from Sanctions," in Hanlon, ed., *South Africa*. See also E. Webster, "Sanctions against Apartheid," *South African Labour Bulletin* 14 (1990). For a critique of these ameliorative corporate measures, see Mangaliso, "Disinvestment by Multinational Corporations."

Part IV

Social Sanctions

10 Diplomatic Isolation
Audie Klotz

International recognition, through diplomatic ties and membership in international organizations, plays an important part in legitimating a state or its government.[1] Opponents of apartheid thus sought to undermine the South African government by promoting diplomatic sanctions. Beginning as early as the late 1940s, many states broke bilateral ties and suspended Pretoria's membership in multilateral institutions. But the National Party (NP) resisted international calls for reform. By the 1960s, South Africa had become a pariah, left out from the everyday interactions that characterize normal international "citizenship."

Diplomatic isolation had mixed results. These relatively mild social sanctions effectively communicated global opinion, regardless of South African intransigence. Exclusion from international organizations publicized apartheid (in part by forcing each country to develop an explicit policy on the issue) and established the normative framework of individual equality within which the international community judged South African domestic race policy. Even though states and institutions automatically lost some or all of their direct leverage once they broke diplomatic ties, South Africa did face increased costs in pursuing its foreign and domestic policies. As this chapter will demonstrate, diplomatic sanctions curtailed Pretoria's global and regional influence, and undermined the Bantustan component of the apartheid system. Furthermore, recognition of and material support for the anti-apartheid movement set the stage for negotiations with legitimate representatives of the majority of the population.

These communicative and framing functions of diplomatic measures are significant because of normative processes of legitimation and delegitimation which go beyond the traditional state-to-state focus of formal diplomacy. In this case, diplomatic sanctions supported domestic opponents of the regime and undermined the internal social and economic foundations of apartheid. These consequences of isolation confirm the need to assess more than the direct effects of sanctions on a government – global and domestic civil societies are also significant targets.

EXCLUDING THE APARTHEID REGIME

Initially, South Africa's domestic racial policies received international attention because of an escalating dispute with India over
discrimination against Indians within South Africa.[2] At the first
General Assembly session in 1946, India brought the issue to the
attention of the United Nations (UN), which became increasingly
involved in monitoring apartheid throughout the 1950s. Despite this
international scrutiny of its domestic policies, South Africa remained
an active member. Not only did it participate fully in the General
Assembly, it even sent troops to Korea as part of UN operations.[3]

Demands for South Africa's diplomatic isolation gained ground
in the late 1950s and early 1960s, notably after the Sharpeville
massacre in 1960. Following India's lead, newly independent African states called for a wide range of multilateral sanctions; many
of them also implemented bilateral measures. For example, India
broke off trade relations with South Africa and withdrew its High
Commissioner (the equivalent of an ambassador) in 1946. It severed diplomatic ties in 1954.[4] Except for Malawi, all African countries (through Zimbabwean independence in 1980) refused to establish
diplomatic relations.[5] Overall, the number of South African missions abroad hovered between 20 and 30, mostly in Western Europe.[6] While this number remained fairly stable, it represented a
dramatically declining percentage of the total number of independent
states.

Following the same general pattern as in the UN, apartheid also
emerged as a contentious issue in the Commonwealth as India and
African states gained a voice by the 1950s.[7] They adamantly rejected the possibility that South Africa retain its membership in a
multiracial organization while explicitly practicing discrimination at
home. Yet the NP defiantly insisted that its segregation laws apply
even to non-white diplomatic representatives.[8] While Britain and
Australia hesitated to criticize, Canada suggested compromise.
Rejecting even modest reforms as unacceptable interference, South
Africa withdrew in 1961, rather than face continuing controversy.[9]
In effect, opponents expelled the apartheid regime.

Bolstered by their success, in 1962 African and Asian states in
the General Assembly called on all members to implement diplomatic and economic sanctions against South Africa, and created a
Special Committee on Apartheid; South Africa objected to the
abrogation of Chapter 2 (7) of the UN Charter.[10] Critics of apart-

heid then mobilized to implement these voluntary measures while continuing to demand mandatory sanctions through the Security Council. African members also tried to eject South Africa from a broad range of international, continental, and regional functional organizations. In settings where rules or constitutions precluded a simple majority vote on the membership issue, activist states used alternative tactics, such as walking out of meetings and denying visas to South African representatives (for meetings in African countries).[11]

Opponents quickly excluded South Africa from numerous groups. For example, the Economic Commission for Africa (a regional off-shoot of the UN Economic and Social Committee) initially included South Africa at its founding in 1958, but by 1963 Pretoria no longer attended meetings. Also in that year, the International Labour Organization ceased inviting South Africa to its meetings. Protests produced comparable results in the World Health Organization, the Food and Agriculture Organization, and other UN affiliates. The Organization of African Unity (OAU), founded in 1963, omit-ted South Africa from membership. The NP responded passively to these African initiatives.[12]

South Africa thus found itself unwelcome in many international organizations – but not all. The most notable exception was the International Atomic Energy Agency, whose members stressed the importance of inspecting South African nuclear sites.[13] Some others, including the World Bank and International Monetary Fund, con-sidered political factors, such as apartheid, to be irrelevant to their economic decisions. And at the UN, where only the Security Council could decide membership issues, the United States (US), Britain, and France consistently blocked formal expulsion by defending the principle of universal membership. Only in 1974 did African states succeed in suspending South Africa from the General Assembly by rejecting its diplomatic credentials.[14]

Momentum for diplomatic isolation flagged by 1965 as activists reached a stalemate in any organizations that still included South Africa. Sanctions advocates shifted their focus to mandatory econ-omic measures through the Security Council and educational ef-forts to raise awareness about racial discrimination in southern Africa. In addition, after 11 November 1965, world attention shifted to mandatory sanctions against Rhodesia's Unilateral Declaration of Independence. Only in the mid-1970s did another spate of countries, primarily in Latin America, withdraw recognition of South Africa.[15]

Although diplomatic pressures did not eliminate white minority rule in southern Africa, isolation did inflict some direct costs on the South African government. Such social sanctions generally are difficult to measure in monetary terms, but the expenses of UN dues and a New York office indicate that South Africa did place a value on diplomatic activity. In the early 1970s, for example, the Department of Foreign Affairs allocated over six percent of its budget to UN activities.[16] In addition, the political and economic costs resulting from the "Muldergate" scandal, which ultimately brought down the Vorster government, demonstrate the importance some NP members placed on international propaganda in defense of apartheid.[17]

Both instrumental and symbolic reasons justify such expenses. For example, participation in everyday international relations provides states with access to information and informal bargaining opportunities; maintaining a UN mission enables pursuit of numerous issues at one location. UN diplomacy, debates, and policies also still directly affected South African interests, especially its control over Namibia. A presence in New York (and to a lesser extent London and Washington) gave Pretoria access to a wide array of diplomats, foreign ministers and heads of state, many of whom did not maintain formal ties with the apartheid government.[18] Such unofficial meetings are standard diplomatic practice.[19] Thus, even after actively considering renouncing its membership in the early 1960s, South Africa remained. Domestic (white) public opinion, furthermore, would have supported withdrawal (as it did withdrawal from the Commonwealth), indicating that the decision to remain served international purposes rather than electoral posturing.[20]

The NP also recognized that the UN confers legitimacy. Pretoria's continued formal membership, for example, made it more difficult for the liberation movements to gain recognition (as will be discussed below). The apartheid government also used access to the UN to keep track of the activities of its opponents and took advantage of access to international media to disseminate its views.[21] Countering the education campaign of the UN Center against Apartheid became a focus for South African foreign policy (with the Department of Information even briefly incorporated into Foreign Affairs after the Muldergate scandal). Thus maintaining a representative to the UN offered South Africa many opportunities to combat the negative consequences of its pariah status.

Exclusion from international organizations also leads to missed opportunities for cooperation in various issues, from scientific research to development aid. The proliferation of international institutions, and scholarly literature analyzing them, reinforces the conclusion that states would not participate in multilateral organizations if they did not perceive gains from cooperation.[22] Many opportunity costs, however, are difficult to measure since they involve assessing counterfactual scenarios: cooperation that never happened, development loans that were never contemplated, influence that never expanded. Pretoria's persistent interest in continental and regional African institutions as avenues for leadership and influence indicates that it placed value on diplomacy.

In the 1950s, for example, South Africa participated in groups such as the Commission for Technical Cooperation South of the Sahara (the precursor of the Economic Commission for Africa).[23] Pretoria also promoted the idea of a regional common market as early as the 1960s and consistently sought to integrate surrounding states, especially Botswana, Lesotho, and Swaziland, into its economic sphere (they were already members of the Southern African Customs Union, established in 1909). By the late 1960s, Pretoria tried to compensate for its growing isolation by seeking conservative African allies such as Ivory Coast and Malawi, and establishing alternative regional groups (in contrast to its initial retreat in response to international criticism).[24] Furthermore, in the late 1970s, South Africa promoted a "Constellation of Southern Africa States" as a counter to the anti-apartheid Southern African Development Coordination Conference; "destabilization" of neighboring countries punished those who persisted in rejecting dependence on South Africa.[25] Given the high level of attention paid to these various initiatives, Pretoria clearly perceived benefits from regional leadership, and surveys of elite opinion in the mid-1980s confirm preference for an Africa-oriented foreign policy.[26] Exclusion thus inflicted material and psychological costs for maintaining apartheid.

Overall, formal diplomatic isolation had mixed results. In the 1950s and 1960s, the costs of diplomatic sanctions were not strong enough incentives to induce the government to reform apartheid. Most state-to-state relations could continue in bilateral or informal settings, albeit at greater inconvenience. South Africa adapted to an increasingly hostile international environment, but its leaders did not fundamentally change their racial views. Especially given the NP's isolationist orientation, diplomatic sanctions remained a relatively weak direct bargaining tool, in part because the UN,

Commonwealth, and OAU lacked normative authority in Pretoria's eyes.[27] Nonetheless, by the 1970s and 1980s, the regime increasingly responded to the opportunity costs of lost influence and economic gains in regional and continental settings.

Such costs, however, had double-edged effects on electoral and bureaucratic politics. For example, South Africa's withdrawal from the Commonwealth in 1961 demonstrated that diplomatic isolation can have unintended negative domestic consequences: a majority of white voters, including those with British ties, supported the traditionally isolationist NP.[28] In the ensuing 25 years, perceptions of international hostility increased, peaking during the "total onslaught" era of the late 1970s and 1980s. Divisions between bureaucrats and politicians increased, with the latter proving more aware of, and sensitive to, the country's isolation.[29] Diplomatic sanctions were one among many causes of these counterproductive perceptions.

REJECTING THE HOMELANDS

Although apartheid is frequently viewed as an ideology evolving out of the isolationist and racist views of (presumably parochial) Afrikaners, in practice international norms played a crucial role in the content of South Africa's segregationist schemes. In particular, its development of "Bantustans" (or "homelands") for disenfranchised blacks paralleled decolonization in the rest of Africa. NP policy moved toward a "national" basis for African representation as Hendrik Verwoerd rose from Minister of Native Affairs to Prime Minister in 1958. The Bantu Self-Government Act of 1959 designated eight territorial units for different tribal nations. Initially, Verwoerd did not foresee these homelands becoming states or even self-governing, but in April 1961, after the Sharpeville killings and increasing international pressure, he announced the ultimate goal of their independence. Generally known for being defiant in the face of critics, he even acknowledged that independence was an attempt to placate foreign pressure.[30]

Apartheid strategists sought recognition for the Bantustans based on international norms of self-determination and sovereignty.[31] Their vision of increased autonomy for Africans paralleled conservative thinking on decolonization, which emphasized very gradual increases in self-government, with prerequisites that would take a generation or more to achieve. Yet independence for Botswana and Lesotho

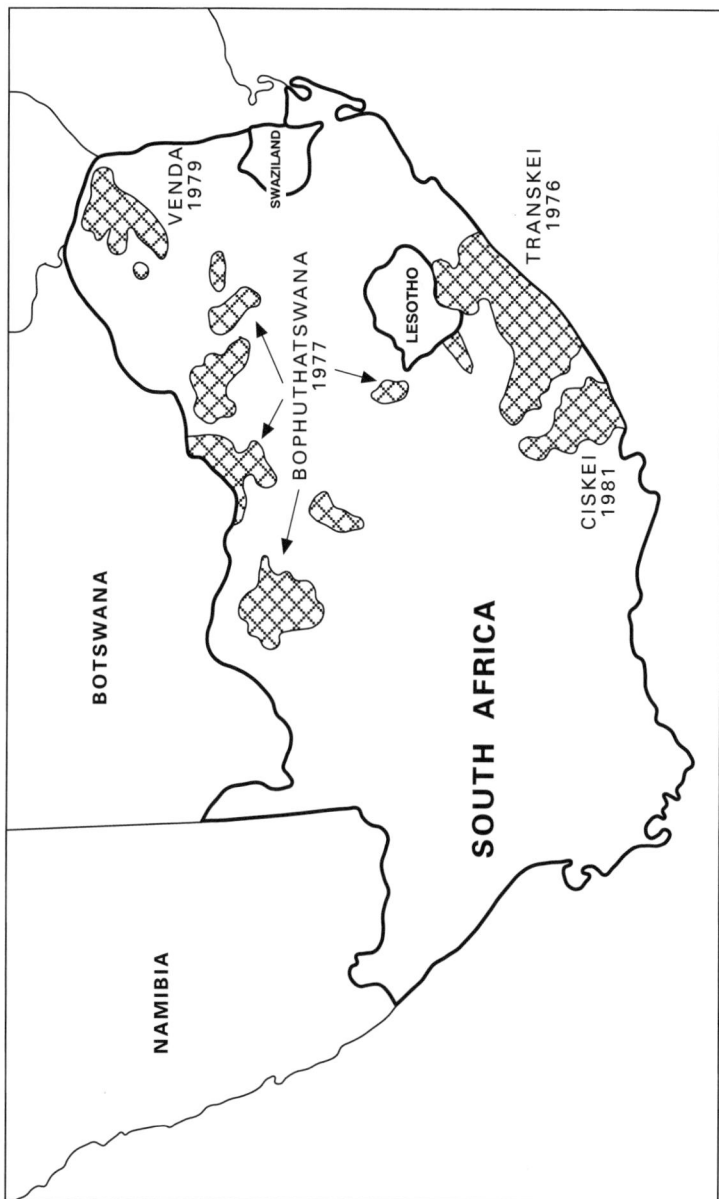

Map 3 "Independent" Homelands

in 1966, and Swaziland in 1968, undermined South Africa's scheme to incorporate these territories (and Namibia) into the apartheid framework.[32] Bantustans did not have the authoritative basis for claiming independence, but that alone would not be enough for denying their legitimacy, since numerous states (especially Botswana, Lesotho, and Swaziland) lacked the political control or economic resources of "classic" states.[33] As decolonization sped through the rest of the continent, South Africa increasingly envisioned faster and more complete autonomy for the homelands.

In principle, independent Bantustans could defuse pressures for non-white political participation, since Africans would exercise citizenship rights, including voting privileges. Setting the precedent for "decolonization," the Transkei declared independence in 1976, cloaked in all the rhetoric of self-determination, including domestic African nationalists claiming to have liberated their territory.[34] Yet it met systematic rejection from the UN and its members, as did the other nominally independent homelands of Bophuthatswana (1977), Venda (1979), and Ciskei (1981). Even South Africa's most steadfast allies refused to accept a scheme that so blatantly furthered the aims of apartheid.[35]

South Africa persisted in creating the trappings of sovereignty, including the creation of parallel governing institutions in these territories. The Transkei, for example, created a "Department of Foreign Affairs and Information" and set up offices in the US, Britain, Denmark, Switzerland, and Zimbabwe.[36] But because South Africa withheld many authoritative functions, independence did not offer control over resources or a real transfer of power.[37] Notably, these faux-states lacked taxing jurisdiction over a range of economic activities, especially white businesses and mines, or the incomes of absentee populations.[38] Defense and police forces remained heavily dependent on South African officers, training and supplies.[39]

The Bantustans became an expensive proposition. In essence, South Africa maintained duplicate bureaucracies, which manufactured costly inefficiencies that contributed to the ideological and institutional crisis of the apartheid state in the 1980s.[40] South Africa needed to give "development aid" if it hoped to keep Africans in these rural reserves; without international recognition, the Bantustans were ineligible for multilateral assistance and had trouble getting foreign investments. Approximately 80 percent of the homelands' budgets came from South Africa, through a combination of a statutory annual payment and yearly parliamentary allocations. In 1975–76, for example, the total statutory outlay of R163.5 million and parliamentary supplement of R86.5 million vastly overshadowed the homelands' direct revenues from taxes, merely R64.6 million.[41] Pretoria also created regional institutions incorporating these faux-states to bolster the appearance of their legitimacy.[42] The South African government justified these expenses as necessary for internal security and alleviation of migration into the cities.[43]

These expenditures failed to forestall political difficulties. Even some of the independent homelands became increasingly sympathetic to the anti-apartheid movement (for various reasons), and some leaders in non-independent homelands used their relative autonomy to challenge the apartheid regime as well. While South Africa had sought to externalize race relations by creating independent Bantustans, in practice this policy increased black opposition on many fronts. Opponents of apartheid insisted on universal suffrage within a unitary state.

In sum, diplomatic sanctions subverted apartheid by rejecting the Bantustan system. Universal lack of recognition undermined the state ideologically and financially. International opponents vociferously attacked these faux-states, and internal devolution of partial authority created new decentralized bases for resistance to apartheid. International non-recognition thus prevented the dismemberment of the country into separate racially based states and foreclosed the possibility of a political dispensation that excluded external and imprisoned opponents of apartheid. The homelands were an expensive and failed proposition that contributed to the crisis which prompted NP reforms in the late 1980s.

RECOGNIZING THE ANTI-APARTHEID MOVEMENT

Diplomatic sanctions also had a substantive effect on the reform process by bolstering the anti-apartheid movement. When the South African government cracked down on its domestic opponents, international organizations and states offered the African National Congress (ANC) and Pan-African Congress (PAC) recognition and resources – the corollary policy to isolating Pretoria. Some created homes for exiled activists, while others tendered diplomatic and financial support. The UN also established publicity and research facilities to disseminate information about apartheid. These measures substantially increased the global strength of the anti-apartheid movement, culminating in the ANC's standing as a government-in-exile and internationally recognized representative of the South African majority, the group with whom the South African government would ultimately negotiate.[44]

This process of international legitimation began in the late 1950s when the South African government cracked down on domestic opposition; it became essential after the both the ANC and PAC were banned and most of their leaders imprisoned in the early 1960s. External financial aid and training for guerrilla action came primarily from African countries, Nordic states, China, and the Soviets.[45] ANC exiles built the organization's external base in London and later in Lusaka, Zambia. Meanwhile, the PAC established its headquarters in Maseru and opened other offices in Africa.[46] Transnational solidarity groups also spread. The two factions increasingly fought between themselves over recognition and finances.

In 1963, the OAU established its Liberation Support Committee, through which it channeled aid to various African groups, including the ANC and PAC. Indeed, financial control led the Committee to arbitrate the legitimacy of contending liberation movements. In the South African case, it recognized both the ANC and PAC.[47] In practice, African financial contributions remained limited, but diplomatic recognition proved crucial.[48] As this "Africa Group" became the core of UN activism on the apartheid issue, the General Assembly followed the OAU's lead.

The UN Special Committee against Apartheid became the centerpiece of the General Assembly's overall campaign for sanctions, publicity about apartheid, education of world opinion, and aid to the victims of apartheid. Originally, the Committee reviewed and reported on apartheid. As its mandate expanded in subsequent years, so too did its budget, from approximately $14 000 in 1969 to over $2 million by 1984.[49] In essence, the Committee promoted the campaign against apartheid for the UN, following the comprehensive program of action proposed in 1966, which advocated sanctions and the general support of the anti-apartheid movement in consultation with the OAU.

The General Assembly authorized the Committee to consult with specialized agencies, regional organizations, states and nongovernmental organizations, especially to target Western countries that resisted sanctions.[50] Thus the Committee worked directly with anti-apartheid movements, especially in Britain and the US, in order to raise consciousness. But anti-apartheid activists could not use UN funds directly. Rather, the Trust Fund for South Africa, established in 1965, functioned as a central locus for donations from governments, organizations and individuals. By 1988, contributions totaled $31 million.[51] After the Soweto uprising in 1976, which increased the number of South African exiles, the UN provided humanitarian assistance, including education, legal aid, and refugee assistance. By 1985, the budget for the Education and Training Program for Southern Africa totaled $2.7 million.[52]

In 1973 the General Assembly formally recognized the liberation movements as "the authentic representatives of the overwhelming majority of the South African people."[53] Direct UN support started in 1974 (the same year it rejected the credentials of the South African government), through various subsidiary organizations.[54] The Committee was also authorized, in consultation with the OAU, to include the liberation movements in its work. The General Assembly also invited them to attend meetings about apartheid.[55] In 1979, the UN budget provided grants to the liberation movements to maintain offices in New York; the annual expenditure mounted to $250 000 per year.[56]

Numerous other factors determined the outcome of the rivalry between the ANC and PAC, not least of which was their relative abilities in reestablishing ties to the resurgent domestic opposition in the mid-1980s. International support treated these two groups relatively equally, but the lack of international recognition for other domestic contenders, notably Inkatha, underlines the importance of OAU and UN recognition. International diplomatic support was one resource which helped to determine the ANC's standing as the NP's primary negotiating partner. By the late 1980s, it had official representation in more capitals than the South African government.[57] Even South African business leaders recognized its standing by initiating a "trek to Lusaka" for consultations.[58]

Thus throughout its years in exile, the ANC gained legitimacy and logistical support through the OAU and UN, without which it probably would not have survived. International recognition reinforced pressures on the shunned South African government to negotiate with legitimate representatives of the majority of the South African people.

CONCLUSION

South Africa's experiences with diplomatic sanctions offer insights into how international recognition works. One important lesson is the limitation of a rational actor, economic cost-benefit, perspective. Many of the consequences of international isolation are not readily measurable in economic (or material) terms. Another conceptual lesson is the need to disaggregate the target beyond the state. Examining solely state-to-state relations, in this case the formal withdrawal of membership rights in a range of international organizations, would obscure the additional effects on the anti-apartheid movement. Diplomatic pressures can operate transnationally by circumventing the state to support the domestic opposition.

To some extent, especially in the early years of international protest, diplomatic sanctions fostered white South Africans' sense of outside hostility and thus perhaps reinforced isolationist tendencies and group solidarity, as described in the classic "rally round the flag" argument. The politics of (il)legitimacy, therefore, tie into perceptions of threat. The Afrikaner leaders' view that apartheid furthered their national survival clouded an "objective" analysis of costs and benefits. But this solidarity effect also should not be viewed out of context. Although sanctions galvanized white support for the South African government, the extra-parliamentary opposition garnered moral and material resources in their struggle to overthrow apartheid. International diplomatic support enabled the anti-apartheid opposition to survive decades of banning, imprisonment, and exile. International organizations offered exiled groups legitimacy and resources which contributed to the negotiated transition to non-racial democracy.

The symbolic politics of legitimacy also had material consequences for the apartheid regime, which consequently expended resources attempting to gain recognition for "independent" homelands. Despite limitations on direct leverage over the apartheid regime, diplomatic sanctions succeeded in subverting the ideological coherence of apartheid by undermining the Bantustan system. The failure of the homeland scheme, especially the inevitable migration of Africans out of these barren areas, contributed substantially to the crisis of the 1980s that convinced National Party leaders of the need for dramatic reforms. As the normative context changed, Afrikaner leaders responded to new opportunities to justify their segregationist policies, ultimately reaching a point of ideological bankruptcy.

Isolating the South African government thus contributed significantly to a negotiated transition to a political system based on universal suffrage in a unitary state. The international community marked its acceptance of the new non-racial democratic government by lifting diplomatic sanctions following Nelson Mandela's election in April 1994. South Africa resumed participation in the UN, rejoined the Commonwealth, and initiated OAU membership, in addition to (re)establishing bilateral ties with numerous states. The power of diplomatic isolation, in other words, resides in the normative foundations of the international system.

Although diplomatic sanctions against South Africa offered little direct bargaining leverage against South African leaders, this type of measure should be more effective against states which are more sensitive to international judgment and place a higher value on international participation. Once our analyses move beyond material and rationalist assumptions, these dynamics will be better understood. Diplomatic isolation may not be the strongest tool of direct international leverage, but its efficacy should be taken seriously. Because international norms establish the context for bargaining, their enforcement through diplomatic isolation establishes the "rules of the game" within which actors then negotiate. Such framing and communicative functions are evident even in the South African transition, an unlikely case for international pressure to succeed, given the country's avowed isolationism.

Notes

Thanks to Neta Crawford and Kim Nossal for detailed comments.

1. I. L. Claude, Jr., "Collective Legitimation as a Political Function of the United Nations," *International Organization* 20 (1966), pp. 367–79. Claude stresses that this process of legitimation is fundamentally political, rather than legal or moral.
2. See A. Klotz, *Norms in International Relations: The Struggle against Apartheid* (Ithaca, NY: Cornell University Press, 1995), ch. 3.
3. J. Barratt, "South African Diplomacy at the UN," in G. R. Berridge and A. Jennings, eds., *Diplomacy at the UN* (New York: St. Martin's, 1985), p. 195; E. Louw, *The Case for South Africa*, ed. H. H. H. Biermann (New York: Macfadden, 1963), p. 13.
4. L. L. Mehrotra, "India's Response," in *India and South Africa: A Fresh Start*, ed., A. B. Sawant (Delhi: Kalinga, 1994), p. 28.
5. Sanctioning South Africa presented more difficulties for countries in

the region than for those which had few ties to South Africa. See G. M. Khadiagala, "Regional Dimensions of Sanctions," in this volume, and Klotz, *Norms in International Relations*, chs. 5 and 8. These states did not need to implement bilateral sanctions, however, in order to be effective advocates of sanctions in multilateral settings.

6. D. Geldenhuys, *Isolated States: A Comparative Perspective* (Cambridge: Cambridge University Press, 1990), p. 159.

7. See Klotz, *Norms in International Relations*, ch. 4.

8. J. Barber and J. Barratt, *South Africa's Foreign Policy: The Search for Status and Security* (Cambridge: Cambridge University Press, 1990), p. 79.

9. See J. D. B. Miller, "South Africa's Departure," *Journal of Commonwealth Political Studies* 1 (1961), pp. 56–74.

10. Resolution 1761 (XVII), 6 November 1962, passed 67–16–23, with Britain, the US, Japan, France, Canada and Australia (among others) voting against; similar drafts had been defeated before. South Africa consistently asserted its right of domestic jurisdiction in the face of international criticism; see Louw, *The Case for South Africa*, esp. pp. 133–52.

11. For numerous examples, see R. E. Bissell, *Apartheid and International Organizations* (Boulder, CO: Westview, 1977). Countries also increasingly denied visas to ordinary South African passport holders, which may have raised white awareness of international condemnation.

12. Ibid., pp. 51–64, 80–94. See also J. Dugard, "Sanctions against South Africa: An International Law Perspective," in M. Orkin, ed., *Sanctions against Apartheid* (Cape Town: David Philip, 1989), p. 119. In most of these cases, South Africa either withdrew or organizational rules allowed suspension; rarely was it formally expelled.

13. South Africa did, nonetheless, eventually lose its seat (as African representative) on the governing board. See Bissell, *Apartheid*, p. 92, and D. Fig, "Sanctions and the Nuclear Industry," in this volume.

14. Resolution 3411 (XXX). See N. Stultz, "The Evolution of the United Nations Anti-Apartheid Regime," *Human Rights Quarterly* 13 (1991), pp. 10–11. The legality of this move was widely contested; see Dugard, "Sanctions," pp. 119–20; and A. Abbott, F. Augusti, P. Brown, and E. Rode, "The General Assembly, 29th Session: The Decredentialization of South Africa," *Harvard International Law Journal* 16 (1975), pp. 576–88.

15. Geldenhuys, *Isolated States*, p. 183.

16. By the late 1970s, South Africa spent negligible amounts. See Republic of South Africa, *Report of the Controller and Auditor-General* (Pretoria: Government Printer, annual), and Barratt, "South African Diplomacy," p. 196.

17. Among their misdeeds, high-ranking officials used government funds to control foreign newspapers, in an attempt to create a more favorable image of South Africa in powerful Western countries. See P. O'Meara, "South Africa's Watergate: The Muldergate Scandals" (Hanover, NH: American Universities Field Staff, 1979), and M. Rees and C. Day, *Muldergate: The Story of the Info Scandal* (Johannesburg: Macmillan,

1980). In more routine uses of the media, Radio South Africa broadcast a favorable view of the regime to Europe and North America, as well as Africa. See D. R. Browne, "Something New Out of Africa? South African International Radio's Presentation of Africa to Listeners in North America," *Journal of African Studies* (1987), pp. 17–24.

18. Thus diplomatic sanctions by Western countries would have been more costly because they could forestall covert diplomacy in their capitals. I thank Margaret Doxey for this point.

19. Even diplomatic visits by states that did retain formal ties decreased (Geldenhuys, *Isolated States*, pp. 226–34), further enhancing the utility of the UN mission. The extent of these secret meetings is impossible to know. See Barratt, "South African Diplomacy," pp. 200–1; G. R. Berridge, *Talking to the Enemy: How States without 'Diplomatic Relations' Communicate* (London: St. Martin's, 1994).

20. Barratt, "South African Diplomacy," pp. 197–8.

21. Ibid., pp. 198–9.

22. For a literature overview, see D. A. Baldwin, ed., *Neorealism and Neoliberalism: The Contemporary Debate* (New York: Columbia University Press, 1993).

23. D. Geldenhuys and D. Venter, "Regional Cooperation in Southern Africa: A Constellation of States?" *International Affairs Bulletin* 3 (1979), pp. 43–5; Geldenhuys, *Isolated States*, pp. 433–5.

24. Various interests underpinned this policy, including economic gains from trade and access to strategic resources; see, for example, J. Brooke, "Pretoria Lends Helping Hand to Friends With Big Airstrips," *New York Times*, 21 October 1987. South Africa also hoped to split the cohesion of the African anti-apartheid movement based in the OAU, but advocates of "dialogue" were defeated by sanctions proponents who insisted that the apartheid government needed to negotiate with internal representatives of the majority; see Barber and Barratt, *South Africa's Foreign Policy*, pp. 143–50.

25. Ibid., pp. 130–5, 259–63; Geldenhuys and Venter, "Regional Cooperation," pp. 45–51; G. M. Khadiagala, *Allies in Adversity: The Frontline States in Southern Africa Security, 1975–1993* (Athens: Ohio University Press, 1994), esp. ch. 7.

26. Alienation from the West also increased. See K. van Wyk, "Foreign Policy Orientations of the P. W. Botha Regime: Changing Perceptions of State Elites in South Africa," *Journal of Contemporary African Studies* 10 (1991), pp. 45–65, esp. pp. 51–2, 55.

27. On views of these international groups, see G. Erasmus, "White South Africans and the United Nations," *International Affairs Bulletin* 9 (1985), pp. 26–40, and K. van Wyk, "Some Elite Perceptions and South Africa's Bilateral Relations: A Comparison of Two Surveys," *Politikon* 16 (1989), pp. 75–85.

28. The (whites-only) referendum in favor of republic status passed by 74.6 percent (with a 90.7 percent turnout), indicating broad-based support even among the English-speaking population; Miller, "South Africa's Departure," 58.

29. For elite opinion surveys, see K. Manzo and P. McGowan, "Afrikaner

Fears and the Politics of Despair: Understanding Change in South Africa," *International Studies Quarterly* 36 (1992), pp. 1–24; K. van Wyk, "State Elites and South Africa's International Isolation: A Longitudinal Comparison of Perception," *Politikon* 15 (1988), pp. 63–89, esp. 69–71; and van Wyk, "Some Elite Perceptions," esp. 78–9.

30. J. Butler, R. I. Rotberg, and J. Adams, *The Black Homelands of South Africa: The Political and Economic Development of Bophuthatswana and KwaZulu* (Berkeley: University of California Press, 1977), p. 31; D. Geldenhuys, *The Diplomacy of Isolation: South African Foreign Policy Making* (New York: St. Martin's, 1984), p. 24.

31. On the normative basis of sovereignty and decolonization, see R. H. Jackson, *Quasi-States: Sovereignty, International Relations and the Third World* (New York: Cambridge University Press, 1990).

32. For an overview of the different perspectives on decolonization, see ibid., ch. 4. At this time, South Africa was coming under ever-increasing criticism for its refusal to grant independence to Namibia. It sought, therefore, to create a scheme that would justify and serve as a model for Namibian incorporation; see R. Southall, *South Africa's Transkei: The Political Economy of an "Independent" Bantustan* (New York: Monthly Review, 1983), p. 49; N. Stultz, *Transkei's Half Loaf: Racial Separatism in South Africa* (New Haven: Yale University Press, 1979), pp. 137–44.

33. Verwoerd emphasized the similarities between the homelands and these newly independent neighbors; Barber and Barratt, *South Africa's Foreign Policy*, p. 128.

34. Southall, *South Africa's Transkei*, esp. pp. 49, 249.

35. For example, General Assembly Res/31/6A, 26 October 1976.

36. Southall, *South Africa's Transkei*, p. 251. While the department's annual budget was less than 0.5 percent of the homeland's total expenditures, this represents one measure of the cost of replicating diplomatic functions. The Department of Defence received approximately 3 percent (during the 1980s). Figures based on Government of Transkei, *Estimate of Expenditure*, annual.

37. Butler et al., *Black Homelands*, p. 222. However, some carved out greater autonomy than others.

38. Ibid., p. 145.

39. G. Wood and G. Mills, "The Present and Future Role of the Transkei Defence Force in a Changing South Africa," *Journal of Contemporary African Studies* 11 (1992), pp. 255–69.

40. S. Greenberg, *Legitimating the Illegitimate: State, Markets and Resistance in South Africa* (Berkeley: University of California Press, 1987). Greenberg focuses primarily on the labor control aspects of the Bantustan policy. Also see H. Giliomee, "Democratization in South Africa," *Political Science Quarterly* 110 (1995), p. 90. For a more quantitative assessment of the costs, see the budget allocations (such as the Department of Foreign Affairs' "Development Cooperation Branch") in the *Report of the Controller and Auditor-General*; also Geldenhuys, *Isolated States*, pp. 435–6.

41. Based on figures from the Department of Bantu Administration, com-

piled in T. Malan and P. S. Hattingh, *Black Homelands in South Africa* (Pretoria: Africa Institute, 1976), p. 93. In defense of the homelands policy, Malan and Hattingh emphasize that South Africa's outlay to the homelands, approximately 2.4 percent of its GNP, far exceeded typical levels of international aid donations (p. 91). (Note that these figures pre-date "independence" and therefore do not include defense appropriations or expenditures.)

42. See Geldenhuys, *Isolated States*, p. 185.
43. Butler et al., *Black Homelands*, p. 145.
44. I use the term "government in exile" loosely, since the liberation movements were not formally recognized as such. They did, however, aspire to overthrow a regime based on claims of authenticity; see Y. Shain, "Introduction: Governments-in-Exile and the Age of Democratic Transitions," in Y. Shain, ed., *Governments-in-Exile in Contemporary World Politics* (New York: Routledge, 1991), pp. 2–3.
45. T. Lodge, *Black Politics in South Africa since 1945* (London: Longman, 1983), pp. 297–8. For the most comprehensive survey of the ANC's years in exile, see S. Thomas, *The Diplomacy of Liberation: The Foreign Relations of the ANC since 1960* (London: I. B. Tauris, 1996).
46. Rivalries within the PAC undermined its effectiveness; infighting over control of money exacerbated other divisions. See Lodge, *Black Politics*, pp. 306–7.
47. Initially, support proved difficult for the ANC to garner because pan-Africanists viewed it with skepticism; see N. Mandela, *Long Walk to Freedom* (New York: Little Brown, 1994), ch. 6. Thus the PAC began the exile period with more credibility in Africa.
48. In 1967, for example, only about $4000 of generous pledges actually materialized; S. Johns, "Obstacles to Guerrilla Warfare: A South African Case Study," *Journal of Modern African Studies* 11 (1973), p. 274, cited in Lodge, *Black Politics*, p. 300, and Thomas, *Diplomacy of Liberation*, p. 90. Shain also emphasizes the distinction between operational aid and legitimacy, and observes that most movements are primarily concerned with legitimacy; Y. Shain, "Governments-in-Exile and International Legitimation," in Shain, ed., *Governments-in-Exile*, pp. 220–1.
49. Figures based on UN budget estimates, as compiled by Stultz, "Evolution," pp. 10–11.
50. United Nations, Department of Public Information, *The United Nations and Apartheid 1948–1994* (New York: United Nations, 1994), pp. 43–5.
51. Stultz, "Evolution," p. 15; UN, *United Nations and Apartheid*, pp. 80–4.
52. Stultz, "Evolution," p. 16. UN activities also included support for Namibian independence. Because the Namibian issue involved additional questions of its legal status as a former League of Nations Mandate territory, I do not include it with my discussion of the South African liberation movements. For an overview of the Namibia question, see R. Dreyer, *Namibia and Southern Africa: Regional Dynamics of Decolonization* (London: Kegan Paul International, 1994).
53. UN, *United Nations and Apartheid*, p. 30.
54. Ibid., pp. 42–3; Bissell, *Apartheid*, pp. 156–8.

55. UN, *United Nations and Apartheid*, pp. 47–8.
56. Stultz, "Evolution," 16.
57. Geldenhuys, *Isolated States*, p. 234.
58. Declining international support following the demise of its eastern bloc supporters in 1989 and its unbanning in 1990 weakened the ANC. Debates persist over the extent to which the end of the Cold War facilitated the transition, particularly the NP's perceptions. See A. Guelke, "The Impact of the End of the Cold War on the South African Transition," *Journal of Contemporary African Studies* 14 (1996), pp. 87–100, as well as Klotz, *Norms in International Relations*, ch. 9.

11 "Not Cricket": The Effects and Effectiveness of the Sport Boycott
David R. Black

Sport is a relatively neglected sphere among students of political science and international relations. In South Africa, however, its political salience has long been apparent, as it became a lightning rod for opponents of apartheid.[1] Several distinctive features made sport a locus of pressure for change. As Rob Nixon observes, modern international sport has a striking capacity to inspire national passions and identities, and thus to facilitate popular mobilization.[2] Hence, the campaign to isolate "apartheid sport" elicited a very high level of national and international passion and participation.

Paradoxically, the assumption prevalent in the West that sport is trivial compared to economic and security affairs – indeed, that sport offers an escape from these preoccupations – enabled groups which recognized its political potential to pursue their agenda relatively free from powerful opposition. Thus, a loose coalition of newly independent African states, South African exiles and anti-apartheid activists in the West precipitated a process of steadily mounting isolation culminating, in the 1980s, in a degree of ostracism unparalleled in the history of modern sport.

If measured in terms of the extent of the country's isolation, the sport boycott was the most "effective" of all sanctions against South Africa. Few other areas targeted by the anti-apartheid movement, Bruce Kidd notes, faced "organizational controls on their freedom of movement, [whereas] all athletes, coaches, and officials, especially at the highest levels of performance, are subject to the discipline of powerful monopolistic associations."[3] This "hierarchical governance of modern sport" meant that, in principle, these monopolistic associations could enforce a very high degree of compliance with sanctions. In addition, the high-minded ideology of sport incorporated a "moral claim that sport be free from racial discrimination."[4] Boycott proponents skillfully exploited this source of normative purchase *vis-à-vis* sports associations.

Nevertheless, answers to the larger questions of how the sport boycott contributed to the sanctions campaign as a whole and to the demise of apartheid remain elusive. A number of sober analysts note how difficult it is to distinguish the effects of mounting isolation in sport from other external and internal sources of pressure for change, and are modest in their estimation of its influence.[5] This chapter aims to be more precise and expansive in its assessment.

One cannot properly understand either the political process of mounting international pressure or the reasons why it "worked" without incorporating the role of sport sanctions. Although other factors had more immediate and direct roles in dismantling apartheid, the campaign around sport contributed significantly to the larger process of change in three principal ways: as a potent form of *punishment* of white South Africans for their racialist political and social practices; as a *delegitimizing* influence on the hegemony of the white state, which corroded white morale and sensitized the white body politic to other forms of pressure; and as a *precedent* both for additional sanctions and for the country's rehabilitation. Following a brief review of the key moments in the rise of the sport boycott, I discuss the impact of sport sanctions in terms of these three mechanisms. Finally, I draw out some of the most salient lessons of this experience for other sanctions campaigns.

THE ROAD TO ISOLATION AND BACK

With a favorable climate and a lifestyle which created ample opportunity for recreation, white South Africans developed a culture in which sport held great prominence, and international success was highly prized. Recognition of the potential for social and political influence through sport began to crystallize in the minds of anti-apartheid activists in the 1950s. Trevor Huddleston wrote in *Naught for Your Comfort* (1956) that "because the Union [of South Africa] is so good at sport . . . isolation would shake its self-assurance very severely. Fantastic though it may sound, it might be an extraordinarily effective blow to the racialism which has brought it into being."[6] In 1958, anti-apartheid activists formed the South African Sports Association to promote non-racial sports bodies as alternatives to "establishment" (racially constituted) organizations. They then launched the South African Non-Racial Olympic Committee (SANROC) in 1962, with the ultimate aim of displacing the white South African Olympic and National Games Association (SAONGA) as the officially recognized affiliate of the International Olympic Committee (IOC). The emerging South African non-racial sports movement confronted both the predominant white establishment organizations and their subordinate African and "Colored" affiliates.

The South African Government responded by banning SANROC's leading members, including its formidable spokesman, Dennis Brutus. After several years of quiescence, however, the organization reemerged fully operational in London. By 1966, SANROC became a leading force in the transnational campaign to isolate South African sport, retaining that role for the next 25 years. In the early 1970s, the non-racial sports movement regrouped inside South Africa, consolidating under the leadership of the South African Council of Sport (SACOS) from 1973. The third key component of the anti-apartheid sports movement were newly independent African states and their national sporting authorities. Unlike their Western counterparts, African leaders quickly recognized the potential influence of international sports boycotts as a weapon against South Africa's deeply offensive racial order. Their unwavering opposition to any form of intercourse with representatives of white South Africa, supported by allies throughout the Third World and the eastern bloc, drove the international boycott forward. Thus, the general contours of the politics of sport sanctions had emerged: the exiled SANROC at the center of a transnational sport boycott movement, most active in the West; African governments and sports organizations promoting the boycott in international and transnational organizations; and South African non-racial sports organizations challenging establishment bodies at home.

The campaign's first major success was barring South Africa from the 1964 Tokyo Olympics based on SAONGA's failure to comply with the egalitarian principles of the Olympic Charter.[7] In 1966, the same year SANROC became fully operational in exile, the African bloc formed the Supreme Council of Sport in Africa (SCSA). The SCSA quickly emerged as an implacable opponent of apartheid sport. According to Shayne Quick, "the creation of SCSA was the single most important factor in wrestling the initiative over South Africa away from the IOC."[8] It mobilized opposition to the IOC's attempt to reinstate South Africa for the 1968 Mexico Olympic Games by threatening a boycott. The resulting rescission of South Africa's invitation to the Mexico Games and the 1970 expulsion of SAONGA from the Olympic Movement were highly visible blows to white South Africa – an early landmark in mounting international isolation.

In the wake of the IOC's decision, international sports federations associated with the Olympics steadily isolated South Africa from membership and competition.[9] The South African Government, in response, initiated a long process of "reform" whereby it explored formulas aimed at winning reacceptance into international competition while conceding as little as possible of the essence of segregation. Establishment sports bodies, too, undertook organizational and policy changes in pursuit of international rehabilitation.

Yet even as white South Africa sought to put a more enlightened face on its sporting practices, it undermined itself through galling instances of racism. Perhaps the most celebrated of these was the "D'Oliveira Affair." A talented "Colored" cricketer who had left South Africa for England in 1960 to pursue his playing career, Basil D'Oliveira was belatedly chosen for the English side due to tour South Africa in 1968 – not long after the country had been forced out of the Mexico Olympics. His selection precipitated Prime Minister John Vorster's decision to cancel the tour. Adrian Guelke argues that this episode did more than any other to bring about South Africa's isolation in international sport.[10]

Yet sporting isolation was never total.[11] Some of the most resilient gaps in sanctions included individual professional sports. Both tennis and golf were very popular in South Africa but hard to tackle politically because tournaments for individual professional athletes were not beholden to national sporting authorities. The most important gaps, however, were in the team sports of cricket and rugby. These two arenas of South Africa's fiercest and most treasured rivalries became major battlegrounds in the sport sanctions campaign of the 1970s and 1980s.

Key moments in this campaign included the protests which dogged the South African Springbok rugby tour of Britain in late 1969 and the resulting cancellation of the Springbok cricket tour scheduled for 1970.[12] Even larger demonstrations greeted the rugby Springboks in Australia in 1971, again precipitating the cancellation of a cricket tour scheduled for later the same year. The African boycott of the 1976 Olympics was precipitated by the presence of New Zealand, whose rugby All Blacks had just toured South Africa in the midst of the Soweto upheavals. The Montreal boycott significantly widened the sanctions campaign, which henceforth targeted not only South African teams and athletes but also representatives of third countries that maintained links with South Africa. The 1977 Commonwealth Gleneagles Declaration became another key landmark and lever, urging member governments to fight apartheid by "withholding any form of support for, and by taking every practical step to discourage contact or competition by their nationals with sporting organizations, teams or sportsmen from South Africa."[13]

A particularly decisive moment in this escalating campaign was the 1981 Springbok rugby tour of New Zealand, the first in over a decade. The drama of a storied rivalry at the pinnacle of world rugby was heightened by the fact that this was the first New Zealand tour to be televised live in South Africa.[14] Sport and television have a peculiarly powerful affinity. Rob Nixon stresses that as a result, television creates unprecedented opportunities for social movement activism to convert politics into "telegenic theater" because of "its ability to concentrate a vast, anonymous community around an event devised to arouse nationalist passions." In the case of the 1981 tour, dedicated Bok supporters witnessed a New Zealand cleaved by the presence of their beloved team. "At their most intense," Nixon observes, "the confrontations between [anti-apartheid] protesters and police [in New Zealand] assumed apocalyptic dimensions. . . ."[15] South African sports correspondent Dan Retief noted that, "clearly, if an objectionable form of apartheid still exists in South Africa when a Springbok tour is again at issue, the Boks will not be seen in New Zealand, or Britain for that matter."[16]

With the exception of the England rugby tour of 1984, the remainder of the decade saw no further major official (versus "rebel") tours to South Africa and no South African tours abroad. The sport boycott movement concentrated on tightening the *cordon sanitaire* around South African sport through this period, with considerable success.[17] In 1989, the International Cricket Conference completely banned participation by players who had competed in South Africa. The International Tennis Federation, motivated by a desire to achieve full Olympic status, suspended the South African Tennis Union and eliminated South African events from the Grand Prix tennis tour. Within South Africa, the non-racial sports movement achieved its greatest success in 1990 when it transformed a high profile "rebel" cricket tour from England into a major failure.[18]

As the global momentum for sanctions generally ebbed in 1990, lifting the sport siege sparked additional controversy. The first public step toward sporting rehabilitation was taken when South African Rugby Board kingpins Danie Craven and Louis Luyt met with officials of their non-racial rival, the South African Rugby Union, and ANC leaders in Harare.[19] This October 1988 meeting yielded an agreement to establish a single non-racial controlling body for rugby. The ANC agreed to use its good offices to ensure that non-racial South African rugby rejoined world rugby, implying that it would accept South African participation in international sport before the establishment of majority rule.[20] This marked a strategic departure from the SACOS principle of "no normal sport in an abnormal society."

Organizational changes in the non-racial sport movement followed. Within South Africa, a new National Sports Congress (later the National and Olympic Sports Congress), formally launched in July 1989, championed the new strategy. This precipitated a split in the non-racial sport movement, with a minority remaining faithful to the uncompromising SACOS line. Similarly, London-based SANROC split, with the majority supporting Sam Ramsamy and the new National Sports Congress. Thereafter, the process of rehabilitation moved rapidly, nowhere more so than in relation to the Olympic Movement. Following a flurry of study visits, the IOC recognized the National Olympic Committee of South Africa in July 1991, leading to the participation of an integrated team in the 1992 Barcelona Olympics.[21]

South Africa's relations with other international sport governing bodies also improved in some cases, even before readmission to the Olympics. Its cricketers toured India in November 1991 as "less controversial" emergency replacements for Pakistan, and in March 1992 participated in the Cricket World Cup in Australia and New Zealand.[22] In January 1993, it was announced that South Africa would host the 1995 Rugby World Cup, signalling rehabilitation in the most controversial of South African sports.

EFFECTS AND EFFECTIVENESS

Some argue that the ANC and its non-racial allies acted precipitously in compromising on sport, foregoing the opportunity to use it to promote societal "transformation." What is clear is that they opted for the more pragmatic, reformist path of negotiated transition, in sport as elsewhere. However, the question remains: how, and how much, did the highly successful campaign to isolate South African sport add to the overall dynamic of change? Sport, I argue, significantly contributed in three ways: punishment, delegitimation, and precedent.

Punishment

Kim Nossal has argued that a principal purpose of sanctions is to *punish* the target for an act of wrongdoing.[23] Based on this understanding, sport sanctions were particularly effective since much of the white (particularly male) population of South Africa suffered an acute sense of pain and loss on their account. Moreover, those opposed to and oppressed by the apartheid state generally took comfort and encouragement from these measures. Indeed, black South Africans could not be much hurt by the loss of that which they had been largely denied! It is in this sense that sport sanctions had, in the words of Peter Hain, a "phenomenal impact"; according to Helen Suzman, they "really [hurt] South Africans where they feel it."[24] Public opinion poll data support these assessments. For example, according to a study published in 1990 by the Investor Responsibility Research Center, 29 percent of whites considered the impact of the sport boycott to have been "very strong," and a further 45 percent considered it to have been "strong." These totals were marginally higher for Afrikaners versus English-speakers.[25]

In this light, persistent efforts of the National Party to maintain international sporting contacts with traditional friends, while maintaining the essence of apartheid, were presumably motivated at least partly by a desire to prevent pain and unhappiness among its white electorate. Politicians not infrequently attempt to capitalize on international sporting triumphs; conversely, international defeat – let alone denial of the opportunity to play the game – can be a political liability.[26] Thus, the South African Government responded to growing isolation in international sport with a series of reforms.[27] In a 1967 policy reversal, Prime Minister Vorster announced that South Africa would be prepared to host racially mixed touring sides from traditional friends, specifically to accommodate a New Zealand rugby side including Maoris. Even this minimal concession stirred controversy within the National Party, leading directly to the first open split in the Nationalist front marked by the emergence of the *Herstigte Nationale Party* in 1970.

The Vorster government then introduced a new "multinational" sports policy in 1971, which permitted visiting teams to include matches against black South African teams. Black sportsmen were also allowed to participate in "open international" competitions in South Africa so long as they were members of sports bodies affiliated with white federations, that is, not associated with non-racial sports bodies. Integration was still not permitted at provincial or club levels, however. Thus South Africa presented itself to the world as permitting multiracial competition, while preserving apartheid at home.

The sporting world was not persuaded. As a result, "multi-nationalism" was extended down to the club level in 1976, albeit in an incoherent and inconsistent manner. The Government wished simultaneously to adhere to the requirements of racial separation and the promotion of Afrikaner identity at home, while being seen to be moving "intelligently toward a normalization of [race] relations" in the eyes of the international sporting community.[28] Finally, in the late 1970s and the early 1980s, the Government adopted a policy of "autonomy" for sport. It abolished the Department of Sport and Leisure in 1982, replacing it with a Directorate of Sport Advancement within the Department of National Education. It also amended the Group Areas Act, the Liquor Act, and the Black Urban Areas Consolidation Act to exclude sporting events from apartheid restrictions. "In effect," as an Australian Department of Foreign Affairs report put it, "decisions about racial segregation were shifted from the Government to local authorities, private bodies, and individuals."[29]

These modifications nonetheless fundamentally failed to alter the racial balance of opportunities in sport. In the wake of the radicalizing events of 1976, SACOS at home and the sport boycott movement abroad rejected these reforms. They encapsulated their demands in the phrase, "No normal sport in an abnormal society," and called for the continuation of sport sanctions until the dismantling of apartheid in society as a whole. As noted above, the boycott movement maintained this position until the late 1980s.

It is important to note that the potency and precise social impact of the punishment inflicted by the denial of international competition varied considerably by sport, underscoring the need to disaggregate the hurts inflicted by different sanctions. Each major sport has its own socio-cultural identities and meanings.[30] Even within the realm of sport, then, complex interrelationships and particular points of vulnerability emerge which a sophisticated sanctions strategy should consider. For example, whites could rationalize away the

Olympic boycott through their implacable anti-communist ideology because of its Third World and eastern bloc instigators. Isolation in cricket and rugby proved more painful and harder to accept, given the dominance of traditional Western allies in these sports. And cricket, though popular, could be sacrificed ahead of rugby in light of the influence of the West Indies, India, and Pakistan and its traditional identification as an "English" sport.

Rugby's prominence in (male) Afrikaner nationalism and popular culture, and the white Western clique dominating the International Rugby Board (Australia, England, France, Ireland, New Zealand, Scotland, and Wales), made it a particular point of socio-psychological vulnerability and a focus of boycott advocates.[31] The ugly and defiant behavior of white rugby fans which accompanied renewed international competition in 1992 provided strong evidence of the extent to which sport sanctions had hurt. In an historic August test match against the New Zealand All Blacks at Johannesburg's Ellis Park Stadium, white rugby fans greeted the call for a minute's silence in memory of the victims of the Boipatong Massacre with a lusty rendition of *Die Stem*, apartheid South Africa's national anthem, and throughout the match defiantly flaunted the old South African flag while vilifying the ANC. This was a disturbing and traumatic moment.[32] But this type of outburst was not repeated at subsequent sporting internationals. With the future of renewed sporting contacts in the balance, cooler heads and more appropriate behavior prevailed. Now keenly sensitive to its traditional image as the sport of the oppressors and fearing a loss of national stature relative to cricket, rugby has significantly strengthened its development effort and adopted new affirmative action principles for its youth sides.[33] The point is that sport-based identities and meanings can be reconstructed over time, in relation to each other and to changing historical dynamics.

The psychic and punitive power of sport is also evident in the controversies surrounding sporting symbols. During the transition period, the non-racial sports movement demanded the abandonment of symbols associated with the old order – the flag, the anthem, and the Springbok. Cricket complied quickly, adopting the Protea flower as its new symbol. But the idea of dropping the Springbok created stormy controversy among white South Africans in general, and rugby fans in particular. In an important compromise, the Bok remained for the 1995 Rugby World Cup, and has subsequently been retained permanently as the rugby symbol.[34]

In sum, sport has been a powerful source of emotive, symbolic meanings and identities, holding the power to both punish and reward. As a form of punishment, these sanctions were "smart" due to sport's hierarchical governance and thus their high degree of enforceability. Targeting specific sports inflicted sharp and direct socio-psychological pain on key white groups, with low costs to both the non-white majority and the sanctioners.[35] Conversely, the sport boycotts gave encouragement to non-racial opponents of establishment sport.

Delegitimation

Sanctioners hoped to promote change as well as to punish, however. Sport boycotts contributed to the delegitimation of the apartheid order, paving the way for profound social change. Efforts by the Government and establishment sport to reverse the tide of isolation cumulatively undermined the ideological basis of white rule. In this way, the boycotts' sustained attack on some of white South Africans' most treasured cultural practices eroded their will to resist other forms of pressure.

This argument draws theoretically on the Gramscian insights that political power is most stable when it rests on broadly based consent throughout state and civil society (the "historic bloc"), and that such a "hegemonic" order is embedded and maintained "through the ordinary experiences and relationships of everyday life."[36] From this perspective, culture and ideology are integral to the process of maintaining class, race, and state power. Moreover, struggle in the cultural and ideological realms is crucial to successfully challenging hegemonic power and constituting a "counter-hegemonic" alternative to prevailing structures.

Sport as a cultural practice may be particularly valuable in hegemonic order because it creates "uniquely gratifying" shared practices and identities, and because it is widely viewed as "nonserious" and therefore not warranting critical scrutiny.[37] Insofar as South African sport reflected and reinforced racialist norms and structures, it "normalized" them – rendering them part of social common sense. By disrupting this everyday realm of activity, then, the sport boycott challenged the normative basis of apartheid, ultimately helping white South Africans prepare for the inevitability of change. As Government sport policies attempted to deny their racialist basis, and as establishment sport bodies portrayed themselves (however disingenuously) as advocates – indeed champions – of racial reconciliation, it became harder and harder to justify racialist social, political and economic structures.

In addition to the public policy reforms already discussed, establishment sport bodies modified their structure and practice in an effort to win international reacceptance. Leading the way was cricket, which established a fully non-racial constitution and a unified administration in 1977. In the first season under this new structure (1977–78), many cricketers previously associated with the non-racial body joined teams under the auspices of the newly "integrated" South African Cricket Union. By the second season, however, many returned to the non-racial South African Cricket Board because "they had not found the playing opportunities they had expected and were revolted by the racism they had encountered."[38] The Cricket Union also took a relatively early and proactive approach to the establishment of development programs in black townships. Although these steps did not win a reprieve from isolation, cricket did position itself well for transition and led the way in renewing international sporting contacts. More generally, many athletes and administrators embraced the notion that sport was in the vanguard in breaking down societal barriers, as reflected in a 1987 *South African Sports Illustrated* editorial: "Sport has led the way in dismantling apartheid laws and breaking down artificial barriers and it is our duty to continue this line. It is every sportsperson's duty to ensure that every single sportsman has an EQUAL OPPORTUNITY to fulfil his/her God-given potential."[39]

Simultaneously, establishment sport bodies also responded defiantly.[40] A series of "rebel" tours in the 1980s provided a substitute for official international events, and challenged the credibility and legitimacy of the boycotts.[41] Corporate sponsors, including South African Breweries, the Yellow Pages, and the National Bank, generously financed the tours. Rebel cricket and rugby players came from England, the West Indies, Sri Lanka, Australia, and New Zealand. Yet these tours could not mask South Africa's isolation and ultimately became counter-productive. As one opposition member of parliament opined, "I am sure all members will agree with me on this . . . we all look forward to the day when we can welcome an All-Black team, an Australian team or Welsh team, *inter alia*, as teams fully representative of their own countries, instead of their finding some clandestine way of coming into the country. How we long for that day!"[42]

Thus, when the costs of maintaining white domination mounted during the 1980s (evident in declining prosperity and increasing personal insecurity), an intellectual or normative defense of the "South African way of life" had already been severely compromised. A wide cross-section of South Africans, including the editors of *South African Sports Illustrated*, had become used to asserting that apartheid must end. In most cases, their meaning fell considerably short of what their opponents had in mind. Nevertheless, there was a large constituency in white society that supported the idea of a *process* of change, and this opening ultimately paved the way for the transition. Sport sanctions thus fostered the preconditions for the transition. Moreover, during the uncertain and violent years between 1990 and 1994, renewed sporting contacts stood as a beacon of the rewards awaiting post-apartheid South Africa in other areas.

Precedent

It is very difficult to weigh precisely the influence of sport because culture and norms are largely unmeasurable. Yet perhaps one reason so many seasoned South African experts failed to anticipate F. W. de Klerk's dramatic reforms is precisely that they did not appreciate the corrosive effects of cultural isolation – most importantly in sports.[43] Nor was the impact of sport sanctions limited to individual or collective consciousness of white South Africans. In at least three ways, sport boycotts set precedents for other forms of sanctions and encouraged advocates of external pressure on the apartheid state. Thus, in Crawford and Klotz's terms, they contributed *indirectly* and *externally* to pressure for change.

First, the Olympic boycott established that South Africa's domestic racial policies were sufficiently offensive to warrant the imposition of international sanctions. Because of the entrenched resistance to any such measures in the West, this precedent marked South Africa as "sanction-worthy," making other measures easier to contemplate. Seen as relatively unimportant and "apolitical," sports sanctions met little resistance from powerful interests.[44] Yet the symbolism proved potent: if South Africa violated norms even in the "untainted" and relatively trivial realm of sport, then surely it deserved punishment in economic and political arenas too. Moreover, the Afrikaner political elite recognized – and feared – the sport precedent. For example, a 1975 communication from the

Broederbond executive to its membership asserted that, "international ties, especially in rugby and cricket, have serious implications at this stage for our country, regarding international trade, national trade, military relationships and armaments, and strategic industrial development."[45] Although overstated, this assessment shows the inner circle's sensitivity to the sport boycott and explains its relatively rapid adoption of sport policy reforms.

The sport boycott also bolstered the anti-apartheid movement, both transnationally and domestically. Prompt reforms by the South African state and establishment organizations undermined the conventional view that sanctions would not work. None of these changes went far enough, but they pointed to the influence of external pressure and added impetus to the international campaign to isolate South Africa. Especially in traditional rivals such as Britain, Ireland, Australia, and New Zealand, protests over South African tours turned into mass mobilizing events, dramatically heightening the profile of the apartheid issue and the anti-apartheid movement.[46] These popular groups, in turn, became determined lobbyists of their own governments for broader sanctions. (This effect is more difficult to appreciate from North America, where sporting links with South Africa were relatively limited.) The sport boycott campaign thus catalyzed the momentum for stronger international pressures.

A third dimension of the precedent-setting importance of sport sanctions was the clear demarcation of criteria for rehabilitation. Specific conditions were set for relaunching international competition and exchange, in particular "the creation of single, democratic, nonracial, and nonsexist governing bodies actively committed to the eradication of inequality [thus implying an active sports development program]; that is, establishment sport must join with the nonracial movement to build unified federations in every sport."[47] The ANC and its internal allies saw in the manipulation of whites' craving for a return to international competition an opportunity to demand full non-racialism and integration at the organizational level, and a tangible commitment to development for disadvantaged South Africans.[48] The ANC also hoped to signal that there were immediate and tangible benefits to be gained by accepting change, in this case the renewal of international sport. Change could thus be linked in the minds of white South Africans not just to danger and loss, but to renewal and opportunity. The most explicit use of sport in this manner was, ironically, by F. W. de Klerk and other proponents of negotiations during the 1992 whites-only referendum.

Proponents of reform skillfully exploited South Africa's success at the Cricket World Cup to promote the benefits of negotiations. As Rob Nixon succinctly summarizes: "With the opportunism that has characterized his political performance, de Klerk temporarily commandeered the boycott issue as an electoral weapon, wielding it against the extreme right, to whom he dealt a sport-aided trouncing. . . ."[49]

Lifting the boycott followed a shift in strategy, described at the time as the "uncoupling" of sport from the overall campaign against apartheid. In fact, however, sport and the wider process of change had not been uncoupled; rather, the order of their rehabilitation had been reversed. The setting and meeting of these aforementioned requirements for rehabilitation – however superficially in practice[50] – powerfully reinforced the norms of acceptable social behavior for a "new" South Africa. Sport sanctions thus reinforced normative change and signalled directly to white South Africans the positive opportunities associated with the ending of apartheid. In their removal, as with their imposition, sport set a highly visible precedent.

IMPLICATIONS FOR THE STUDY AND PRACTICE OF SANCTIONS

Sport sanctions inflicted significant socio-psychological pain on the dominant (white) elite, thereby undermining the legitimacy of the South African racial order and strengthening new norms of behavior.[51] They also heightened the susceptibility of white South Africans to other external and internal pressures for change. While the influence of sport should not be overstated – apartheid did not crumble in *direct* response to sport boycotts – one cannot understand either the sanctions campaign as a whole or the South African transition without an appreciation of the role played by the sport boycott.

A number of implications flow from this analysis. First, success in the South African case indicates that if the principal aim of sanctioners is punishment, sport sanctions are likely be particularly effective. They can impose a painful "hurt" without causing significant deprivation either to "ordinary citizens" in the target or to powerful interests in the sanctioning country. Of course, some athletes suffer, so these sanctions should not be imposed lightly.

But where important principles or interests are at stake, sport boy-cotts should be given serious consideration. Moreover, while there are obviously situations in which this form of pressure would work more and less well, depending on the degree to which societies are as "sports mad" as the South Africans, a good many societies are "mad" about one sport or another, and therefore potentially vul-nerable in this area.

The bigger obstacle to the more routine use of sport sanctions is the entrenched commitment of international sports organizations to the principle of universalism. There is probably no higher prior-ity for organizations such as the IOC than to maximize participa-tion in events under their authority. They will, therefore, resist any efforts to limit competition.[52] What distinguished South Africa, then, was not its vulnerability but the coalition of forces that precipi-tated the imposition of sanctions in this area. But as sport becomes ever more heavily commercialized, emulating the long-established patterns in tennis and golf that so frustrated sports activists, the strategic opportunity created by its hierarchical governance struc-tures is being eroded. As a result, it may become all the more difficult to mobilize a coalition that can overcome the weight of entrenched interests to successfully deploy the "sports weapon."

Second, where the goal of sanctions goes beyond punishment to the precipitation of change, sophisticated sanctions strategies should also incorporate culture in general and sport in particular. I do not mean, however, that sanctioners should seek to isolate the tar-get society in these areas in an undifferentiated manner. Rather, targeted cultural isolation can catalyze and reinforce the impact of other pressures, and can influence the direction of social change. Moreover, lifting cultural sanctions can provide incentives for re-form, while other coercive pressures are maintained. The incorpo-ration of culture thus expands the range of tools the sanctioner can deploy and, if deftly used, can multiply the impact of the whole ensemble.

However, the South African case also suggests that such a so-phisticated, multifaceted strategy will most likely require a substantial time period to work. It may take years for the corrosive effects of cultural isolation to be felt and for their delegitimizing consequences to become apparent. This is not to say that one must anticipate a 25–30 year process (roughly the time between South Africa's ban-ning from the Tokyo Olympics and the beginning of the "end game" in 1990). But one of the political challenges for would-be sanctioners is that a comprehensive strategy must be (able to be) sustained over a significant period of time.

Finally, the wider point – hardly new but worth reiterating because it defies conventional wisdom – is that influence is exercised on an issue-specific or contextual basis.[53] In this case, through sport, an improbable coalition of South African exiles, Western activists, and newly independent African governments was able to induce telling pressure on an entrenched and determined South African regime. Thus, there are often openings for agency by those whom most conventional views dismiss on account of "weakness."

Notes

1. Many have written about how and why sport achieved a prominent place in the campaign to isolate South Africa. See, for example, R. Lapchick, *The Politics of Race and International Sport* (Westport: Greenwood, 1975); R. Archer and A. Bouillon, *The South African Game* (London: Zed, 1982); A. Guelke, "Sport and the End of *Apartheid*," in L. Allison, ed., *The Changing Politics of Sport* (Manchester: Manchester University Press, 1993); A. Guelke, "The Politicization of South African Sport," in L. Allison, ed., *The Politics of Sport* (Manchester: Manchester University, 1986), pp. 118–48; B. Kidd, "The Campaign Against Sport in South Africa," *International Journal* 43 (1988), pp. 643–64; and B. Kidd, "From Quarantine to Cure: The New Phase of the Struggle Against Apartheid Sport," *Sociology of Sport Journal* 8 (1991), pp. 33–46.
2. R. Nixon, *Homelands, Harlem and Hollywood* (New York: Routledge, 1994), pp. 131–54. Of course, the "nation" invoked by sporting events remains selective and partial, experienced very differently by various segments of a country's population – no more so than in South Africa.
3. Kidd, "The Campaign Against Sport," p. 642. See also Nixon, who contrasts sport with the "exasperatingly baggy and diffuse political target" of other forms of culture (*Homelands, Harlem, and Hollywood*, p. 156).
4. Kidd, "From Quarantine to Cure," 38, and Kidd, "The Campaign Against Sport," pp. 648–52.
5. See, for example, A. Payne, "The International Politics of the Gleneagles Agreement," *Round Table* 320 (1991), p. 428; Guelke, "Sport and the End of *Apartheid*," p. 168; and A. Grundlingh, "Responses to Isolation," in A. Grundlingh, A. Odendaal, and B. Spies, *Beyond the Tryline, Rugby and South African Society* (Randburg: Ravan, 1995), pp. 99–100.
6. Cited in Guelke, "The Politicization of South African Sport," p. 121.
7. See S. P. Quick, "'Black Knight Checks White King': The Conflict Between Avery Brundage and the African Nations over South African Membership of the IOC," *Canadian Journal of History of Sport* 21 (1990), esp. pp. 20–4; and D. Macintosh, H. Cantelon, and L. McDermott, "The IOC and South Africa: A Lesson in Transnational

Relations," *International Review for Sociology of Sport* 28 (1993), pp. 377–83.

8. Quick, "Black Knight," p. 26. Also on the SCSA, see "Ganga Happy Boycott is About to be Lifted," *City Press* (South Africa), 31 March 1991, featuring an interview with leading African sports official and Congolese Cabinet Minister Jean-Claude Ganga.

9. See Kidd, "From Quarantine to Cure," 39.

10. See Guelke, "The Politicization of South African Sport," pp. 130–1; and Lapchick, *The Politics of Race and International Sport*, pp. 126–9.

11. Guelke, "Sport and the End of *Apartheid*," p. 152.

12. See P. Hain, *Don't Play with Apartheid* (London: George Allen and Unwin, 1971).

13. Cited in Payne, "The International Politics of the Gleneagles Agreement," p. 421. See also D. Macintosh, D. Greenhorn, and D. Black, "Canadian Diplomacy and the 1978 Edmonton Commonwealth Games," *Journal of Sport History* 19 (1992), pp. 26–55.

14. The South African government (belatedly) allowed (censored) television in 1976. For a broader discussion of television, culture, and sanctions, see N. Mangaliso, "Cultural Boycotts and Political Change," in this volume.

15. Nixon, *Homelands, Harlem and Hollywood*, pp. 145, 148.

16. D. Retief, "Curtain is Drawn on Overseas Tours," *Cape Times*, 12 September 1981. Note his recognition of the need for significant change but also the implication that a "non-objectionable" form of apartheid would suffice!

17. Kidd, "From Quarantine to Cure," p. 40. The information in the remainder of this paragraph is drawn from this source.

18. On the importance of the "Gatting tour," see Guelke, "Sport and the End of *Apartheid*," pp. 154–6.

19. Prior to the Harare meeting, a few clandestine meetings had been held between representatives of the establishment Rugby Board and the ANC in Europe. See P. Dobson, *Doc: the Life of Danie Craven* (Cape Town: Human and Rousseau, 1994), pp. 178–81. Board representatives hoped the meeting would help them secure an international tour to mark its centenary in 1989. My thanks to Douglas Booth for this insight.

20. Guelke, "Sport and the End of *Apartheid*," p. 161. The process of negotiating rugby "unity" subsequently stalled and was not completed until 1992.

21. See Macintosh, Cantelon, and McDermott, "The IOC and South Africa," pp. 385–8.

22. Nixon, *Homelands, Harlem, and Hollywood*, p. 151.

23. K. R. Nossal, "International Sanctions as International Punishment," *International Organization* 43 (Spring 1989); and *Rain Dancing: Sanctions in Canadian and Australian Foreign Policy* (Toronto: University of Toronto Press, 1994).

24. Cited in G. Jarvie, *Class, Race, and Sport in South Africa's Political Economy* (London: Routledge and Kegan Paul, 1985), p. 6.

25. J. Hofmeyr, *The Impact of Sanctions on South Africa: Whites' Political*

Attitudes (Washington: Investor Responsibility Research Center, March 1990), pp. 30–1.

26. For examples, see Nixon, *Homelands, Harlem, and Hollywood*, pp. 152–3, and T. Monnington, "Politicians and Sport: Uses and Abuses," in Allison, ed., *The Changing Politics of Sport*, pp. 125–50.

27. The following account is drawn particularly from Guelke, "The Politicization of South African Sport," and W. A. Munro, "The State and Sports: Political Maneuvering in the Civil Order," in W. James, ed., *The State of Apartheid* (Boulder, CO: Lynne Rienner, 1987).

28. Munro, "The State and Sports," p. 129.

29. Department of Foreign Affairs and Trade (Australia), "Race and Rugby in South Africa," *Australian Foreign Affairs Review* 59 (1988), p. 141.

30. See D. Lewis, "Soccer and Rugby: Popular Productions of Pleasure in South African Culture," *Southern African Political and Economic Monthly* 6 (1992/1993), pp. 13–17.

31. J. Nauright and D. Black, "It's Rugby that Really Matters: New Zealand–South Africa Rugby Relations and the Moves to Isolate South Africa, 1956–1992," in Wilcox, ed., *Sport in the Global Village* (Morganstown, WV: Sports Information Technologies, 1994); and Archer and Bouillon, *The South African Game*, esp. pp. 294–301. On rugby's role in Afrikaner nationalism and popular culture, see Grundlingh, "Responses to Isolation," pp. 100–3, and A. Grundlingh, "Playing for Power: Rugby, Afrikaner Nationalism and Masculinity in South Africa," in Grundlingh et al., eds., *Beyond the Tryline*. While the role of sport in fostering racial identities and hierarchy in South Africa has been widely recognized, its role in fostering gender identities and hierarchy among *all* racial groups has been relatively neglected. The enormous popularity and cultural centrality of sport is a powerful socializing influence in a deeply patriarchal society. See J. Nauright and D. Black, "'Hitting Them Where it Hurts': Springbok-All Black Rugby, Nationalism, and Counter-Hegemonic Struggle, 1959–1992," in T. Chandler and J. Nauright, eds., *Making Men: Rugby and Masculine Identity* (London: Frank Cass, 1996).

32. For poignant commentaries on this incident, see S. Johnson, "Inside the Protected Citadel," and "We Are All Sore Now," in his *Strange Days Indeed* (London: Transworld, 1993), pp. 213–19. See also J. Nauright, "'A Besieged Tribe'? Nostalgia, White Cultural Identity and the Role of Rugby in a Changing South Africa," *International Review for Sociology of Sport* 31 (1996), pp. 63–77.

33. See "South African Rugby Development – A Statement by Edward Griffiths, Chief Executive, SARFU," May 1995. The South African Rugby Football Union is the non-racial successor to both the establishment Rugby Board and the SACOS-affiliated Rugby Union. Of course, both rugby and cricket are playing catch-up to soccer, the national game of the majority.

34. See D. Booth, "Mandela and Amabokoboko: The Political and Linguistic Nationalization of South Africa?" *Journal of Modern African Studies* 34 (1996), pp. 459–77.

35. On the limited effects of the boycott on black South Africans, see

Guelke, "Sport and the end of *Apartheid*." Sanctioners too were not totally unscathed, as the trauma inflicted on New Zealand society by the 1981 Springbok tour demonstrated; see *56 Days: A History of the Anti-Tour Movement in Wellington* (Wellington: COST [Citizens Opposed to the Springbok Tour], 1981).

36. J. Hargreaves, "Theorizing Sport: An Introduction," in J. Hargreaves, ed., *Sport, Culture, and Ideology* (London: Routledge and Kegan Paul, 1982), p. 14. For a Gramscian interpretation of South African sport, see Jarvie, *Class, Race, and Sport.*
37. Hargreaves, "Theorizing Sport," p. 16.
38. Archer and Bouillon, *The South African Game*, p. 261.
39. "Editorial: 1987 – Sports Watershed," *South African Sports Illustrated*, January 1987, p. 3.
40. Grundlingh, "Responses to Isolation," p. 98.
41. Guelke, "Sport and the End of *Apartheid*," p. 157.
42. M. A. Tarr, Progressive Federal Party spokesman on sport, in the South African *Hansard*, 16 April 1986, p. 3449.
43. On isolation in other cultural realms, see N. A. Mangaliso, "Cultural Boycotts," the next chapter in this collection.
44. Guelke, "The Politicization of South African Sport," p. 144.
45. From H. Strydom and I. Wilkins, *The Broederbond* (New York: Paddington, 1980), p. 250; cited in Munro, "The State and Sports," p. 128. The *Broederbond* was an elite male secret society committed to the promotion of the "Afrikaner nation," which was tightly intertwined with the National Party government.
46. Canadian and particularly Australian policymakers proved keenly sensitive to the implications of sport sanctions. See D. Black, "Australian, Canadian, and Swedish Policies Towards Southern Africa: A Comparative Study of 'Middle Power Internationalism'" (PhD diss., Dalhousie University, 1992).
47. Kidd, "From Quarantine to Cure," p. 41.
48. Nixon, *Homelands, Harlem and Hollywood*, p. 149.
49. Ibid., p. 152.
50. The transition in sport has been neither as complete nor as profound as non-racial sports advocates had hoped. See D. Booth, "South Africa: Elite Sport is Winning," *Southern Africa Report* (1995), p. 28.
51. Hofmeyr, *The Impact of Sanctions*, pp. 42–9.
52. On the ideological internationalism of the IOC, see J. Hoberman, "Towards a Theory of Olympic Internationalism," *Journal of Sport History* 22 (1995), pp. 1–37. On the IOC as a transnational organization with its own priorities and influence, see Macintosh, Cantelon, and McDermott, "The IOC and South Africa."
53. See D. A. Baldwin, "Power Analysis and World Politics: New Trends versus Old Tendencies," *World Politics* 31 (1989).

12 Cultural Boycotts and Political Change

Nomazengele A. Mangaliso

The extensive documentation and literature on economic and political anti-apartheid pressures (as presented in the other chapters in this volume) contrasts with the scarce attention paid to cultural boycotts. This paucity is understandable since economic and political issues tend to be more observable and tangible. And because those with economic power often have political power, economic means should, logically, bring about political ends. Culture, on the other hand, is abstract, incorporating a wide variety of elements ranging from the aesthetics of a nation to philosophical ideas. Definitions of culture reflect this breadth.[1]

Some elements of culture are potentially vulnerable targets of sanctions because intercultural interaction between nations encourages comparisons; isolation fosters cultural autarky, either out of conviction or necessity.[2] Arts (theater, literature, architecture, and so forth) are an aesthetic expression of a nation's identity. Culture is also linked to a society's structural factors: art emanates from particular classes and conveys political ideas.[3] Since apartheid influenced every aspect of people's lives in South Africa, the struggle for its removal was waged on all fronts, including culture.

This chapter analyzes the impact of the international community's boycott of South African culture during apartheid by examining two elements: performing arts (music, theater, television, and film) and academic exchanges. These areas were among the main targets of sanctions.[4] For example, the General Assembly of the United Nations (UN) discouraged any support of South African performing and fine arts, and any exchange of ideas and scholarship. In addition to requesting that member states cease any artistic and academic collaboration, the UN also appealed to writers, artists, and musicians to boycott South Africa, and urged academic and arts institutions to sever links.[5] In practice, the performing arts and academic boycotts were selective, in part because the ANC encouraged flexibility.

Outside South Africa, these cultural restrictions raised public awareness about apartheid. But South African arts flourished, even while relatively unknown to the rest of the world; music as a commodity, for example, simply became less available on the international market. Within South Africa, the academic boycott in particular increased the isolation of whites – both opponents and supporters of apartheid. Some black South Africans were hurt by the cultural boycotts but others received assistance, such as scholarships. In general, the boycott created physical and psychological isolation from both the West and the rest of the African continent. As this chapter demonstrates, however, these effects varied considerably, both in terms of the dynamics of each boycott and their differential consequences for societal targets.

THE PERFORMING ARTS BOYCOTTS

The cultural boycott emerged in the late 1950s as part of the call for sanctions from anti-apartheid activists such as Trevor Huddleston and Albert Luthuli. Initially, British musicians, actors, and writers joined the boycott. In 1965, the American Committee on Africa presented a star-studded list of performing artists and actors who joined together to sign the "We Say No to Apartheid" pledge; signatories included Harry Belafonte, Leonard Bernstein, Sammy Davis Jr., Arthur Miller, Sidney Poitier, and Nina Simone.[6] In the 1970s, the Dutch Anti-Apartheid Movement initiated a campaign to abrogate a cultural treaty with South Africa, on the grounds that it forged a link with the wrong partners – mainly apartheid propagandists.[7]

The cultural dimension of anti-apartheid sanctions gained urgency after the 1976 Soweto riots, because South African students rejected Afrikaans as the language of the oppressor. In 1980, the UN called for a complete boycott, irrespective of the artists, their subject matter, or their relationship to the struggle within South Africa.[8] The UN Anti-Apartheid Committee monitored compliance with these measures through a list of international artists who performed in South Africa. Those blacklisted became objects of pickets, boycotts of their performances, and negative publicity.[9] The cultural boycott also received strong support from various liberation movements within South Africa. In March 1981, for instance, the Azanian People's Organization called for a worldwide boycott of artists who performed in South Africa. Other organizations advocating sanctions included the Congress of South African Students, the Music, Drama, Art and Literature Institute, and the Port Elizabeth Black Community Organization.[10]

Boycotts targetted both international artists exporting culture to South Africa and artists bringing South African culture abroad. The purpose was to add psychological pressures on white South Africans, who enjoyed the highest standards of living, including comfortable theaters, while the majority of blacks lived under adverse conditions. Furthermore, the boycott sought to deny whites the legitimacy of normal relations with the West.[11] Musical exchanges between South Africa and neighboring African states, in contrast, were already curtailed by apartheid laws which restricted movement between these countries; African music remained virtually unknown in South Africa until recently. In addition, most African countries deplored apartheid enough to support (if not instigate) the UN cultural boycott.[12] The consequences of these measures varied in different cultural industries, as the following sections explain.

Music and Theater

The US boycott focused most intensely on music because of the influential 1985 *Sun City* record album and video, which were aggressively publicized by activist artists. The project sought to educate performers and audiences. For example, several world-renowned artists performed at Sun City because promoters characterized it as a multiracial vacation resort located in a neighboring state – these artists did not understand the difference between the South African homeland of Bophuthatswana and the neighboring independent country of Botswana. Musicians involved in this consciousness-raising project included Bob Dylan, Bruce Springsteen, Kenny Loggins, Miles Davis, Little Steve Van Zandt, Afrika Bambataa, and others. Some also testified at the UN and appeared on American talk shows, such as *Phil Donohue*, to educate audiences about the impact of apartheid and to publicize their call on all music artists not to perform in South Africa.

The timing of *Sun City* also proved critical in keeping international attention on apartheid during a period of increasing censorship in South Africa. While the Botha government blocked media coverage of political uprisings, the music video broadcasted images of apartheid around the world. Within the US, other causes adopted the project's style of fund-raising; similar charity events included *Live Aid, Band Aid, Farm Aid,* and *We Are The World,* demonstrating the extent to which the mobilizing concept had succeeded.[13]

Certainly the *Sun City* production did not convince all musicians not to perform in South Africa, but many artists did refuse lucrative deals. For example, singer Roberta Flack reportedly rejected a $2.5 million offer. The late Phyllis Hyman also turned down an invitation, declaring that her moral commitment superceded money. Other artists who passed up similar offers included Ben Vereen, Gladys Knight and the Pips, the Floaters, The Jackson Five, Diana Ross, Barry White, The Commodores, The Third World, Lena Horne, Tony Bennett, Odyssey, Bross Townsend, and Betty Wright. The Newport Jazz Festival also refused to perform in South Africa.[14]

Those who violated the boycott faced blacklisting, and thus threats to their sales. The UN also monitored a variety of artists who, having once performed in South Africa, agreed never to return; these included Tina Turner, Elton John, Liza Minelli, Julio Iglesias, George Benson, Chicago, Barry Manilow, David Essex, Nana Mouskouri, Max Bygraves, Kenny Rogers, Shirley Bassey, and Rod Stewart. The late Frank Sinatra, having defended his right to play anywhere he liked, eventually submitted to the pressure not to perform in South Africa again.[15] Three cases illustrate the (varying) consequences of abrograting the boycott: Ray Charles, the Temptations, and Paul Simon.

In the late 1970s, Ray Charles violated the boycott. Appearing on the South African Broadcasting Corporation, he defended his action. The music boycott, he argued, was senseless because all countries had problems of some sort. Did that mean that they should all the boycotted? Furthermore, he claimed that South Africa's problems had nothing to do with him personally. Although his position did not affect his performances, record sales, or his popularity in the US, some South African audiences commented that not only was he blind physically, he was also "blind" mentally. In contrast, the Temptations, who also visited South Africa in the late 1970s, returned to the US to find their performances boycotted by disgruntled fans. To save their tarnished image, they gave a public apology for having violated the cultural boycott.

By the 1980s, public awareness of the cultural boycott had spread, embroiling musician Paul Simon in international controversy as a result of his *Graceland* album, a project involving South African artists Ladysmith Black Mambazo. He defended his tour, which took place in Zimbabwe, and defied criticism that he simply sought to boost his sagging career by popularizing a talented but disadvantaged South African group. Simon noted that he had helped disadvantaged South Africans, and he stressed the important distinction between performing at live concerts in Sun City or white areas of Johannesburg, as opposed to playing privately and recording with black musicians in South Africa. Furthermore, he pointed out that he had turned down offers to play in Sun City and that he had gone to South Africa at the invitation of black musicians.

The controversy over *Graceland* drew several responses from South African musicians. Ray Phiri, the lead guitarist, praised the project as the best thing that ever happened to South African music. For Ladysmith Black Mambazo, the album served as their gateway to the rest of the world. Hugh Masekela, a renowned exiled trumpeter and anti-apartheid activist, argued that *Graceland* was a development project for South African artists. Defending its non-political lyrics, he compared the music to works of creative artists like Duke Ellington, Count Basie, and Miles Davis, who gave the world access to African-American culture without directly challenging racism.[16] Eventually, Simon was removed from the UN blacklist.

Foreign musicians like Paul Simon were only one target. The UN Anti-Apartheid Committee also urged that all performances by South African actors and musicians – black, white, or multiracial – be boycotted. But support for an indiscriminate boycott of all South African performers was stronger in Britain than the US, and treatment varied depending on the degree to which artists addressed the conditions faced by blacks under apartheid. For example, Juluka, a multiracial band which also incorporated African dance, often received a warm reception in the US but not from local musicians and political organizations in Britain.[17] Mahlathini and Mahotella Queens, an all-African music group that also danced, received acclaim in the US even at the height of apartheid. And despite the apolitical nature of their songs, Ladysmith Black Mambazo's performances were never boycotted; indeed, until recently, they enjoyed more popularity and recognition in the US than in South Africa. Similarly, Mbongeni Ngema's musical, *Sarafina*, performed by an African cast plus one African-American member, got positive reviews in the US, as did several of Athol Fugard's plays.

But not all South African artists escaped censure so easily. In 1973, Welcome Msomi's *uMabatha*, a Zulu version of *Macbeth*, encountered opposition in New York. Ultimately the cast disbanded.

Objections to the show focused on its silence about the poor conditions of blacks within South Africa, even though the all-African cast had themselves suffered under apartheid. Another of Msomi's plays, *Ipi Ntombi*, which presented African traditional practices, met a similar fate. The 1977 production, by white South African director Bertha Egnos with an all-African cast, depicted a "happy homeland black," a theme that supported South African government propaganda.[18]

There is no indication that the work of exiled South Africans was targetted for boycotts, since it challenged the South African government and educated audiences about apartheid. However, talented artists like Letta Mbuli, Caiphus Semenya, Hugh Masekela, and Miriam Makeba worked in relative obscurity for years. In particular, Miriam Makeba found sales of her music curtailed in the US – perhaps also because of her association with (avowed communist) Stokely Carmichael. Nonetheless, exiled artists faced a double burden. In the US, sanctions may have contributed to the obscurity of some artists, while most faced a competitive music industry whose audiences were not encouraged to support any aspects of South African culture. At the same time, their music remained inaccessible within South Africa, either because of apartheid laws which banned them or because the local music industry (and state-run media) ignored them.

Television and Film

Because of apartheid censorship laws, television was belatedly introduced into South Africa in 1976, and even then the government hoped to use the new medium to defend its ideology of separate cultures. Ironically, access to television made the South African population more aware of cultural sanctions.[19] But attempts to stop the flow of programs generally remained uncoordinated. The British Equity union interdicted the British Broadcasting Corporation from supplying South Africa with programs that featured its members, but most US television companies made their programs available. Shows like *Dallas* appealed to surburban Afrikaners, while black township youths found inspiration in *A-Team* and *V*.[20] *The Cosby Show*, a program featuring a black middle-class family, spoke to the aspirations of South African blacks; it also exposed South African whites to the possibility of affluent blacks elsewhere in the world. Despite this widespread availability of US programs, a small number were cancelled. For example, at Archbishop Tutu's prompting, Bill Cosby withdrew his show in 1987, despite its popularity. Lorimar Production Company stopped access to *Knots Landing*, while the stars of *Cagney and Lacey* made a political statement by donating their South African earnings to the ANC.[21]

South Africa also relies heavily on imported films, since few are produced locally. No systematic sanctions took hold. One exception was the US audience boycotts of Jamie Uys' *The Gods Must Be Crazy*. This film, shot in Namibia (governed by South African apartheid laws), was criticized for being apolitical, making a mockery of indigenous people ("bushmen"), and portraying a black government and freedom fighters as highly incompetent.[22] Even the film *Gandhi*, which raised international awareness of apartheid by portraying the life of the Mahatma under racial discrimination and his role in challenging it, was not totally immune to boycotts. Its director, Sir Richard Attenborough, cancelled plans to attend its showing in South Africa in April 1983, and a South African delegation was forced to leave a Capri film festival in September 1983.[23] In contrast, the film *Shaka Zulu*, produced in South Africa with heavy support from the South African government, was well received by US audiences and media. Perhaps one difference is that *Shaka Zulu* involved a large number of African actors portraying a brave defense against British invasion. (Ladysmith Black Mambazo also toured the US in a bus marked "Shaka Zulu.")

These sporadic boycotts in film and television contrast with even weaker measures in literature and graphic arts. Well-known authors like Nadine Gordimer, who showed an international audience how both black and white South Africans were all victims of the apartheid system, remained unaffected. And few black South African writers ever escaped apartheid laws; those who challenged the system had their work suppressed or banned. Photo-journalist Peter Magubane also gained popularity in the US and all over the world for his graphic images that captured quite vividly the experiences of apartheid.[24]

Thus, in practice cultural sanctions against South Africa were very selective. Even the ANC modified its commitment to a blanket boycott. Pointing to an alternative people's culture emerging within South Africa, Oliver Tambo recommended in 1987 that sanctioners discriminate among their potential targets.[25] Not all South African artists ought to be boycotted, he argued, and in particular not those who, regardless of their racial background, challenged apartheid. Artwork which overlooked political conditions – especially any that apologized for the South African government – became the primary targets of boycotts. Overall, despite gaps in the enforcement of sanctions, this process of scrutiny and evaluation raised awareness of apartheid around the world.

THE ACADEMIC BOYCOTT

Ordinarily, educational institutions take academic freedom for granted.[26] But in South Africa, apartheid fundamentally limited academic freedom. For example, separate Ministries of Education, established for each of apartheid's racial groups, determined curricula at segregated schools and universities. The academic boycott, therefore, generated spirited discussion. Proponents of sanctions argued that academic freedom was a poor defense for privilege; they questioned the morality of a mythical free flow of ideas in a society marked by government censorship. Furthermore, they refused to make a special case for academics in calls for the comprehensive isolation of South Africa.[17] In contrast, boycott opponents argued that intellectual freedom was essential to academic life and that restrictions promoted parochialism in scholarship. Even some anti-apartheid activists saw the boycott as benefitting the South African government by restricting the flow of radical or progressive ideas that could hasten apartheid's demise. In 1986, Conor Cruise O'Brien became one particularly notable proponent of this view, when some students at the University of Cape Town prevented his lecture series on campus.[28]

Anti-apartheid activists called for restrictions on academic, professional, and scientific exchanges, including "educational, cultural and scientific meetings, and other opportunities for the exchange of information and knowledge, the purpose of such restrictions being to protest the social and political policies of government."[29] The boycott also used law, custom, or agreement to withold information by restricting scholarly exchange, in order to ostracize "offending" collegues.[30] Strategies included banning the distribution of publications to South Africa; rejecting papers submitted by South African scholars to international journals; avoiding meetings in, visits to, or collaboration with colleagues in South Africa; denying opportunities for South African scholars to participate in conferences outside South Africa; and failing to lend scholarly material from libraries in other countries to institutions in South Africa.[31] Although the publishing industry was not a boycott target, a number of publishers (of their own volition) blocked publication or sales in South Africa.[32]

In practice, the academic boycott curtailed South Africans' participation and membership in international scholarly associations. Some groups, such as the World Archeological Congress, banned South African membership or participation. Others, including the American Psychological Association, also established special subsections, like "Psychologists against Apartheid," whose members focused not only on the academic boycott of South Africa but also on the implications of living under apartheid. Advocates of bans noted the need both to avoid disruptions at their meetings by anti-apartheid groups (a particularly prevalent tactic in Britain) and to prevent a loss in participation from countries who would boycott to protest any South African presence. Implementing the boycott also signalled these associations' solidarity with the anti-apartheid movement.[33] In most instances, blocking membership and participation specifically targeted whites who have historically dominated South African scholarly activities. How to treat the few blacks in these associations was a matter of debate and remained at the discretion of the office-bearers.

International support for black South African students and academics, such as scholarship programs, further underscored the isolation of white academics. For example, in 1965, the UN established its Education Program for South Africans (both refugees and passport holders) to address the lack of educational opportunities for blacks. It operated until 1992, when the UN shifted its focus to providing education opportunities within South Africa.[34] Fulbright scholarships offered opportunities for qualified academics of all races to study in the US. As part of its "constructive engagement" policy, the US also provided scholarships to blacks under the auspicies of the Johannesburg-based Equal Opportunities Council and the New York-based Institute of International Education. The Commonwealth offered similar opportunities. These programs aimed both to compensate for the deprivations of discrimination and to prepare blacks for leadership roles after the abolition of apartheid.

Thus the academic boycott primarily targetted the white elite within South Africa because apartheid already curtailed the careers of black academics. Sanctions may have raised the consciousness of some white scholars who could have gone on with their routine work unmindful of the negative repercussions of apartheid. For example, the Council for Scientific and Industrial Research and the Human Sciences Research Council, with direct links to the South African government, funded ongoing research projects at various South African universities. By the early 1990s, these institutes hired a small number of black academics and researchers.[35] In sum, the academic boycott sent a signal to privileged white South African academics that no one could pursue "business as usual" in an abnormal society.

CONCLUSION

Although far from comprehensive, the arts and academic boycotts primarily targetted whites who enjoyed privileged access to international cultural and educational ties. One result was a heightened awareness of international rejection of apartheid. With the exception of the careers of specific black artists, the majority of South Africans remained unharmed by these social sanctions, because apartheid already restricted their expression and educational opportunities.

As a consciousness-raising component in the sanctions campaign, these cultural boycotts may have increased the social and pyschological costs of maintaining the apartheid system. But lack of access to international music or films certainly did not overthrow institutionalized racial segregation. Rather, these measures supplemented the array of economic and strategic restrictions facing South Africa in the 1980s. Cultural boycotts are most likely to be effective when used in conjunction with other measures.

Some forms of social sanctions will be easier to organize, monitor and enforce. Differences between types of culture may significantly affect the utility of these measures. Music and television will be strongly influenced (and possibly constrained) by market considerations. Academia, in contrast, can enforce restrictions more effectively through professional associations. The degree of censorship in the target country, furthermore, would also affect the extent to which populations are influenced by – or even aware of – restrictions.

Despite the sporadic application of cultural boycotts in the South African case, these measures show promise as a potentially effective means of signalling international opposition to a target state, mobilizing societies for sanctions, and inflicting social and pyschological costs on ruling elites – with little harm to majority populations. Social sanctions, therefore, deserve more systematic attention from both analysts and policymakers.

Notes

1. Compare, for example, J. J. Macionis, *Sociology*, 5th ed. (Englewood Cliffs, NJ: Prentice Hall, 1995); K. Marx, *Das Kapital* (New York: Random House, 1973); C. Geertz, *The Interpretation of Cultures* (New York: Basic Books, 1973).
2. A. Mazrui, *Africa's International Relations: The Diplomacy of Dependency and Change* (London: Westview, 1977), p. 99.
3. B. Breytenbach, *End Papers: Essays, Letters, Articles of Faith, Workbook Notes* (New York: Farrar, Straus and Giroux, 1986).
4. Another primary target for cultural boycott was South African sports; see D. Black, "'Not Cricket': The Effects and Effectiveness of the Sport Boycott," previous chapter in this volume.
5. Resolution 35/206E of 16 December 1980, in *Yearbook of the United Nations 1980* (New York: United Nations Department of Public Information), p. 231.
6. C. Braam and F. Geerlings, "Towards New Cultural Relations: A Reflection on the Cultural Boycott," in W. Campschreur and J. Divendal, eds., *Culture in Another South Africa* (London: Zed, 1989), p. 173.
7. Braam and Geerlings, "Towards New Cultural Relations," pp. 173–4.
8. L. Shore, "The Cultural Boycott of South Africa," in R. E. Edgar, ed., *Sanctioning Apartheid* (Trenton, NJ: Africa World Press, 1990), p. 408.
9. Ibid., pp. 406–7.
10. *The United Nations and Apartheid 1948–1994* (New York: United Nations Department of Public Information, 1994), p. 376.
11. Shore, "Cultural Boycott," p. 399. Similar intentions motivated sports sanctions; see Black, "Not Cricket."
12. On the role of African countries in the sanctions movement, see G. M. Khadiagala, "Regional Dimensions of Sanctions," in this volume.
13. R. Nixon, *Homelands, Harlem and Hollywood: South African Culture and the World Beyond* (New York: Routledge, 1994).
14. *The United Nations and Apartheid*, p. 377.
15. Nixon, *Homelands, Harlem and Hollywood*, p. 163.
16. Ibid., p. 166.
17. Shore, "Cultural Boycott," p. 406.
18. Ibid., p. 411.
19. On the effects of the availability of televised sport, see Black, "Not Cricket."
20. Nixon, *Homelands, Harlem and Hollywood*, p. 160.
21. Ibid.

22. Shore, "Cultural Boycott," p. 411.
23. *The United Nations and Apartheid*, p. 376.
24. Shore, "Cultural Boycott," p. 406.
25. Braam and Geerlings, "Towards New Cultural Relations," p. 178.
26. *Academic Freedom and Human Rights Abuses in Africa: An Africa Watch Report* (New York: Human Rights Watch, 1991).
27. L. Haricombe, "The Effect of an Academic Boycott on Academics in South Africa" (diss., University of Illinois at Urbana–Champaign, 1992), p. 68.
28. Vice Chancellor's Report 1994, University of Cape Town, p. 2.
29. World Health Organization, *Apartheid and Health* (Geneva: World Health Organization, 1983).
30. *Yearbook of the United Nations 1945–1995*, Special UN 50th Anniversary Edition (The Hague: Martinus Nijhoff, 1995).
31. Haricombe, "The Effect of an Academic Boycott."
32. Shore, "Cultural Boycott," p. 401.
33. P. Ucko, *Academic Freedom and Apartheid* (London: Gerald Duckworth, 1987).
34. *The United Nations and Apartheid*, p. 83.
35. Haricombe, "The Effect of an Academic Boycott," p. 70.

Part V

Implications

13 Regional Dimensions of Sanctions

Gilbert M. Khadiagala

My country trades with South Africa. In fact, it has traded with South Africa since we became independent in 1964. The problem was that while the facts and figures showed that trade was in fact going up, the political language was such that there wasn't any trade. The previous government called for sanctions while employing third parties to trade with South Africa. The results were that in the process we paid more than we would have done. By opening up a trade mission in South Africa, we are trying to get rid of the third parties for the good of our country. And all we want is our language to match our practices.

(Frederick Chiluba, President of Zambia)[1]

While a lot of countries have lifted sanctions against South Africa, I am not sure we had any sanctions against it. Economic activity has always been carried out behind closed doors.

(Edmund Chawira, Trade Export Manager of Zimbabwe)[2]

The post-apartheid consensus on sanctions captured in Zambian president Chiluba's Washington address and by Zimbabwe's head of export trade summarizes the ambivalent position of small states caught in the uncomfortable position between sanctioners and targets. Constrained by economic and political weakness, South Africa's neighbors sought global sanctions to induce change in South Africa even as a majority of them maintained close economic ties with the pariah. Their experiences illustrate the double-edged nature of sanctions policies. States that attempt to influence political change in the target state often confront competing political, economic, and security interests.[3]

The puzzle of these intermediary states, which play active roles in sanction regimes yet are subject to retaliation by the target, raises conceptual questions akin to those discussed by Kim Nossal in his analysis of middle power participation in international sanctions.[4] Nossal argues that Canadian and Australian sanctions primarily reflected oscillations in domestic and coalition politics. Because sanctions sustain the appearance of action, "all the participants feel better – but nothing of substance is actually accomplished."[5] Economic interests restrain these states from sanctioning, but assorted domestic and external pressures force their involvement, often at significant cost.

Smaller neighbouring states confront similar pressures from local and global constituencies. Their economic dependence on the target state makes them maneuver between accommodation and guarded support for international measures. As targets of retaliatory sanctions, these neighbors may also display a siege mentality, which promotes national solidarity. Alone or in concert, they might alert external actors to their existential vulnerability, with the hopes of gaining assistance.

Following on Nossal's analysis of middle powers, this chapter discusses the ambiguous position of the Frontline States (FLS) and Southern African Development Coordination Conference (SADCC) as mobilizers for international anti-apartheid sanctions and as targets of South Africa's retaliatory sanctions. I argue that, in the context of profound regional economic and political vulnerability, sanctions had three outcomes. First, they allowed postcolonial elites to build their domestic power bases. Second, as instruments of South Africa's regional hegemony, retaliatory sanctions propelled southern African states to construct overarching structures of regional cooperation. Third, and more significantly, regional mobilization for international sanctions permitted the entry of powerful external actors to counterbalance South Africa's regional economic and military hegemony.

IN THE SHADOWS OF RHODESIA: FORGING A SANCTIONS POLICY

In Africa, sanctions against South Africa embraced two contradictory features. On one hand, regional leaders perceived sanctions as a tool for decolonizing southern Africa; a postcolonial region would, in turn, afford them more geographical space, organizational leverage, and a moral victory over apartheid. On the other hand, states bordering the white minority-ruled territories of Rhodesia, Mozambique, Angola, and Namibia, bore tremendous costs that compromised their long-term ability to challenge South Africa. While

Map 4 Southern Africa

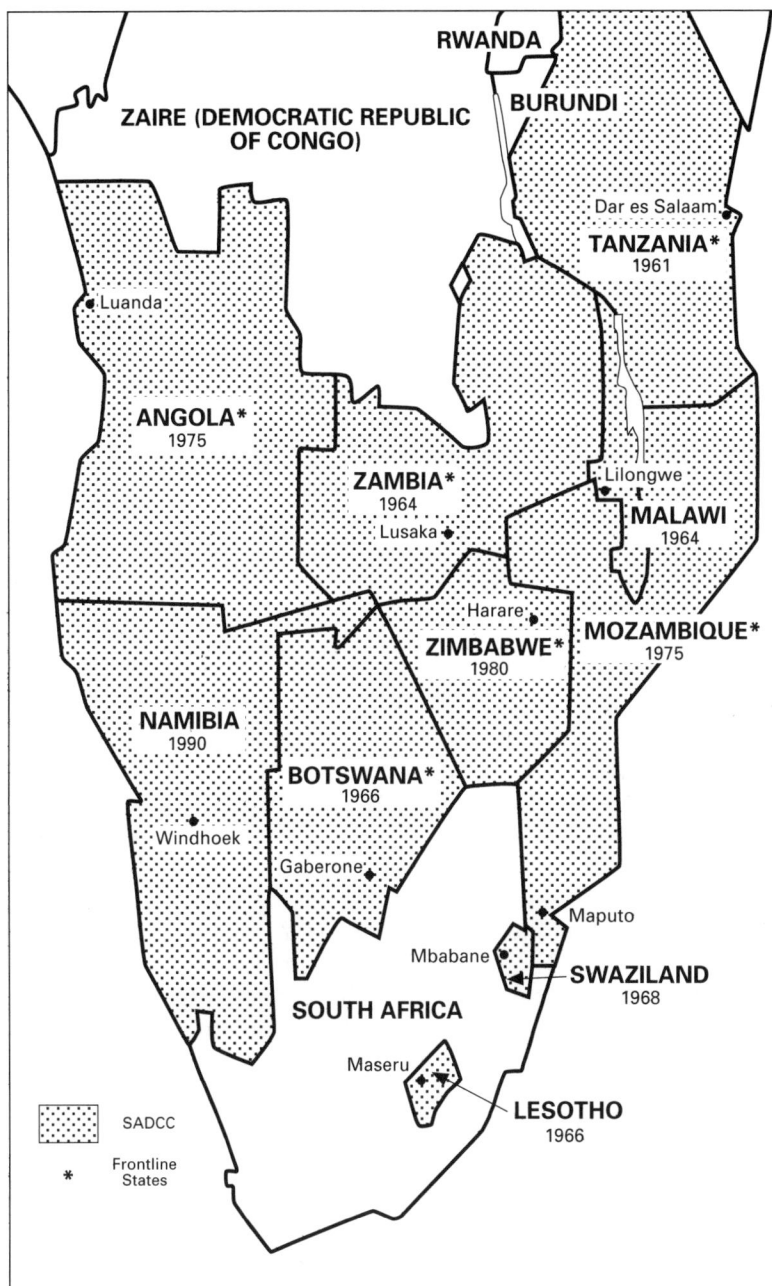

decolonization produced the political infrastructure for change, it left insurmountable obstacles in its wake. Southern African leaders thus faced an ineluctable geopolitical quandary: location gave them a natural advantage over distant states in the implementation sanctions, but proximity bred economic and political vulnerability to retaliatory measures. Intricate structures of economic dependency on the targets of sanctions, Rhodesia and South Africa, compounded their predicament.

The Rhodesian Unilateral Declaration of Independence (UDI) in 1965 set the broader parameters for regional sanctions.[6] African states first called on the British government to assume responsibility for its colony and then used United Nations (UN) machinery to garner international action. Zambia quickly declared sanctions against Rhodesia. Ironically, in the short term, these measures also increased its trade links with South Africa.[7] For instance, imports from South Africa rose from $48.2 million in 1965 to $82 million in 1969. Attempts to diversify trade failed because South Africa proved the cheapest source of supply for crucial imports.[8]

UDI also generated significant pressures on external actors' policies toward the region.[9] African states expected Western countries, universally perceived as both silent partners of minority regimes and sanctions laggards, to offset the economic costs of colonialism and apartheid. Zambia's search for external assistance to ease the burdens of sanctions reflected its inordinate dependence on external actors.[10] UN Security Council Resolutions 253 (1968) and 277 (1970) recommended that Zambia be compensated for its "special economic hardships as a result of the decision to implement fully the mandatory sanctions."[11]

Zambia's 1973 decision to divert its copper exports away from Rhodesian railroads, as part of the sanctions package, pushed it in the direction of transport collaboration with Tanzania. Starting with the construction of a road and pipeline, the search for alternative transport routes culminated in the Chinese-built Tanzania–Zambia Railway (Tazara), the first organizational foundation for long-term regional economic integration.[12] This approach evolved initially as a compromise between two broad visions represented by Tanzania's activism and Zambia's moderation. From the mid-1960s, Tanzania's relative isolation gave it regional leadership that complemented Zambia's geopolitical overexposure. Over time, domestic mobilization for national unity and development by single-party bureaucratic systems became indistinguishable from the regional politics

Map 5   Regional rail transport routes

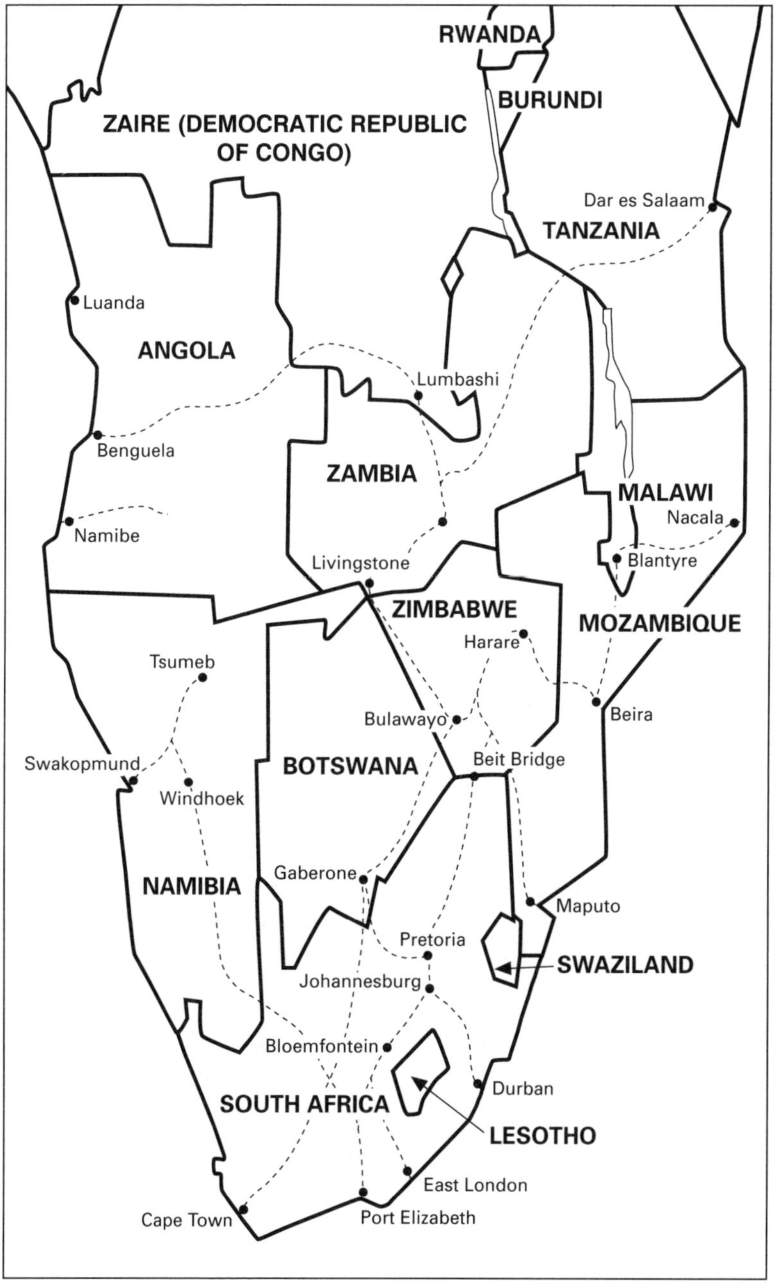

of decolonization. Julius Nyerere's African socialism and Kenneth Kaunda's humanism (later combined with Afro-communist regimes in Angola and Mozambique) worked in tandem as mobilizing ideologies for nation- and state-building, and for southern African liberation.[13]

Initially, sanctions against Rhodesia failed to bring down the Smith government, which shifted to import-substitution industrialization and aggressive export promotion to Western markets via South Africa and colonial Mozambique. Meanwhile, Zambia's economy declined, as rapid diversification of transport routes had been achieved at a great sacrifice.[14] In July 1974, the UN Assistance Program for Zambia estimated that the border closure cost 186.7 million kwacha (K), of which international assistance contributed only K40 million.[15] In 1978, after years of coping with UDI and collapsed copper prices, Zambia reversed its policy by reopening the southern border with Rhodesia in the name of economic survival.[16]

Sanctions against the Smith regime began to bite only after the collapse of Portuguese rule in Mozambique in 1975. Samora Machel's Front for the Liberation of Mozambique (Frelimo), infused by socialist activism, imposed transport and economic sanctions against Rhodesia in March 1976, with devastating impact. More pertinent, Mozambique's provision of military and logistical bases for Zimbabwean liberation movements made it a dependable link in the overall decolonization strategy of the FLS.

Like Zambia before it, Mozambique imposed sanctions at immense economic costs. Participation in Zimbabwe's liberation spawned destabilization and military pressure from the Smith regime, with far-reaching consequences. Furthermore, Mozambique's sanctions dramatized the dilemma of continued reliance on international economic compensation. While the UN Security Council launched an international aid program to compensate Mozambique for the losses sustained from sanctions, a 1976 UN report underscored the inadequacy of this assistance:

The direct costs to Mozambique of applying sanctions may be estimated at between $139 million and $165 million for the next twelve months, and between $108 million and $134 million for the following 12 months. Thereafter the costs are likely to be in the region of $106 million to $132 million annually. The appeal for international aid has so far generated aid totalling approximately $100 million, but most of this is to be spread over several years, and almost all is in the form of loans that will add to Mozambique's long-term external debt.[17]

For Mozambique, sanctions against Rhodesia compounded problems of postcolonial transition. Portugal's hasty withdrawal thrust Mozambique deeper into South Africa's economic ambit, long before Pretoria's destabilization policy of the 1980s.[18]

The cumulative effect of Mozambique's sanctions was to intensify Rhodesia's dependence on South Africa in security, trade, finance, and transport. Until the border closure, Rhodesia shipped about half of its exports via Mozambican ports; the closure forced Smith to reroute over 1.5 million tons of export goods per year through South Africa, at great expense. Similarly, for the first ten years of Rhodesian sanctions, South African refineries processed the bulk of its oil; after the Mozambique border closure, South Africa took over the transport network, supplying oil to Rhodesia through a hastily constructed rail line.[19]

These structural links subsequently compromised the ability of the Zimbabwean government to take part in sanctions against South Africa after independence in 1980. Hopes that a "socialist transition" would undo its dependence foundered on the imperatives of postcolonial reconstruction and regional instability. Zimbabwe's cautious stance toward the apartheid regime in the 1980s essentially mirrored Zambia's well-trodden path. These structural constraints, however, did not preclude the Robert Mugabe government from using sanctions as a tool for domestic mobilization and legitimation.[20]

SANCTIONS IN THE 1980s

With Zimbabwe's decolonization, the African sanctions movement concentrated on South Africa. Yet there was growing realization that few regional states would impose new sanctions. Though most states had already imposed diplomatic, cultural, and sports restrictions, economic measures did not appear to be on the horizon. The protracted nature of Zimbabwean decolonization reinforced the view that the FLS would not endure years of confrontation with South Africa because of their structural and institutional dependence. As Jesmond Blumenfeld observed, "Few people, even among the FLS governments themselves, seriously expect them to 'apply' (let alone enforce) anything more than token economic sanctions. . . . It is widely assumed that the FLS would have to be excused from participation in most significant sanctions."[21]

In light of their incapacity, regional states decided to construct collective mechanisms that would insulate them from the potential effects of both international sanctions and South African retaliatory measures. Building on the political infrastructure of FLS cooperation, Angola, Botswana, Lesotho, Malawi, Mozambique, Swaziland, Tanzania, Zambia, and Zimbabwe established SADCC in 1980 to foster regional development through sectoral economic coordination. The Lusaka Declaration that created SADCC identified four broad objectives: to reduce economic dependence, particularly (but not only) on South Africa; to forge links to create genuine and equitable regional integration; to mobilize resources to promote the implementation of national, interstate, and regional policies; and to act in concert to secure international cooperation for economic liberation.[22]

As a mechanism for regional integration, SADCC's fate from the outset was tied to its ability to attract international attention to its members' geopolitical plight. Some regional states also used SADCC to mobilize for comprehensive international sanctions against South Africa. SADCC's dual strategy of external assistance and sanctions succeeded because South Africa was the sole source of regional insecurity. As Simba Makoni, SADCC's secretary general, emphasized, "Foreign support for SADCC projects within the countries most severely affected by South Africa's war of destabilization is one way to cushion the impact of sanctions. For SADCC, it is sanctions *by* South Africa rather than *against* South Africa that are the main concern."[23]

South Africa's destabilization repertoire included retaliation to keep its neighbors endemically weak, to raise the costs of their support for liberation movements, and to demonstrate the fallacy of decolonization.[24] As Blumenfeld characterized it, "Pretoria views the FLS both as its hostages and as its escape route in the wider international sanctions campaign. . . . Pretoria uses destabilization both to keep the FLS ambivalent in their own attitudes to sanctions and to demonstrate to the rest of the world that escalating sanctions will bring dire consequences for the rest of the region."[25] By supporting anti-government rebels in Angola and Mozambique, destabilization embraced surgical military attacks on FLS capitals, economic sabotage and blockades, and propaganda broadcasts. As an integral weapon in South Africa's armory, economic sanctions complemented the policy of military intervention that targeted strategic assets such as power lines, dams, and roads in the FLS.

But by making SADCC states even more vulnerable via destabilization, South Africa complicated the policies of its ardent allies. Before the 1980s, Western powers had, with varying degrees of success, engaged South Africa and the FLS to find mutual solutions to the Zimbabwe and Namibia problems. For the most part, they also hoped to preclude punitive economic sanctions. Instead, South Africa launched its policy of Total Strategy, designed to counter a perceived communist Total Onslaught. This shift scuttled initiatives on Namibian decolonization and South Africa's shaky rapprochement with some of its neighbors.[26]

The ferocity of South Africa's military and economic pressures galvanized SADCC's efforts. In the face of sabotage, their strategy in the mid-1980s was to invest in and secure the transport routes through Mozambique, Angola, and Tanzania that would delink the region from South Africa.[27] Military training and security became a logical part of overall economic coordination, most notably the joint Mozambican–Zimbabwean operations that secured the Beira and Nacala railroads, and the Malawi–Zimbabwe highway.[28] The UN estimated that destabilization by proxy war cost 1.5 million lives between 1980 and 1988, including 925 000 children (primarily in Angola, Namibia, and Mozambique). In 1990, Malawi hosted over 800 000 Mozambican refugees. Cumulatively, the economies of SADCC suffered losses estimated at $60.5 billion.[29]

To mitigate some of these costs, Western and multilateral donors organized as SADCC's "partners" to provide an estimated $2.6 billion in annual aid between 1980 and 1990. Towards the late 1980s, even the more conservative Reagan and Thatcher administrations, which were at the forefront of opposition to economic sanctions, joined hands with the Scandinavians to promote SADCC's economic viability as a long-term counterweight to South Africa.[30] External assistance prevented the collapse of regional economies, but it could not radically change the imbalances. Yet SADCC achieved only partial successes in its major goals of reducing transport and trade dependence on South Africa.[31] The irony, as Blumenfeld noted, "is that as SADCC relies more and more on foreign aid to make good the damage caused by South Africa's destabilization policies, so Pretoria has even less need to heed the consequences of its actions. . . . [F]oreign aid continues to provide SADCC countries with the wherewithal to pay for their imports from, and their use of the transport routes through, South Africa.[32] Furthermore, as Robert Davies and Judith Head observed, "patterns of economic interaction [were] modified to the disadvantage of neighboring states."[33]

Nonetheless, destabilization fuelled the anti-apartheid sanctions movement. South Africa's regional military intervention clearly demonstrated the inability of the apartheid regime to sell its domestic reform policies, particularly the tricameral parliament.[34] When the South African townships exploded in the mid-1980s, Botha exported these crises via regional subversion.[35] This coincidence of internal pressures and regional aggression underlined the urgency of international sanctions as a mode of jump-starting fundamental change. Since SADCC's pro-sanctions stance was often an invitation to South African retaliation, regional states benefitted from this shift in focus to insurrection in the townships. Internal repression and militarization of society intensified global pressures for economic sanctions and disinvestment. Powerful actors formerly set against sanctions, including the US, Britain, members of the European community, and some international bankers and corporations, now challenged white supremacy.[36]

SADCC and the FLS renewed global activism for sanctions. The Commonwealth assumed a central role in this diplomacy, offering the FLS a low-cost forum for sustaining the sanctions debate.[37] Through the Commonwealth, the African underdogs, in Nyerere's apt description, "embarrass[ed] the Thatcher government in its anti-sanctions stance."[38] After the Commonwealth adopted a package of sanctions in 1985, Kaunda and Mugabe became the most dynamic regional proponents of comprehensive economic sanctions; even when South Africa warned of the dire effects of an economic embargo, Zambia and Zimbabwe committed themselves to the Commonwealth sanctions package. In Mugabe's words, "We must be determined to bear the burden our own way, to counteract the measures South Africa will impose against us. It is just like war. Let us prepare for it."[39]

But Zambia and Zimbabwe failed to convince their SADCC counterparts to join them. At the Luanda summit in August 1986, southern African leaders reaffirmed their long-established position that economic dependence upon South Africa left them in no position to impose sanctions against South Africa.[40] Makoni summarized his group's position: "Although we recognize that individual member states may not be in a position to impose sanctions, SADCC supports the imposition of sanctions against South Africa by those within the organization and outside who are in a position to do so. The vulnerability of SADCC countries cannot be used as an excuse by those in a position to impose not to do so. SADCC member states will cooperate to minimize the effects on their economies of the imposition of sanctions."[41]

Whenever the FLS used the Commonwealth to promote anti-apartheid sanctions, South Africa retaliated. For example, Pretoria implemented selective oil and trade embargoes against Zambia and Zimbabwe in 1986 and 1987, at the height of the Commonwealth sanctions crusade. Mugabe's description of these measures as a "declaration of economic war" underscored the predicament of the southern African states.[42]

GLOBAL SANCTIONS IN THE REGIONAL EQUATION

In the mid-1980s, SADCC states tried to woo foreign investors who were disinvesting from South Africa. But even though the South African economy had become, in the words of the *Financial Times*, an "economic cul-de-sac," no massive financial flows shifted to the SADCC economies.[43] Some firms merely relocated to South Africa's near-periphery, composed of Botswana, Lesotho, Namibia, and Swaziland.[44] As members of the Southern African Customs Union (SACU), these states enjoyed common protective tariffs, which allowed duty-free movement of goods and a revenue-sharing scheme but which also ensured captive markets for South African industry.[45] In the context of global anti-apartheid trade sanctions, these countries absorbed most of South Africa's relatively low-quality and uncompetitive manufactured goods, allowing South Africa to garner hard currency. Beyond SACU, Zambia's trade relations with South Africa typified the persistence of links despite sanctions: imports from South Africa rose from 16.9 percent in 1986 to 29.58 percent in 1992.[46] Similarly, Zimbabwe extended its preferential trade agreement with South Africa and opened a trade mission in Johannesburg in 1989.[47]

South African companies also used the region as part of an intricate web of sanctions-busting and evasive measures that protected the apartheid regime from international pressure. For example, long-established interlocking institutional links enabled South African companies to negotiate false documents with intermediaries in the region to camouflage their products.[48] Other activities included "unconventional trade agreements," a strategy that targeted vulnerable regional states as go-betweens in circumventing the oil embargo, and elaborate schemes by South African companies to route goods circuitously via SADCC states to major international markets. Some South African companies established last-stage assembly plants in Botswana, Lesotho, and Swaziland, allowing them to label products in a way that disguised their South African components. Primary products such as citrus, wood, pulp, coal, and asbestos also reached the outside world as products of other countries.[49] And South Africa's 1986 treaty with Lesotho that launched the Highland Water Scheme was one of the most visible examples of international lenders circumventing anti-apartheid sanctions.[50]

The inability of the FLS to participate wholeheartedly in sanctions played into the hands of opponents of sanctions. For example, Margaret Thatcher could variously point to the "hypocrisy" of Mugabe and Kaunda in justifying Britain's anti-sanctions stance.[51] In testimony to US House of Representatives in 1986, Deputy Assistant Secretary of State John Whitehead noted SADCC's reassessment of the effects of both sanctions and South African retaliatory measures, which fostered regional trade and relegated sanctions rhetoric to the margins of international meetings. He reiterated that US "regional diplomacy is committed to reducing these states' economic vulnerabilities and to easing misunderstandings and tensions in their dealings with South Africa."[52]

External opponents of sanctions, though, were unable to use SADCC's vulnerability to deter the groundswell of anti-apartheid sanctions, in part because of South Africa's own reluctance to promote profound internal change and to reduce its regional militarism. At the 1989 Kuala Lumpur Commonwealth summit, even Thatcher – still refusing to acknowledge that sanctions influenced Pretoria – agreed that their abatement should wait for signs of "clear and irreversible change" in South Africa.[53] Ultimately, South Africa's attempts to deter regional states from their global sanctions campaign became moot when internal repression isolated the apartheid regime and undermined its economy, as the other chapters in this volume detail.

CONCLUSION

Optimism about the region's potential role in sanctioning South Africa, engendered by the independence of Angola, Mozambique, and then Zimbabwe, gave way to pessimism in the wake of destabilization. Yet these weak states straddled successfully the delicate lines between economic dependence and international mobilization for sanctions, a testimony to their ability to survive in a hostile geopolitical context. South African aggression and destabilization legitimated the calls for universal action to end apartheid, reinforcing the southern African states' persistent claims that sanctions would promote both internal transformation and the preemption of regional conflicts. Nyerere summarized this view succinctly: "All the major non-white leaders of the anti-apartheid struggle demand that economic sanctions be imposed against the regime. They are not stupid. . . . But they believe that sanctions will weaken the South African apartheid system. . . . We know that South Africa's retaliation may well be directed against neighboring African states. But we also know that our freedom and economic development will remain under constant threat until apartheid is defeated."[54]

Although SADCC's gains were modest, its institutional mechanisms formed the basis for ongoing post-apartheid transition to a comprehensive Southern African Development Community (SADC), created in 1992. Conceptually, SADC enshrines the long-sought goal of a South Africa taking its rightful place as the center for economic growth and development in a decolonized southern Africa. Institutionally, it reflects both the endurance of South African economic hegemony and, to the small states, the long-term mechanisms for regional restabilization.

These experiences of the FLS and SADCC demonstrate that neighboring states can be crucial players in mobilizing international sanctions, but at a potentially devastating cost. Neighboring states can determine both the moral and material efficacy of global attempts to influence the target. And as sanctioners weigh the costs and benefits of such measures, they should consider consequences beyond the target's borders. Small states in the region may gain or lose, both economically and politically. A sophisticated – and more successful – approach to sanctions will incorporate this regional dimension.

Notes

1. "Speech by President Frederick Chiluba of Zambia to the National Press Club," *Federal News Service* (Washington, DC), 19 February 1992.
2. Quoted in "Southern Africa: Keeping Friends among the International Donors," *Inter Press Service*, 2 December 1992.
3. See N. C. Crawford and A. Klotz, "How Sanctions Work: A Framework for Analysis," in this volume.
4. K. R. Nossal, *Rain Dancing: Sanctions in Canadian and Australian Foreign Policy* (Toronto: University of Toronto Press, 1994).
5. Ibid., p. 29.
6. L. T. Kapungu, *The United Nations and Economic Sanctions Against Rhodesia* (London: Lexington, 1973), pp. 94–6.
7. R. Weiss, "South Africa: The Grand African Economic Design," in C. Legum, ed., *Africa Contemporary Record: Annual Survey and Documents, 1970–1971* (London: Rex Collings, 1971), p. A13.
8. "British Territory: Rhodesia," in C. Legum, ed., *Africa Contemporary Record: Annual Survey and Documents, 1970–1971* (London: Rex Collings, 1971), p. B232.
9. H. R. Strack, *Sanctions: The Case of Rhodesia* (Syracuse, NY: Syracuse University Press, 1978), pp. 61–8.
10. See Kapungu, *United Nations*, pp. 94–6; and M. P. Doxey, *Economic Sanctions and International Enforcement* (New York: Oxford University Press, 1980), pp. 110–12.
11. "The Political and Economic Assessments of the Situation by the UN Mission," 5 March 1973; quoted in C. Legum, ed., *Africa Contemporary Record: Annual Survey and Documents, 1971–1972* (London: Rex Collings, 1972), p. C49.
12. Strack, *Sanctions*, pp. 178–80.
13. See R. Hall, *The High Price of Principles: Kaunda and the White South* (Harmondsworth, UK: Penguin, 1973); D. G. Anglin, *Zambian Crisis Behavior: Confronting Rhodesia's Unilateral Declaration of Independence, 1965–1966* (London: McGill University Press, 1994); C. M. Morris, *A Humanist in Africa* (Nashville: Abingdon, 1966); G. M. Khadiagala, *Allies in Adversity: The Frontline States in Southern African Security, 1975–1993* (Athens: Ohio University Press, 1994).
14. G. Arnold, "Rhodesia: Increasing the Effectiveness of Sanctions," in O. Stokke and C. Widstrand, eds., *Southern Africa: The UN-OAU Conference*, vol. 2 (Uppsala: Scandinavian Institute of African Studies, 1973), pp. 163–72; R. Renwick, *Economic Sanctions* (Cambridge: Harvard University Press, 1981), pp. 43–9.
15. "Zambia," in C. Legum, ed., *Africa Contemporary Record: Annual Survey and Documents, 1973–1974* (New York: Africana, 1974), p. B336.
16. R. H. Green, *South Africa: The Impact of Sanctions on Southern African Economies* (London: Africa Bureau, 1981), p. 11.
17. UN Economic and Social Council [ECOSOC], *Assistance to Mozambique, Report no. E/5812*, April 1976, pp. 3–4.
18. See M. J. Azevedo, "A Sober Commitment to Liberation? Mozambique and South Africa, 1974–1979," *African Affairs* 79 (1980), pp.

571–80; H. Campbell, "War, Reconstruction, and Dependence in Mozambique," *Third World Quarterly* 6 (1984), pp. 839–67; and "Mozambique," in C. Legum, ed., *Africa Contemporary Record: Annual Survey and Documents, 1976–1977* (London: Africana, 1977), pp. B301–4.

19. R. B. Sutcliffe, "The Political Economy of Rhodesian Sanctions," *Journal of Commonwealth Political Studies* 7 (1969), pp. 113–25; E. Windrich, *Britain and the Politics of Rhodesian Independence* (London: Croom Helm, 1978), p. 216; and W. Minter and E. Schimdt, "When Sanctions Worked: The Case of Rhodesia Reexamined," *African Affairs* 87 (1988), p. 207.

20. See Green, *South Africa*, p. 10; A. Klotz, "Race and Nationalism in Zimbabwean Foreign Policy," *Round Table* 327 (1993), pp. 255–79; H. Patel, "Regional Security in Southern Africa: Zimbabwe," *Survival* 30 (1988), pp. 38–58; and S. M. Davis, "Facing Goliath: Zimbabwe's Role in Conflict Resolution in South Africa," *South Africa International* 21 (1991), pp. 244–55.

21. J. Blumenfeld, "A Cautionary View of Economic Sanctions and Southern African Peace and Security," in International Peace Academy, *Southern Africa in Crisis: Regional and International Responses*, Report No. 28, 1987, p. 195.

22. A. Tostensen, *Dependence and Collective Self-Reliance in Southern Africa: The Case of SADCC* (Uppsala: Scandinavian Institute of African Studies, 1982); C. Hill, "Regional Cooperation in Southern Africa," *African Affairs* 82 (1983), pp. 215–39; and R. Weisfelder, "Collective Foreign Policy Decision–Making Within SADCC," *Africa Today* 38 (1991), pp. 5–17.

23. Quoted in P. G. Moll, "Economic Sanctions: Part One," *South African Outlook* 117 (1987), p. 54.

24. J. Hanlon, *Beggar Your Neighbor: Apartheid Power in Southern Africa* (London: James Currey, 1986); C. Desmond, "Economic Sanctions: South Africa's Own Sanctions," *Third World Affairs 1987* (London: Third World Foundation, 1989), pp. 104–14; P. Johnson and D. Martin, *Apartheid Terrorism: The Destabilization Report* (Bloomington: Indiana University Press, 1989); and J. Saul, *Recolonization and Resistance: Southern Africa in the 1990s* (Trenton: Africa World Press, 1993), pp. 59–60.

25. Blumenfeld, "A Cautionary View," p. 196.

26. See K. W. Grundy, "Pax Pretoriana: South Africa's Regional Policy," *Current History* 84 (1985), pp. 150–4; S. Metz, "Pretoria's 'Total Strategy' and Low Intensity Warfare in Southern Africa," *Comparative Strategy* 6 (1987), pp. 437–69; and N. C. Crawford, "South Africa's New Foreign and Military Policy," *Africa Today* 42 (1995), pp. 94–6.

27. G. Maasdorp, *Economic Cooperation in Southern Africa: Prospects for Regional Integration* (London: Conflict Studies Paper No. 253, 1992); C. Stoneman and C. Thompson, "SADCC: The Realistic Hope for Southern Africa," *The Courier* (Brussels) 34 (1992), pp. 74–6.

28. R. Martin, "Regional Security in Southern Africa: More Angolas, Mozambiques or Neutrals?" *Survival* 29 (1987), pp. 387–402; M. Holland, *The European Community and South Africa: European Political Cooperation Under Strain* (London: Allen and Unwin, 1988).

29. United Nations, *South African Destabilization: The Economic Cost of Frontline Resistance to Apartheid* (New York: UN, 1989), pp. 1–56; UNICEF, *Children on the Frontline: The Impact of Apartheid, Destabilization and Warfare on Children in South and Southern Africa* (Geneva: UN, 1988); P. Johnson and D. Martin, eds., *Destructive Engagement: Southern Africa at War* (Harare: Zimbabwe Publishing House, 1986), p. 271; and R. H. Green, "Sanctions and the SADCC Economies," *Third World Affairs 1987* (London: Third World Foundation, 1989), pp. 115–23.

30. A. M. Hawkins, "Economic Development in the SADCC Countries," in G. Maasdorp and A. Whiteside, eds., *Toward a Post-Apartheid Future: Political and Economic Relations in Southern Africa* (New York: Macmillan, 1992), p. 106.

31. N. Thede, "SADCC: Autonomy or Submission?" in N. Thede and P. Beaudet, eds., *A Post-Apartheid Southern Africa?* (New York: St. Martin's, 1994), pp. 43–5; L. Thompson, "Of Myths, Monsters, and Money: Regime Conceptualization and Theory in the Southern African Context," *Journal of Contemporary Southern African Studies* 10 (1992), pp. 72–5; Green, "Sanctions and SADCC Economies," pp. 118–19; and Hawkins, "Economic Development," pp. 116–20.

32. Blumenfeld, "A Cautionary View," p. 198.

33. R. Davies and J. Head, "The Future of Mine Migrancy in the Context of Broader Trends in Migration in Southern Africa," *Journal of Southern African Studies* 21 (1995), p. 446. See also R. Davies, "South Africa's Economic Relations with Africa: Current Patterns and Future Perspectives," in A. Adedeji, ed., *South Africa and Africa: Within or Apart* (London: Zed, 1996), pp. 170–3.

34. S. Nolutshungu, "South Africa's Position in the World," *Southern African Political and Economic Monthly* (1993), pp. 46–9; S. Nolutshungu, "Recent Developments in Southern Africa: Reform, Repression, and Democratization," in International Peace Academy, *Southern Africa in Crisis*, pp. 1–17; T. M. Shaw and M. M. Sejanamane, "Southern Africa: Path-Breaking and Peace-Breaking," *Third World Affairs* (London: Third World Foundation, 1989), pp. 165–70.

35. C. Jenkins, "Sanctions: An Economic Analysis," *South African Outlook* 16 (1986), pp. 12–26; P. Gillespie, "Botswana: Beleaguered Oasis," *Southern African Report* 1 (1986), pp. 9–10; Shaw and Sejanamane, "Southern Africa," pp. 165–70; H. Campbell, "Beyond Sanctions and Destabilization: Toward Popular Mobilization," in International Peace Academy, *Southern Africa in Crisis*, pp. 151–67.

36. See the chapters on economic sanctions in this volume.

37. See L. Freeman, "All But One: Britain, the Commonwealth, and Sanctions," in M. Orkin, ed., *Sanctions Against Apartheid* (New York: St. Martin's, 1989), pp. 142–56; A. Klotz, *Norms in International Relations: The Struggle against Apartheid* (Ithaca: Cornell University Press, 1995), chs. 4 and 8.

38. Quoted in *West Africa*, 9–17 July 1985, p. 838.

39. Quoted in D. G. Anglin, "The Frontline States and Sanctions Against South Africa," in R. Edgar, ed., *Sanctioning Apartheid* (Trenton:

Africa World Press, 1990), p. 266. See also Davis, "Facing Goliath," p. 251.
40. *Africa Economic Digest*, 30 August 1986, p. 25.
41. *Southern African Economist*, February–March 1988, p. 31.
42. *Africa Research Bulletin*, 31 August 1986, p. 8307.
43. P. Gawith, "The Sanctions Debate: Western Policy Flounders as Trade with South Africa Flourishes," *Financial Times*, 22 June 1990, p. 4.
44. R. Davies, *Trade Sanctions and Regional Impact in Southern Africa* (London: Africa Bureau, 1981); L. J. Chingambo, "SADCC and South Africa: Limits and Realities of Integration Under Destabilization," *Round Table* 308 (1988), pp. 387–403; J. Hanlon, "Successes and Future Prospects of Sanctions against South Africa," *Review of African Political Economy* 51 (1991), pp. 91–3; J. Hanlon, "Post-Apartheid South Africa and Its Neighbors," *Third World Quarterly* 9 (1987), pp. 437–49.
45. J. Hanlon, "On the Frontline: Destabilization, the SADCC States, and Sanctions," in Orkin, ed., *Sanctions Against Apartheid*, pp. 181–2; G. Maasdorp, "Trade Relations in Southern Africa – Changes Ahead?" in Maasdorp and Whiteside, eds., *Toward a Post-Apartheid Future*, pp. 142–4.
46. S. Yalemana, "Chiluba Looking for Security in South Africa," *Southern African Political and Economic and Monthly*, September 1993, p. 16.
47. R. Riddell, "Zimbabwe in the Frontline," in Edgar, ed. *Sanctioning Apartheid*, p. 366.
48. J. Blumenfeld, "The Economics of South African Sanctions," *Intereconomics* (1987); H. S. Kibola and A. L. Nyange, "Problems of Enforcing Multilateral Sanctions Against South Africa," in International Peace Academy, *Southern Africa in Crisis*, pp. 169–88.
49. J. Daniel, "Sneaking Around Sanctions," *Southern African Report*, May 1989, pp. 22–3. For analysis of other sanctions evasion mechanisms such as air links and the role of regional states as conduits for sanctions-busting, see J. P. Hayes, *Economic Effects of Sanctions on Southern Africa* (London: Gower, 1987), and *Africa Confidential*, 20 August 1986.
50. J. H. Cobbe, "Economic Aspects of Lesotho's Relations with South Africa," *Journal of Modern African Studies* 26 (1988), pp. 71–89; J. Danisweski, "South Africa – Water," *South African Press Association Feature*, 5 March 1994.
51. Hanlon, "On the Frontline," p. 180.
52. J. C. Whitehead, "The Potential Impact of Imposing Sanctions Against South Africa," *Department of State Bulletin*, August 1988, p. 58. See also the discussion in T. J. Redden, "The US Comprehensive Anti-Apartheid Act of 1986: Anti-Apartheid or Anti-African National Congress?" *African Affairs* 88 (1989), pp. 595–605.
53. "The Commonwealth: A Leaky Boat," *Financial Mail*, 27 October 1989, p. 62.
54. Quoted in Hanlon, "On the Frontline," p. 180.

14 Making Sanctions Work: Comparative Lessons
Audie Klotz

The struggle to eliminate apartheid encompassed many facets of social, economic, and political reform, including demands to outlaw explicit social discrimination, institute equal political rights and propagate peace in the region. Most of the chapters in this volume demonstrate that international pressures contributed to these goals. Sanctioners strengthened the anti-apartheid movement, and added political and economic incentives for the ruling National Party (NP) to repeal apartheid laws and enter into negotiations with the extra-parliamentary opposition. Numerous strategic, economic, and social sanctions also weakened the regime's ability to maintain apartheid, even undermining its ideological foundations. Yet some of the chapters also show that sanctions produced counterproductive effects. The militarization of government and society increased; import-substitution industrialization developed; an isolationist spirit crystallized among the white electorate.

The South African democratic transition thus offers many insights into the interrelationship between international sanctions and domestic politics, rather than providing one overriding lesson about international economic coercion. The legacies of sanctions continue in the post-apartheid era, serving as a reminder that there is also no sharp cut-off point for evaluating the impact of international pressures; hopefully other scholars will extend our study of the South African case to include these longer-term consequences as they become apparent in subsequent years. The complexity of the sanctioners' cumulative goal of total political, economic, and social transformation of the apartheid system precludes a unitary measure of utility, in part because no single discrete policy decision existed against which to gauge the efficacy of international influence. Consequently, making a simple assessment of sanctions against South Africa is impossible. Policymakers should not expect sanctions to be the sole tool for achieving political change.

This conclusion, therefore, synthesizes our empirical evidence in order to reach a balanced evaluation of both the positive and negative consequences of international pressures. While our analytical frame-work in Chapter 2 stressed the importance of disaggregating types of sanctions, this chapter recognizes the synergies and contradic-tions among these tools of influence. The strategic, economic and social measures covered in the three parts of this volume demon-strate diverse impacts on states, economies, and societies, both within the target country and globally. Two themes are particularly strik-ing in the contribution of sanctions to the South African transi-tion: the dynamic nature of the sanctions process and the persistence of the anti-apartheid opposition – not least the majority popula-tion's willingness to suffer the consequences of sanctions. Table 14.1 offers a typology of tools and targets, which the following sec-tion explains in more detail.

Based on the implications of this one case, I then draw out broader lessons for both practitioners and international relations theorists. Throughout the volume as a whole, we reject the sharp distinction between domestic and international politics which flows from the state-centrism of conventional sanctions analyses (and international relations theory more generally). South Africa and other potential targets of sanctions are fundamentally integrated into a global economy and society, as well as a system of interstate relations. Sanctions will be more useful in other cases if policymakers recog-nize these complex connections. While sanctions may not always be appropriate, I argue that international pressures can be effec-tive under the right conditions.

SANCTIONS AGAINST SOUTH AFRICA

In drawing together the sectoral analyses in this volume, I look at three dimensions of the target: government, economy and society. Unlike in our initial framework, however, I now integrate "spillover" and "externalities" into each category because of the strong inter-connections between domestic, regional, and global dimensions. Thus the discussion of the government includes alliances, and I stress fundamental links between domestic, regional, and global econ-omies. The transnational nature of the anti-apartheid movement reinforces a global, rather than narrowly domestic, conception of society. I end this section with an overall assessment of sanctions for the South African transition.

Table 14.1   Tools, targets, and consequences

	Strategic sanctions	Economic sanctions	Social sanctions
Government and Interstate System	Arms embargoes created shortages of spare parts and weapons Technology boycotts shifted regional and global alliances	International bankers pressured for reforms Threat of economic isolation changed patterns of regional dependency	Diplomatic isolation increased costs of maintaining regional and global ties Lack of global recognition contributed to the failure of the Bantustan system International recognition supported exiled liberation movements
Domestic and Global Economy	Growing mililtary-industrial complex strengthened mining and key industrial interests Stockpiling oil and other strategic resources increased costs to the economy Import-substitution in arms industries created some new jobs but also increased pressures on economic aspects of apartheid	Higher prices for oil, international capital and other embargoed imports exacerbated recession Various sanctions led to job losses in some sectors but gains in others Efforts to circumvent sanctions benefitted some neighboring states but hurt others	Lack of recognition limited regional integration and trade opportunities Intellectual isolation inflicted professional costs, especially on white elite Boycotts precluded potential markets for cultural exports
Domestic and Global Society	Regional tensions spurred militarization and mobilization of (white) society Global isolation reinforced "laager" mentality and culture of secrecy	Growing global divestment and sanctions movement spurred domestic resistance through solidarity Circumvention of some economic embargoes – but not finance – bolstered white resolve Declining economic conditions spurred "trek to Lusaka" by white elites to negotiate with the ANC	Sports boycotts inflicted psychological costs on white elites Protests by entertainers and sports fans raised global awareness of apartheid Various cultural measures bolstered resolve of anti-apartheid movement

Government and Interstate System

Conventional strategic analyses generally view sanctions as a tool of foreign policy to influence the behavior of a target government. While other dimensions are important, we should not underestimate the direct effects on the strength of the state (defined either as elite decision makers or as a cluster of institutions). Analysts should also consider the implications for interstate relations because strategic, economic and social sanctions can significantly alter regional and global alliances.

Chapters 3, 4, and 5 demonstrate that sanctions aimed at strategic resources had a significant impact upon South Africa's military capabilities. Neta Crawford shows that arms embargoes proved substantially debilitating over the long run by creating crucial shortages of spare parts for aircraft and a general inability to modernize.[1] One result was South Africa's declining air superiority in the region, especially in its war against Angola. But Gilbert Khadiagala's assessment of regional implications reminds us that the apartheid government still maintained enough military force to destabilize its neighbors. Its aggressive regional policies, however, backfired to the extent that they spurred global opposition to apartheid, even among steadfast allies. For example, David Fig's study of access to nuclear technology indicates that suppliers shifted as anti-apartheid pressure grew in the US and Britain. Nevertheless, European and Israeli connections enabled South Africa to acquire the bomb. Overall, strategic sanctions weakened South Africa directly by undermining its military capabilities and straining its key alliances, but the state remained strong enough to respond to perceived regional security threats. Unfortunately, these measures tended to reinforce aggressive and isolationist tendencies rather than encouraging elites to solve the country's security problems through negotiations.

In contrast to military measures, economic restrictions did successfully create a range of international and domestic incentives for reform. In Chapters 6, 7, 8, and 9, Meg Voorhes, Mzamo Mangaliso, Xavier Carim, Audie Klotz, Olivier Lebleu, and Tshidiso Maloka all document detrimental consequences of economic isolation. Investor confidence declined as shareholder and consumer pressures escalated, leading both public and private financial institutions to demand political (as well as economic) reforms. In combination, divestment, disinvestment, "bankers' sanctions," partial trade embargoes and other economic sanctions undermined growth, making the government increasingly vulnerable to domestic political pressures and escalating sanctions. Even the benefits of import substitution, emphasized in Crawford's analyses of oil and arms, could not buoy the economy through recession and worker unrest. As a result, both international financial pressures at the height of the country's debt crisis in the late 1980s and growing dissatisfaction of domestic business leaders created unavoidable demands for the government to implement political reforms.

Growing ideological contradictions, in part brought on by social sanctions, exacerbated the state's economic vulnerability and undermined the foundations of the apartheid system. Diplomatic isolation, Audie Klotz argues in Chapter 10, cost South Africa opportunities to project its political and economic influence abroad. Furthermore, by rejecting independence for the homelands, the international community subverted the "grand" apartheid plan. Simultaneous support for the anti-apartheid movement in exile combined to force the government to acknowledge the need to negotiate with legitimate representatives of the majority population. Thus social sanctions pressured the South Africa government through a process of delegitimation.

Collectively, these measures directed at the state undermined its ability to defend white minority-rule, both from resistance within and opposition abroad. Restrictions on the flow of arms gradually affected South Africa's capacity to use force and may have constrained its military operations in the mid- and late 1980s. Economic restrictions forced the government to bargain with international bankers over the elimination of apartheid, and social sanctions undermined the legitimacy of the regime. None of these measures alone toppled apartheid, but the evidence from the South African case is more positive than skeptics acknowledge. Most notably, our analysis emphasizes economic and social – rather than solely military – dimensions of state vulnerability.

The ruling NP's decision to negotiate cannot be explained at the governmental level alone. Pressures from the anti-apartheid movement and business elites – partly the indirect consequence of sanctions – also contributed to the external pressures for reform. A more complete picture of the South African transition, therefore, requires looking beyond the realm of the state to the economic and social targets of sanctions.

Domestic and Global Economy

The prevailing tendency among sanctions analysts is to examine only the economic consequences of economic measures. The South African case calls for a more expansive assessment. The broad array of military, economic, and social sanctions all had economic consequences, including in the region.

The economic sectors connected to military industrialization and oil import substitution remained most insulated from concerns about the costs of sanctions. As Crawford and Fig demonstrate, the government spent substantial sums developing domestic replacements for embargoed weapons, technology, spare parts, and oil. White South Africans bore the brunt of those costs. On the other hand, import substitution in response to oil, nuclear, and conventional arms sanctions bolstered the strength of key mining and industrial interests. Overall, the economic costs of strategic embargoes did not translate into pressures for political reforms. But such was not the case in other economic sectors.

Although South Africa succeeded in circumventing many specific trade embargoes, most notably oil, it paid dearly for covert trade. Goods imported at premium, sanctions-busting prices exacerbated inflation and other recessionary conditions. While the sanctions-specific employment consequences appear to be mixed (according to Crawford and Maloka, some import-substitution sectors expanded while other embargoed sectors contracted), the perception of recession being connected to sanctions further damaged investor confidence. Faced with an impending crisis, including escalating domestic strikes and political protests, business elites increased their demands for political reform. As Carim, Klotz, and Lebleu document, frustration with the government ran high, provoking many elites to open direct talks with the African National Congress (ANC) in exile, creating even more extra-parliamentary pressure for reform.

South Africa's inability to expand into Africa exacerbated its economic difficulties. At the continental level, diplomatic isolation reduced benefits from regional trade and integration, as Klotz argues. Some degree of economic cooperation continued due to structural ties such as railways, domestic politics within neighboring states, and other factors examined by Khadiagala, but the South African economy lost greater opportunities for lucrative continental expansion. Cultural boycotts, described by Nomazengele Mangaliso in Chapter 12, reinforced these barriers to the rest of Africa.

While the overall economic effects of these sanctions are a far cry from total destruction, the political consequences indicate growing pressure from business elites for reform. Import substitution failed to protect the economy, and ultimately the government. Some economic sectors, notably finance, offered more direct bargaining leverage. Thus the conventional economic-devastation theory falls short of explaining South Africa's response to sanctions but it rightly points to growing popular unrest and dissatisfaction among the business community as critical components.

Yet the connections between domestic and global opposition need to be explained in order to understand the dynamic nature of the sanctions process. A combination of domestic unrest, business pressure, and escalating sanctions fostered persistent demands for reform. With the alienation of the conservative flank of the Afrikaner community, the NP had little to lose by trying to implement "power sharing" to preclude the one person, one vote system that both domestic and international critics demanded.

Domestic and Global Society

The societal impact of international pressure is the most neglected dimension in the literatures on both sanctions and the South African transition. In particular, the transnational (rather than purely domestic) nature of the anti-apartheid movement highlights the global and domestic implications of demands for reform. In addition, the multitude of racial, ethnic, class, and other divisions within the country requires a multidimensional perspective on South African society. Particularly notable for the sanctions debate, Afrikaners proved to be more vulnerable than analysts anticipated. The effects of international influence reached deep into the fabric of society, undermining the legitimacy of apartheid among white South Africans while bolstering that of the anti-apartheid movement.

As skeptics would lead us to expect, some cultural consequences proved counterproductive. Restrictions on arms and technology spurred the militarization and mobilization of white society. As Fig shows, scientists within South Africa's nuclear establishment revelled in the challenge of circumventing sanctions. But such policies proved costly, in both financial and social terms. Resistance to militarization mounted, evident in the establishment of the End Conscription Campaign, escalating white emigration, and a general growth in liberal political opposition. Censorship and persecution of anti-apartheid activists could not conceal the deepening fissures within the white community.[2]

Although the economic consequences of corporate policies may have had less influence than proponents of either disinvestment or corporate codes of conduct hoped, as both Voorhes and Mangaliso explain, mobilization for divestment in industrialized countries strengthened anti-apartheid resistance. At the same time, South African perceptions of the failure of specific sanctions also bolstered the confidence and resolve of some members of the ruling elite. Overall, the barrage of economic sanctions exacerbated increasing divisions among whites, including Afrikaners. Conservatives, especially in the rural areas, remained defiant in the face of international criticism, but many business leaders (and other professionals) joined the "trek to Lusaka" to meet with the exiled ANC.[3] The NP proved belatedly attuned to its core constituency, instituting increasingly substantive reforms throughout the 1980s, culminating in de Klerk's dramatic measures in the early 1990s.

Of the sanctions directed against apartheid society, sports boycotts proved most directly damaging to whites. As David Black explains in Chapter 11, exclusion from world-class competition in cricket and rugby inflicted socio-psychological pain and undermined the ideological foundation of the apartheid system, including South Africa's deeply mythologized ties to European culture. Furthermore, Mangaliso shows that entertainment and academic boycotts raised the consciousness of the world and bolstered the resolve of the anti-apartheid movement. Both of these dimensions of sanctions targeted white elites and left the majority of blacks relatively unscathed – demonstrating the potential for "smart" sanctions.

On the whole, the mobilization for economic sanctions and the imposition of restrictions strengthened the resolve of the anti-apartheid movement, domestically and globally. The social consequences for whites proved contradictory. The arms embargoes exacerbated the "laager" mentality, and some circumvention of trade boycotts bolstered confidence, yet sports boycotts and financial sanctions fuelled divisions in white society. The result was a crisis in apartheid ideology, sharpened divisions within the Afrikaner community, and escalating demands for reform. On balance, these social consequences undermined the foundations of white minority-rule and strengthened the commitment of blacks to suffer in the short term to achieve the elimination of apartheid. These effects refute the conventional wisdom that sanctions necessarily lead to solidarity in the target society. While some elements of "rallying round the flag" are evident in the South African case, both elite fracture and social movement mobilization proved more important.

Cumulative Consequences for the South African Transition

In the 1980s, external pressures combined especially with domestic labor mobilization to create conditions that required dramatic political and economic change. Reform proved to be a process – rather than a discrete outcome – as the regime attempted a series of insufficient amendments to apartheid before finally recognizing the need for its elimination. Each of the chapters in this volume details the effects of a particular type of sanction on this reform process. Such sectoral analyses are crucial for improving the implementation of restrictions, but at the same time can miss the cumulative and dynamic nature of sanctions. Here, therefore, I pull together these various strands of influence on the South African transition.

Demands for boycotts and embargoes by international organizations, states, corporations, cities, unions, and others, began with social movements in South Africa and expanded abroad.[4] These international pressures in turn stimulated popular resistance against the apartheid regime. After its initial defiance in the 1950s, the government sought to preserve apartheid through partial reforms. Granting "independence" to the homelands, legalizing black unions, including "Coloreds" and "Asians" in the new 1983 constitution, relaxing influx control, and abolishing many aspects of "petty" apartheid social segregation highlighted contradictions in the apartheid system, exacerbated disagreements within the Afrikaner leadership, and thereby presented political openings for resistance. Repression in reaction to persistent popular opposition stimulated additional international sanctions, leading to a point where both the NP leadership under de Klerk and two-thirds of the white minority (as evident in the 1992 referendum) recognized the urgent need to create a more inclusive political system. It is this mutually reinforcing nature of social movement mobilization and international sanctions – not one or the other alone – that led to negotiations between the government and legitimate representatives of the majority.

Sanctions did not dictate democratic terms for the post-apartheid constitution, but several aspects of international pressure promoted the relatively peaceful transition and its moderate outcome.

Fear of additional isolation, for example, may have precluded more brutal repression. The conditions set forth in sanctions packages, in addition, listed specific reforms, including the elimination of the legal pillars of apartheid and the release of Nelson Mandela, that guided the de Klerk government step by step. Notably absent from this set of international expectations, however, were conditions of economic reform or redistribution, thus sealing the moderate, capitalist, nature of the transition.[5]

This assessment of the interaction between international and domestic pressures is necessarily preliminary since the purpose of this project is to explore the effects of sanctions rather than to offer a complete explanation of political change in South Africa. Our evidence clearly indicates that sanctions contributed to the democratic transition, but not in the direct ways most often articulated by sanctions theorists. Economic and social conditions mediated the influence of international pressures, with the most critical effects being on the anti-apartheid movement and white elites outside government. Practitioners seeking to replicate the positive lessons of the South African experience would do well, then, to focus on the indirect consequences of sanctions, especially in target societies.

SANCTIONS AFTER SOUTH AFRICA

The relative success of sanctions against South Africa stands out historically and has spurred the proliferation of similar measures against other countries, including Haiti, Burma (Myanmar), China, and Nigeria. The apartheid case need not be unique, but our analysis indicates that the utility of international pressure remains contingent on particular international and domestic military, economic, and social contexts. Drawing out implications from the South African experience through brief comparisons with other cases leads to a cautiously optimistic forecast for the use of sanctions in the post–Cold War era. In seeking more general lessons for the larger sanctions debate, I focus on three areas: international norms; domestic characteristics of the target; and timeframes for applying and lifting sanctions. Throughout, I stress the need for sanctioners to decide whether they are trying to coerce, induce, or teach the target to change and then to choose appropriate means accordingly.

International Norms

International institutions, states, and non-state actors have adopted sanctions for centuries in pursuit of a wide array of goals. Some measures aimed to provoke a particular behavioral response from a clearly identifiable agent; others sought broad social transformation not directly tied to the specific actions of individuals. In the post–Cold War era, many observers of international relations point to increased normative consensus over capitalism, democracy, and liberal codes of human rights leading to the increased adoption of multilateral sanctions to promote these goals.[6] Especially as the new conventional wisdom trumpets it as a success case, South Africa serves as a precedent and potential model for norm-based multilateral actions.

Yet some norms may be impossible to promote with the use of sanctions. Opposing military aggression, for example, may indeed require the target to be as vulnerable to economic coercion as it would be to armed assault. The South African experience confirms the limited utility of strategic measures in the absence of a credible threat of force. Similarly, the initial UN response to Iraqi abrogation of Kuwaiti sovereignty in August 1990 reinforces skepticism about collective security.[7] Weaknesses first evident in the League of Nations framework continue to plague the use of sanctions as an alternative to armed conflict. Rather than preventing violence, many observers have rightly pointed out that in some circumstances sanctions may require the threat of war. Other observers, however, stress that the violence inflicted by sanctions is not necessarily any less harmful than the consequences of war, further challenging the (implicit or explicit) ethical claims of sanctioners.[8]

Sanctions, therefore, may be an inappropriate response to armed aggression precisely because they cannot replace military force. Nonetheless, in such cases sanctions can still serve as a warning and complement to other measures. For example, arms and economic embargoes combined with NATO airstrikes against the former Yugoslavia apparently brought its leaders to the negotiating table in Dayton.[9] Weapons proliferation is another fruitful area. Since the 1991 Gulf War, sanctions have moderated (but not completely eliminated) Iraqi efforts to acquire prohibited weapons.[10] Successful issue-linkage between inspections of North Korean nuclear facilities and economic aid in the mid-1990s also confirms the utility of sanctions for enforcing norms embedded in non-proliferation regimes.[11]

Alternatively, other norms may be impossible to enforce through coercive means because the goal requires social transformation, as in South Africa. For example, the UN and US discovered in both Somalia and Haiti that military occupation cannot create and enforce democracy. Where the international community hopes for a fundamental change in domestic institutions and attitudes, such as the adoption of a norm of racial equality, a slower process of socialization through selective sanctions may be required for strengthening reformist actors and promoting peaceful solutions to internal conflicts. For example, calibrated incremental measures against China – reminiscent of the bargaining between international bankers and the apartheid regime – appear to have procured release of political prisoners and improved conditions in prisons. Threats of broad economic sanctions against Asian states in response to human rights abuses generally appear less effective than specific reforms tied to modest and specific sanctions measures.

Ideally, consensus on international norms, such as human rights, would enable sanctioners to focus on the calibration of measures. But in practice, international actors are bound to disagree on the value of particular norms, the seriousness of their abrogation, and the costs they are willing to bear for enforcement. Sanctions against South Africa proved effective in part because of their wide range and broad adoption driven by consensus on a norm of racial equality. Diplomatic sanctions against Haiti (enabling deposed President Jean-Bertrand Aristide to maintain a government in exile) worked in part because of regional support through the Organization of American States.[12] In contrast, sanctions against Nigeria for human rights abuses failed to generate concerted African, not to mention global, support.[13] Similarly, Southeast Asian states refuse to support sanctions against the Burmese military government.[14] The Chinese, Nigerian, and Burmese cases illustrate critical differences between a norm of racial quality (which garnered global support) and codes of human rights (which have been rejected by many as Western cultural imperialism). Countries with high degrees of cultural autonomy will remain fairly insulated from international normative pressures. But as the anti-apartheid sport boycott demonstrates, most societies have social vulnerabilities. Even the Chinese government proved vulnerable to the International Olympic Committee's choice of Sydney over Beijing for the 2000 games.

One of the most striking features of the apartheid case is the grassroots origin of demands for sanctions – first within South Africa and African states, then spreading to solidarity movements throughout the world, and finally taking hold in critical advanced industrial states by the mid-1980s. Others have sought to replicate this mobilization. Drawing most directly on its own experiences responding to white minority-rule in Southern Africa, the US lobbying group TransAfrica worked with the Congressional Black Caucus in championing sanctions against Haiti and garnering support for its exiled leader in the early 1990s.[15] A similar coalition in the mid-1990s demanded US action against the military government in Nigeria.[16] Students, stockholders, and other activists throughout the US and other major trading partners have coordinated calls for divestment, oil sanctions, and other trade restrictions against Burma, Nigeria, China, Indonesia, and in other instances of human rights abuses.

However, increasingly institutionalized coalitions and experience in mobilizing international public opinion will not automatically lead to more sanctions, since corporations have also become more sophisticated players in these debates, as exemplified by the Mobil Corporation's series of anti-sanctions advertisements in major US newspapers.[17] Nor does public demand for sanctions necessarily mean these measures will be effective. US sanctions against Cuba, for example, respond primarily to domestic political pressures from the exile community in Florida. Rather than being the basis for global mobilization and consensus, however, US measures, especially the most recent Helms-Burton provisions which seek to sanction third countries which circumvent the primary boycott, infuriated Canada, Mexico, Spain, and other critical allies.[18] The European Union and Japan reacted in a similar fashion to sanctions against Burma.[19] Battles ensue in the World Trade Organization over the legality of extraterritorial restrictions on trade, highlighting the dangers of pursuing unilateral policies in an increasingly global economy.

While comprehensive implementation may not be a prerequisite for successful sanctioning, multilateral coordination ensures greater legitimacy and thus creates more compelling international normative pressure. As international institutions govern more political arenas in the post–Cold War era, practitioners would do well to include normative consensus-building on their list of optimal conditions for the success of international pressures.

Domestic Characteristics

The success of the sanctioning process also depends on the domestic setting of the target government. More attention to economic and social context is crucial for understanding how sanctions indirectly influence key decision makers and state institutions. On the societal dimension, political institutions link the state to opposition parties, social movements, and other non-governmental actors. In some countries, therefore, the personalities of leaders will be most important, but in others the broader social impact of sanctions will be more significant. The degree to which the target country has a market economy will create further variations in the indirect impact of sanctions on the state.

In some circumstances, individual decision making will be a critical determinant of the potential success of sanctions. Under coercion and bargaining perspectives, actors change their behavior or transform domestic institutions to accord with international demands in response to external threats and incentives. Views that emphasize socialization, alternatively, stress that decision makers may internalize or "learn" new values. For example, while some white South Africans abandoned apartheid because they thought it had failed or become too expensive, others more profoundly rejected the principle of racial discrimination. In particular, cultural boycotts and other social sanctions communicated international opinion. In contrast to fracturing white solidarity in South Africa, the imposition of UN sanctions against Rhodesia actually fostered consensus over segregation.[20] Furthermore, sports boycotts were unlikely tools to stop genocide in the former Yugoslavia.[21] These variations in the mechanisms that connect sanctions to domestic decision-making processes need to be taken more seriously, because different methods of influence will only work in some contexts.

The degree of bureaucratic centralization within the target state will also determine the salience of both external and internal pressures. Some observers have stressed the importance of the parliamentary system for whites in South Africa, which left national leaders at least partially vulnerable to public opinion.[22] In contrast, military regimes remain insulated from electoral demands. Sanctions designed to target Nigerian public opinion, therefore, are unlikely to succeed, but measures which could undermine the late General Sani Abacha's patronage system might have seriously threatened his regime's position. More centralized political systems also make the personalities of the leaders, such as Saddam Hussein, Raul Cedras, Slobodan Milosevic or the late Deng Xiaoping, a more critical characteristic of the target. Of course, it is much more difficult to gauge the potential effectiveness of sanctions when individual quirks become the focal point for the promotion of political change; the existence of institutionalized decision-making processes make general lessons more applicable.

The relationship between the state and the economy will also create significant variations in the impact of sanctions, even across different sectors within the same target. For example, South Africa's financial crisis offered particular opportunities for international leverage because of the set of market incentives driving bankers' behavior in combination with the role of the Reserve Bank. Other sectors lacked direct links between economic pressures and demands for political reform. The successful application of sanctions, therefore, requires a careful assessment of the complexities of political economies. In the case of Haiti, for example, some observers pointed out that restricting flights from Port-au-Prince to Miami was more likely to influence the military rulers than an oil blockade which dramatically affected the poor population (and enriched smugglers).[23] Military governments in Haiti, Nigeria, and especially Burma also have relied significantly on revenues from the illicit drug trade, substantially weakening any leverage from divestment or sanctions on legal commercial deals. Sanctioners also need to consider more carefully the societal impact of international pressures, including the economic and humanitarian costs to the general population.[24] At minimum, a more just application of sanctions would include compensation for unintended domestic and regional targets of international pressures, as the Frontline States pleaded in the South African case.

No simple formula will determine which types of sanctions are best suited to influence particular target groups. Yet in their attempts to adopt more calibrated measures, sanctioners need to be clearer about whether government leaders, economic elites, or the general population are the targets of pressure. Combined with a more sophisticated understanding of the political and economic institutions that link societies to states, international advocates of political change can better choose methods of pressure that are suited to the most likely mechanisms of influence on decision making processes.

Timeframes

Anti-apartheid sanctions highlight the long-term nature of social transformation. Yet we should not overemphasize the time lag between the implementation of the first multilateral measures in the early 1960s and the elimination of apartheid in the early 1990s. Embargoes and boycotts against South Africa spanned almost 50 years because of the need to battle the conventional wisdom that sanctions would not work. But once this entrenched skepticism was overcome by the mid-1980s, sanctioners quickly implemented substantial restrictions and threatened further, tougher, actions. With the popular new post-apartheid view that sanctions do work, the Commonwealth and others took action within days of Nigeria's execution of political opponents in 1995. Other human rights abuses around the world now bring about immediate calls for international isolation. As the number of these cases increases, multilateral institutions in particular develop precedents and enforcement procedures, further reducing the implementation time for, and thereby increasing the effectiveness of, sanctions. On this dimension of timing, therefore, the South African case opened the floodgates by serving as a convincing precedent.

In addition, skeptics overemphasize the length of time needed to provoke a response from the target. Indeed, South Africa responded quickly once the international community adopted stringent measures in the mid-1980s. However, it is also important to identify those measures, such as financial restrictions, which are best suited to more immediate bargaining leverage; others, such as cultural isolation, are likely to take longer to influence the social fabric of the target. Thus practitioners and analysts need to appreciate that different measures require different lengths of time to be most productive. Assessing the effectiveness of sanctions by the time period between imposition and target response also raises serious questions of measurement bias. Incidents where the mere threat of sanctions brings about the desired change in the target are generally not even included in databases. Thus timing should not be too strong a criterion of evaluation. Overall, since some goals require an immediate response while others entail slower social transformation, sanctioners should adopt measures most appropriate for the type of behavioral, institutional or societal change they seek.

A third dimension of the timing question is the point at which to lift sanctions – that is, how to use them as incentives and rewards rather than just as threats and punishments. Here the evidence from the South African case is sketchy but nonetheless suggestive. In sports, for example, ending boycotts offered the potential for redemption and the implied promise of rewards in other areas. The end of (almost all) economic restrictions by 1991 quickly signalled international approval of de Klerk's reforms. But lifting sanctions too quickly – particularly in areas where they may be difficult to reimpose – can be risky. Efforts to ameliorate harsh conditions for the Iraqi population (by allowing oil sales strictly for importing humanitarian aid) enabled Saddam Hussein to revive attempts to secure arms and other embargoed goods. The timing of lifting sanctions promises to remain contentious. So far, little scholarly attention has been paid to this dimension of the sanctioning process, but the South African case offers a promising example of the benefits of clearly stated criteria.

CONCLUSION

On balance, the South African experience demonstrates that international sanctions can play a constructive role in domestic political change. Although there are no simple generalizations about whether, when and how to adopt effective measures, the evidence from this project suggests three overarching lessons. First, we should consider a broader range of targets of influence beyond governments, especially social movements. The successful use of sanctions will also draw upon a more comprehensive array of mechanisms for influencing these diverse targets, including along social dimensions. Finally, at least in cases relating to international human rights norms, sanctions appear to be particularly appropriate for achieving political change through a process of socialization, rather than coercion.

Most of the comparative cases surveyed in this chapter focus on human rights issues. These general lessons should also be applicable to other issue-areas, especially the environment, but may have less relevance where sanctions are adopted to enforce economic practices. In these latter areas, market dynamics will take on a substantially larger role than in the sectors and cases considered in this volume. These are all areas worthy of further study. Additional systematic and detailed comparisons between South Africa and other cases of the use of sanctions will help guide theorists and practitioners in identifying the best targets and their potential vulnerabilities. Sanctioning will remain a disputed political act, but the lack of sweeping generalizations does not alter the reality that they can be creative and effective instruments of international influence.

Notes

I am indebted to David Black and Kim Nossal for ongoing discussions about sanctions in comparative perspective as well as their detailed comments on drafts of this chapter. Neta Crawford also offered helpful suggestions. This chapter elaborates on ideas first published in the conclusion to "Norms and Sanctions: Lessons from the Socialization of South Africa," *Review of International Studies* 22 (1996), pp. 173–90.

1. Also see G. Cawthra, *Securing South Africa's Democracy: Defence, Development and Security in Transition* (Basingstoke, UK: Macmillan, 1997).
2. On the militarization of society, see J. Cock and L. Nathan, eds., *War and Society: The Militarization of South Africa* (Cape Town: David Philip, 1989).
3. For fascinating interviews with various members of these delegations, see J. Goodwin and B. Schiff, *Heart of Whiteness: Afrikaners Face Black Rule in the New South Africa* (New York: Scribner, 1995), ch. 12.
4. In addition to the brief overview of anti-apartheid mobilization for sanctions in our introduction, see A. Klotz, *Norms in International Relations: The Struggle against Apartheid* (Ithaca, NY: Cornell University Press, 1995).
5. D. R. Black, "The Long and Winding Road: International Norms and Domestic Political Change in South Africa," in T. Risse, S. C. Ropp, and K. Sikkink, eds., *The Power of Principles: International Human Rights Norms and Domestic Change* (Cambridge: Cambridge University Press, 1999).
6. For example, D. Cortright, and G. A. Lopez, *Economic Sanctions: Panacea or Peacebuilding in a Post-Cold War World* (Boulder, CO: Westview, 1995); J. Stremlau, *Sharpening International Sanctions: Toward a Stronger Role for the United Nations*, Report to the Carnegie Commission on Preventing Deadly Conflict (New York: Carnegie Foundation, November 1996).
7. F. Halliday, "The Gulf War 1990–1991 and the Study of International Relations," *Review of International Studies* 20 (1994), pp. 109–30.
8. For example, see L. Buck, N. Gallant, and K. R. Nossal, "Sanctions as a Gendered Instrument of Statecraft: The Iraqi Case," *Review of International Studies* 24 (1998, pp. 69–84); and K. R. Nossal, *Rain Dancing: Sanctions in Canadian and Australian Foreign Policy* (Toronto: University of Toronto Press, 1994).
9. Stremlau, *Sharpening International Sanctions*, p. 28.
10. Ibid., p. 23.
11. The effectiveness of sanctions in such cases will depend largely on the

technicalities of the regimes and their associated treaties. See J. S. Nye, Jr., "Nuclear Learning and US-Soviet Security Regimes," *International Organization* 41 (1987), pp. 371–402; and A. Chayes and A. H. Chayes, *The New Sovereignty: Compliance with International Regulatory Agreements* (Cambridge: Harvard University Press, 1995).

12. For an overview of regional reactions to the Haiti situation, see D. A. Acevedo, "The Haitian Crisis and the OAS Response: A Test for Effectiveness in Promoting Democracy, " in L. F. Damrosch, ed., *Enforcing Restraint: Collective Intervention in Internal Conflict* (New York: Council on Foreign Relations, 1993), pp. 119–55.

13. D. R. Black, "Echoes of Apartheid? Canada, Nigeria, and the Politics of Norms," paper presented at the annual meeting of the International Studies Association, March 1997.

14. S. Mydans, "Burmese Sanctions Get Little Asian Backing," *New York Times*, 25 April 1997, A5; S. Erlanger, "Asians Are Cool to Albright on Cambodians and Burmese," *New York Times*, 28 July 1997, A7.

15. Tactics included full-page advertisements in major US newspapers; see, for example, *New York Times*, 23 March 1993, A11.

16. Activists ended up in a battle of full-page advertisements with the Nigerian government; see *New York Times*, 20 April 1995, 19 October 1995, 3 November 1995, 6 December 1995, 22 January 1997.

17. See, for examples, advertisements placed simultaneously in the *New York Times* and the *Wall Street Journal*, 17 July and 24 July 1997.

18. *New York Times*, 14 March 1997, 13 June 1996, 13 February 1997, 21 February 1997, 17 July 1997.

19. *In These Times*, 17 February 1997.

20. See A. Klotz, "Race and Nationalism in Zimbabwean Foreign Policy," *Round Table* 327 (1993), pp. 260–5; A. Klotz, "Norms and Sanctions: Lessons from the Socialization of South Africa," *Review of International Studies* 22 (1996), p. 189.

21. See Rob Nixon's contrast between Serbs and Afrikaners in *Homelands, Harlem and Hollywood: South African Culture and the World Beyond* (New York: Routledge, 1994), pp. 233–54.

22. I thank Kim Nossal for bringing this issue to my attention.

23. For a survey of debates over specific sanctions measures against Haiti, see Acevedo, "Haitian Crisis," p. 134.

24. Nossal, *Rain Dancing*, pp. 261–7; Stremlau, *Sharpening International Sanctions*, pp. 40–5; L. F. Damrosch, "The Civilian Impact of Economic Sanctions," in Damrosch, ed., *Enforcing Restraint*, pp. 274–315; T. G. Weiss, D. Cortright, G. A. Lopez, and L. Minnear, eds., *Political Gain and Civilian Pain: The Humanitarian Impacts of Economic Sanctions* (Boulder, CO: Rowman and Littlefield, 1997).

Appendix: Chronology of Sanctions Against Apartheid*

1944: Prime Minister Smuts joins the Manhattan Project's search for uranium.

1946: Newly founded UN considers South African domestic discrimination (against Indians); this agenda item expands in the 1950s to include apartheid. India withdraws its High Commissioner (ambassador) from South Africa.

1948: Malan's National Party defeats Smuts' United Party and institutes policies of apartheid. UN adopts the Universal Declaration of Human Rights.

1954: India formally severs diplomatic ties, and other countries follow, especially newly independent African states (from the late 1950s). Father Trevor Huddleston pleads for the international community to boycott South Africa. First crude oil refinery opens in Durban.

1955: South Africa opens Sasol I, a coal-to-oil conversion plant, in Sasolburg.

1957: South Africa and US agree on nuclear cooperation.

1958: ANC President Albert Luthuli calls for sanctions. The (non-racial) South African Sports Association is formed.

1959: Select ANC members go into exile in London and launch the Boycott South Africa movement in Britain.

1960: Sharpeville killings produce international outrage. African states call for sanctions. The Anti-Apartheid Movement founded in London; American Committee on Africa begins sanctions campaign in US. South Africa institutes financial rand system.

1961: After Sharpeville, many opposition leaders are banned, jailed or go into exile. South Africa withdraws from the Commonwealth, in the face of anti-apartheid pressures. Luthuli receives Nobel Peace Prize. US company Allis Chalmers contracts to build South Africa's first experimental nuclear reactor, SAFARI-1.

1962: UN General Assembly calls for diplomatic, economic, and military sanctions. South African Non-Racial Olympic Committee forms.

1963: UN Security Council adopts voluntary arms embargo (resulting in varying degrees of compliance); US announces end to military sales to South Africa. At its founding, the OAU excludes South Africa and supports sanctions. Many other international organizations reject South African participation.

1964: Britain bans arms exports to South Africa. Japan bans direct investment in South Africa. South Africa excluded from Tokyo Olympics.

---

* The editors compiled this chronology from the chapters.

1965: UN establishes its Trust Fund for South Africa and the Education Programme for South Africans. Artists and actors sign the "We Say No to Apartheid" pledge. Students in the US demonstrate at Chase Manhattan's headquarters to protest its loans to South Africa, starting first wave of divestment movement. Rhodesian Unilateral Declaration of Independence and resulting sanctions (including a UN arms embargo) increase attention and pressure on South Africa.

1968: South Africa excluded from Mexico Olympics.

1970: South Africa expelled from the Olympic Movement. Throughout the 1970s, some banks and governments ban investments in and loans to South Africa.

1971: Rev. Leon Sullivan advocates the withdrawal of General Motors from South Africa.

1972: *The Ethical Investor* urges university administrations to follow principles of socially responsible investing; numerous universities divest throughout the decade.

1973: UN General Assembly recognizes the liberation movements as "authentic representatives" of the South African majority. The Zulu version of *Macbeth*, *uMabatha*, boycotted in New York City. The Arab oil embargo adds to South Africa's energy problems, spurring nuclear power and coal-to-oil developments.

1974: UN General Assembly suspends South Africa. Coup in Lisbon results in independence in 1975 for Portuguese territories of Angola and Mozambique. South Africa increases overt and covert military activity in the region.

1976: Soweto uprising; number of exiles dramatically increases. Banks and governments increase restrictions on loans. Africans boycott Montreal Olympics. Transkei declares independence but is not recognized internationally. Bophuthatswana, Venda, and Ciskei meet a similar response in 1977, 1979, and 1981, respectively. Israel signs an agreement to increase scientific cooperation with South Africa.

1977: US increases efforts to restrict nuclear technology transfer; in August, the World Conference for Action Against Apartheid urges states and firms to cease all assistance and cooperation enabling South Africa's acquisition of nuclear capability. South Africa removed from IAEA governing board. Israel supplies South Africa a small quantity of tritium in exchange for shipments of uranium. Commonwealth adopts Gleneagles Declaration against apartheid in sport. Second wave of large US student protests; more colleges and universities adopt divestment policies. Sullivan Principles announced as a guide to corporate conduct in South Africa, with 12 initial US endorsers. New York performance of the musical *Ipi Ntombi* is boycotted. UN Security Council adopts mandatory arms embargo in November.

1978: European and Canadian codes of corporate conduct established. US tightens restrictions on support to military and police in South Africa and South West Africa/Namibia.

1979: UN General Assembly, in January, calls on the Security Council to consider measures that prevent South Africa from developing nuclear weapons. SADCC is established to counter South African destabilization and economic dominance in the region. Iran halts oil exports to South Africa; South Africa opens an oil storage facility in Saldanha Bay. US satellite detects what is thought to be a small nuclear explosion in the South Atlantic on 22 September; South Africa denies it conducted a nuclear test.

1980: The UN General Assembly calls for a total cultural boycott. Sasol II opens in Secunda.

1981: US announces policy of "constructive engagement," including the relaxation of previously imposed sanctions. Springbok tour of New Zealand is last of the apartheid era. UN and OAU International Conference on Sanctions against South Africa calls for sanctions in response to South Africa's acquisition of nuclear weapons capability. South African activists call for a boycott of artists who performed in South Africa.

1982: Connecticut becomes the first US state to legislate a divestment policy for its pension funds. Sasol III opens in Secunda.

1983: US Congress passes Gramm Amendment, blocking IMF loans to states practicing apartheid. Sir Richard Attenborough, director of the film *Gandhi*, cancels plans to attend its showing in South Africa, in support of the cultural boycott. UN General Assembly adopts in December a Programme of Action against Apartheid which urges all governments to refrain from nuclear technology transfer, nuclear cooperation, delivery of reactors and fissile material to South Africa.

1984: New South African constitution establishes a tricameral parliament with separate chambers for coloreds and Indians but leaves out blacks. Widespread protests and violence erupt in the black townships. Sullivan Principles expand to press for the repeal of all apartheid laws. Prominent South African anti-apartheid campaigner Bishop Desmond Tutu is awarded the Nobel Peace Prize. The Free South Africa Movement is launched at South African Embassy in Washington, DC. UN Security Council expands scope of military boycott to a ban on importing South African-made weapons and ammunition.

1985: In response to township violence, South Africa declares a state of emergency and rules out significant power-sharing with blacks. In July UN Security Council resolution 569 urges all member states to prohibit new nuclear-related contracts with South Africa. Chase Manhattan and other international banks refuse to "roll over" their loans in July; in August South Africa declares a moratorium on repayment of some of its commercial debt. Australia, in August, bans exports to South Africa of weapons and computer equipment that could be used for security purposes and banned imports of South African arms. A month later, Britain bans imports of South African-made weapons. The Commonwealth passes an initial package of economic sanctions in October, including a ban on purchases of South African uranium and Commonwealth exports of enriched uranium and nuclear technology. Australian and Japanese codes of corporate conduct established. The US Corporate Council on South Africa representing 100 US corporations is formed to oppose apartheid from within South Africa. The third and most intensive wave of US student anti-apartheid activism begins; divestment increases; group of university presidents also urge sanctions against South Africa. Several major cities adopt selective contracting provisions. The record album and video *Sun City* is produced and aggressively publicized by US anti-apartheid activist artists. US, European Community, and other countries implement additional sanctions measures. Anglo-American and other South Africa business leaders begin talking with the ANC in exile.

1986: France bans imports of South African-made arms and places controls on weapons exports in January. US Congress enacts, over President Reagan's veto, the Comprehensive Anti-Apartheid Act in October. Commonwealth adopts additional economic sanctions. European Community votes to ban imports of iron, gold coins, new investments in South Africa. Japan bans imports of iron and steel but not iron ore. General Motors leads a flood of US companies which announce their withdrawal. First Interim Agreement between South Africa and its creditors reached in March, covering repayments through June 1987. Barclays Bank ends loans to South Africa in response to customer pressure in May and withdraws from South African operations in November. Other banks follow suit. South African students protest abrogation of academic boycott by Dr. Conor Cruise O'Brien, a leading member of the Irish Anti-Apartheid Movement, at the University of Cape Town.

1987: US retirement funds begin sponsoring shareholder resolutions asking companies to withdraw from South Africa. Rev. Sullivan withdraws from the Sullivan Principles program and calls for economic sanctions against South Africa, spurring university and municipal divestment policies. Second Interim Agreement on debt repayment reached in February, covering through June 1990. ANC president Oliver Tambo proposes a selective boycott of South African culture and academics. US removes the tax-exempt status from firms operating in South Africa.

1988: South African Rugby Board and ANC representatives meet in Harare. Commonwealth report on the potential of financial sanctions starts circulating widely.

1989: Mobil and Goodyear – the largest remaining US companies – withdraw from South Africa. Third Interim Agreement on debt repayment reached in October, covering through December 1993, just prior to the Commonwealth summit meeting in Kuala Lumpur. National Sports Congress formed; split within non-racial sport movement. De Klerk succeeds Botha and announces his intentions to repeal several key apartheid laws, to release select political prisoners, and to unban some political organizations.

1990: Nelson Mandela released after 27 years in prison. ANC and other opposition groups are unbanned; the process of return from exile begins. South Africa orders end of its nuclear weapons program and dismantling of existing weapons.

1991: IOC recognizes (non-racial) National Olympic Committee of South Africa. US, Britain, and European Community lift most sanctions.

Key pension funds stop sponsoring anti-apartheid shareholder resolutions. South Africa signs NPT; IAEA inspection.

1992: Whites-only referendum validates de Klerk's reforms. South Africa participates in Cricket World Cup and returns to the Olympic Games at Barcelona. South Africa selected as host of the 1995 Rugby World Cup. UN shifts its focus to providing educational opportunities within South Africa. South African government begins destruction of 12 000 documents (including blueprints) and sensitive components.

1993: In March de Klerk admits that South Africa acquired nuclear weapons. Mandela calls for end to some economic sanctions. In October, UN General Assembly lifts sanctions.

1994: Mandela elected in South Africa's first democratic national elections, calls for end to remaining sanctions eight days after his inauguration on 10 May. US colleges and universities repeal divestment policies. South Africa begins the process of rejoining international organizations and re-establishing diplomatic ties.

1995: In March South Africa decommissions its large uranium enrichment facility, the Z-plant. In April and May, South Africa attends the 25-year review conference of the NPT in New York, supporting indefinite extension of the Treaty.

1996: Treaty of Pelindaba creating an African Nuclear-Weapons-Free Zone opened for signature in Cairo.

1998: US arms embargo ends.

Index